Fodor's

green travel

Fodor's

green travel

The world's **BEST** eco-lodges
& earth-friendly hotels

✳

Fodor's Travel Publications
New York • Toronto • London • Sydney • Auckland

www.fodors.com

Contents

Foreword by Richard Hammond

WE are on the verge of a new era in travel. From no-frills European city breaks to package holidays in the sun, we are travelling further and in far greater numbers than ever before. We trek the highest mountains, dive the world's coral reefs and venture deep into the heart of tropical rainforests. Each year there are some 800 million tourist trips worldwide. But that is just the beginning; by 2020, it is predicted that this figure will have doubled to 1.6 billion.

Tourism has enormous potential to bring significant economic development, particularly to the poorest parts of the planet. Yet ill-conceived tourism can also inflict damage to the very places we return to year after year – coastal areas that have been turned into mass holiday resorts, mountain paths that have become overrun by trekkers, and sites of cultural significance that become so swamped with visitors that they have lost their sense of magic.

There has never been a more urgent need to travel more responsibly, especially given the onslaught of climate change. Just as there is a need to count the carbon cost of household emissions, so we have to consider the environmental cost of flying on holiday. Aviation is one of the fastest growing contributors to greenhouse gases, whereas opting to go by train and bus will substantially lighten the carbon footprint of

A train passing through Yorkshire, England; Fiordland Crested Penguins, Awaroa Lodge

a holiday. Where this is impossible, it becomes even more important that the flight is used to its best advantage, by choosing to stay in those places that give something back to the destination.

Thankfully there are an increasing number of green places to stay designed to impact less on the local environment. These innovative places reduce their draw on energy and use renewable forms of power, they conserve water, and they reduce the amount of waste they create through re-using and recycling. Many too have important social policies that mean that the money from your holiday will help benefit local communities – through using local produce and employing local people. It's easy to forget that our holidays are often the doorstep of people that live there all year round; we visit their bars and restaurants, their national parks and beaches, and so by staying at locally run hotels, buying locally produced goods and shopping at local markets, we're giving something back to these places we so love to visit.

Compared with the vast scale of the tourism industry, a single holiday might seem inconsequential, but every trip does make a difference – to the local environment and to the local community. This book showcases a large variety of eco-friendly and ethical places to stay as well as the growing availability of green holiday experiences around the world that make it easier for us to travel more responsibly. Above all, it provides a host of inspirational ideas for anyone looking to be part of an enlightened, greener way to holiday.

Richard Hammond writes the 'Clean Break' eco-travel column in the *Guardian* and is the editor of greentraveller.co.uk.

Hoopoe Yurt Hotel; local woman on the village walk, Kalmatia Sangam Himalaya Resort

Introduction

'Travel is more than the seeing of sights; it is a change that goes on, deep and permanent, in the ideas of living.'
— Miriam Beard

The best kind of travel can change the way you see the world. It challenges your ideas, inspires you and provides you with an understanding not only of other cultures, but also of yourself. Immersing yourself in another way of life — and gaining an insight into the local environments, traditions, cultures, languages and cuisines that unfold before you as a traveller — is mind-opening and profoundly rewarding. Who wouldn't want to experience this?

Exactly. Tourism is not just big business, it is the world's largest service industry, employing one in every 11 people on the planet. Rapidly growing alongside it is the aviation industry, bringing us the ability to fly anywhere — to the most isolated, the most extreme, and the most beautiful pockets of the world. Tourists can now access every part of the planet, and those with the bank balance of a wealthy oligarch can even venture into space. Thanks to the low-cost airline revolution, it has never been more affordable to travel.

The 'inconvenient truth' about tourism

Flying may be inexpensive, but it's clear that the environmental cost of our enhanced mobility is high. Aviation currently accounts for more than 3 per cent of global greenhouse emissions, and growth in the industry is predicted to soar. Air travel is currently the fastest-growing contributor to man-made CO_2 emissions and is set to become the single leading contributor to global warming by 2020. A return flight from London to Sydney, for example, generates about 5 tonnes of CO_2, which alone surpasses the sustainable carbon footprint of one person per year (3–4 tonnes). There's also the fact that flying actually does far more damage than its 3 per cent when it is taken into account that, at altitude, the negative effects of greenhouse gases are three times as damaging as those released on the ground.

Once we're off our flight, the environmental impact of our travel continues. We want to be accommodated, entertained, pampered and indulged on our holidays. Room must be made for us, often at the expense of the local environment and displacement of local people. Golf courses spring up, causing chemical pollution, demanding water and replacing natural growth; artificial snow machines allow skiers to stay on the pistes while ignoring the reality of global warming; ugly hotel developments dominate coastlines, placing a huge strain on energy and natural resources in order to meet their guests' expectations. The UN has claimed that 'the average tourist uses as much water in 24 hours as a third-world villager would use to produce rice for 100 days'. It is all too obvious that the demands of this kind of tourism are unsustainable.

The idea that, despite all of this, the tourism industry is good for local economies must also be examined more closely. Studies have shown that, of the money paid for a standard package holiday, only one-fifth will trickle down into local economies. The lion's share often ends up in a country other than the destination, being soaked up by the airline, the tour operator and the imported products tourists demand. The jobs created by tourism are notoriously exploitative, with bad pay and conditions not uncommon, particularly in developing countries. There is also little job security for workers in the industry. Employment is often offered on a seasonal, casual basis, effectively denying workers job protection in the case of a natural disaster, threat or scare that affects tourism to the area. The gains invariably flow in one direction, and tourists and the people who serve them rarely engage on a mutually beneficial level.

Leaf-tailed geckos, O'Reilly's Rainforest Retreat; tent interior, Guludo Beach Lodge

Can you travel and still be green?

Taking into account all the negative effects of tourism, it may be hard to see travel as a positive force in the world. But much depends on the way we travel, and on our awareness of the impact we are having on the local people and the environment. In recent years, there has been a huge shift in the way people think about travel. Green travel doesn't have to involve hardship and deprivation and it's not all about hugging trees and saving the whales; it's a practical alternative that any thoughtful individual might consider – travel that respects the places being visited and the people who live there.

The green accommodation and experiences included in this book are just a taste of the wide range of places you can stay and things you can do to make your travel a positive contribution, whether you're staying in a city or a natural area, whether you want to lie on a beach or climb a mountain, and whether you're looking for a budget bed or a luxury suite. The demand for green accommodation is growing, and this makes perfect sense. Why stay in a hotel that exploits its workers when you can choose one that is locally owned and provides long-term economic benefits to the local community? Why stay at an insensitively managed development that pollutes your destination when you could opt for a low-impact ecolodge that works to conserve the environment? And why ignore the local culture or support tokenism when you could engage and interact with the local people on a meaningful level?

There are three overriding considerations that define a responsible approach to travel:

• **Environment and conservation** The impact on the environment should be minimized (through the use of energy-efficient technolo-

A pod sitting above the clouds, Whitepod; education sponsored by Anjajavy l'Hôtel

gies, and reduced waste and pollution), and positive contributions should be made to local conservation and biodiversity projects.

- **Social and cultural awareness** Local cultures, traditions and values and rights should be respected and conserved, and travellers and locals should try to engage in a way that promotes understanding, and that develops cultural pride and confidence.
- **Economic benefits** There should be long-term financial benefits for the local community through tourism based on the principles of fair trade, including fair wages, fair working conditions and a fair distribution of the income from tourism. Money should remain within the community through the use of locally owned accommodation, employment of local people and support of local services. This money can then be put towards funding local community initiatives, providing training and empowering the community economically.

The accommodation and experiences in this book are not faultless examples of responsible tourism. Some do well environmentally, such as Whitepod in the Swiss Alps, which packs up its pods each year, leaving little evidence of ever having been there. Others do well culturally, such as Gunya Titjikala in Australia, where travellers are taught to understand the forms of the land and skies through the eyes of the indigenous Titjikala people. And yet others do a great job economically, such as Guludo Beach Lodge in Mozambique, which was developed with the goal of using tourism to relieve the poverty in the area sustainably. There's a great deal of cross-over between these areas. Many green businesses address a little from each column, and all of the places in this book are making a real effort to maximize the environmental and social benefits of your visit.

Flying and carbon emissions

We should all be making efforts to reduce our carbon emissions. Staying closer to home and finding greener ways to get to your destination are the best ways to do this, but when flying is the only practical and realistic option, what should we do? Travelling more responsibly is a matter of weighing up the economic, environmental and social benefits of your travel against its the negative environmental impact.

Flying is probably the single most polluting thing you can do in a short space of time, but it makes up only part of your carbon footprint. A larger portion of your personal carbon footprint can be attributed to your energy use at home, the car you drive and the manufacture of the products you buy. If you make some changes around your home and in your daily life towards achieving a low-carbon lifestyle, you may be able to put some of the carbon you 'save' towards a flight. But installing one energy-efficient light bulb in your house will not cover a long-haul flight. In fact, to 'pay' for such a trip, you might need to get rid of your car. When you have done everything you personally can to minimize your footprint, you could also think about offsetting your flight through a credible scheme (see pages 154–5). Carbon-offsetting schemes can play an important role in helping us to curb emissions.

To minimize the impact of your air travel:

- Fly less by cutting down on short trips and by staying for longer.
- Try to fly direct rather than stopping over, as take-off and landing use a large proportion of a plane's fuel.
- Fly economy class, keeping emissions per person as low as possible.
- Pack light, as a lighter plane will burn less fuel.
- Make changes to your lifestyle at home to reduce your overall personal carbon footprint.
- Offset your flight.

While the damaging effects of flying are a serious issue, it is also worth considering the positive effect your trip may have. Tourism is the chief export for a third of developing nations. Many of the world's poorest

countries rely on tourism and have few other economic alternatives. If you consider carefully how best to use your flight, and go on trips that are of benefit to the destination, you can make a positive contribution that outweighs the environmental impact of your flight.

Carbon-offset figures in this book

The carbon emissions and offset costs throughout this book have been calculated with the assistance of the UK offsetting company of Climate Care. While we have tried to be as accurate as possible, we cannot account for all stopovers and variations in flight routes, so figures should be used as a guide only. Costs have been rounded to the nearest 5¢/5p. Carbon emissions, measured in tonnes (metric tons) of CO_2, have been calculated as follows:

- **Scheduled and chartered flights** The distance between two airports is calculated on the basis of their coordinates and in a curve (for further information, see www.climatecare.org/living/calculator-data).
- **Non-scheduled flights** Based on a Dash 8 twin-engine turboprop.
- **Car** Based on 0.30kg CO_2 per km (0.48kg CO_2 per mile), the figure supplied by the UK's Department for Environment, Food and Rural Affairs (DEFRA) for a petrol car with engine sized 2L or more.
- **Bus** Based on the DEFRA figures of 0.09kg CO_2 per passenger per km (0.14kg CO_2 per passenger per mile).
- **Ferry** Based on figures of 0.002kg CO_2 per passenger per km (0.003kg CO_2 per passenger per mile).
- **Train** Emissions for train travel vary significantly from country to country. The figures for UK train travel are based on the DEFRA figure for train travel, 0.06kg CO_2 per passenger per km (0.1kg per passenger per mile). Figures in France are based on SNCF's carbon calculator. Other international train figures are not available.

All CO_2 figures are based on return journeys. Where more than one transfer option is given, offset costs are based on the form of transport that generates the most carbon emissions.

Responsible travel tips

'If you reject the food, ignore the customs, fear the religion and avoid the people, you might better stay at home.'
– James Michener

The following guidelines have been developed by the UK-based charity Tourism Concern. Following them will help you to get more out of your travel, give something back to locals and benefit your destination:

- **Learn about the country you're visiting** Start enjoying your travels before you leave by tapping into as many sources of information as you can. Researching the culture, religion, environment, history and politics of a country can be rewarding, and knowing a few basic words of the language is always appreciated.
- **The cost of your holiday** Think about where your money goes, and be fair and realistic about the cost of your travel. Try to put money into the hands of local people – drink local beer or fruit juice rather than imported brands, and stay in locally owned accommodation.

Walking in the Kumaon district and meeting the local villagers, Kalmatia Sengam Himalaya Resort

Haggle light-heartedly and without aggression. Pay what something is worth to you and remember how wealthy you are compared to local people.

- **Culture** Open your mind to new cultures and traditions – it will transform your experience. Think carefully about what's appropriate in terms of your clothes and the way you behave. You'll earn respect and be more readily welcomed by local people if you do so. Respect local laws and attitudes towards drugs and alcohol, which vary in different countries and communities.

- **Your carbon footprint** Minimize your environmental impact by considering what happens to your rubbish. Take biodegradable products and a water-filter bottle with you. Be sensitive to limited local resources such as water, fuel and electricity. Help preserve local wildlife and habitats by respecting rules and regulations, such as sticking to footpaths, not standing on coral, and not buying products made from endangered plants or animals.

- **Guidebooks** Use your guidebook as a starting point, not the only source of information. Talk to local people and discover your own adventure.

- **Photography** Don't treat people as part of the landscape, and remeber that they may not want to have their picture taken. Put yourself in their shoes, ask first and respect their wishes.

www.tourismconcern.org.uk **TourismConcern**

A local Berber woman and her child in Chenni, Tunisia; prayer flags flutter on the wind in Nepal

Selection criteria

Working out whether a place is green or just greenwash can be a tricky business. There are plenty of hotel operators trying to cash in on the 'eco' label who will install a few low-energy light bulbs and call themselves green. The accommodation and experiences that have been included in this book are genuinely committed to a better, greener kind of travel. The Ecofiles in this book contain a responsibility section that outlines, in a nutshell, how each business is making a difference.

In its purest form, responsible travel has minimal impact on the local environment and works towards conserving it. It also has social and cultural benefits for the local community, and provides long-term economic advantages (see pages 10–11). These have been summarized in the Ecofiles under two main categories of responsibility:

- **Environmental** Includes environmentally sensitive technology and conservation efforts.
- **Social** Includes the social, cultural and economic benefits that the accommodation brings to the local community.

Each property has been given a rating out of five, shown as ∅, in these two categories, according to the criteria listed below.

Environmental

In order to rate the accommodation in terms of its environmental impact, we asked the following questions:

- What materials were used in the construction of the building? Are they natural and sustainable?
- What is the overall environmental impact of the building on the land?
- Are there any special architectural features that make it green (such as a green roof, effective insulation, natural ventilation to eliminate air conditioning, minimal use of concrete)?
- What is the visual impact of the building on the land? Does it fit in with the surroundings or is it an eyesore?
- Are any water-saving devices in place?
- Is greywater (second-hand water from washing machines) or rainwater recycled and reused? Is bore water (groundwater) used?
- Are towels and bed linens washed unnecessarily often?
- Is there a swimming pool? If so, what kind of chemicals, if any, are used in it and what effect do these have on the environment?
- Is waste treated in an environmentally friendly way?
- Is the toilet a composting type? If it is of the flushing variety, does it have a half-flush button and is the wastewater treated naturally?

- Are the cleaning products and toiletries biodegradable?
- Are renewable energy sources used to run the accommodation?
- Are guests encouraged to turn off lights? Are sensor lights and low-energy bulbs installed?
- How is the building heated?
- Is waste recycled and composted as much as possible?
- Are there any projects that work towards conserving the local wildlife and environment?
- Is information provided about local wildlife?
- Is the food served grown locally and organic?

Social

In order to give the accommodation a social responsibility rating, we asked these questions:
- Is the accommodation locally owned and managed?
- Are local staff employed? Are they given training, paid fairly and provided with good working conditions? Is this employment stable? Does it help to alleviate poverty and unemployment in the area?
- Does money from the accommodation go towards local community projects?
- What is the economic benefit of tourism to the local community?
- If guides are employed, are they local?
- Where does the food come from? Is it locally sourced and do local farmers/fishermen benefit?
- What information is available to guests about the local culture, people and customs?
- Are there any locally organized cultural activities? Are these bogus performances of 'traditional' dances or are they authentic local experiences?
- What kinds of activities are on offer? Are they a way to connect with the local people and culture?

We hope that the selection of accommodation and responsible travel experiences in this book will provide an insight into what some green businesses are achieving around the world, and will encourage you to start asking these questions wherever you go.

When you choose to travel in a more responsible way and seek experiences that benefit the environment and local communities, travel stops being just a personal indulgence and starts being a wonderful way to make a difference to your destination and the people who live there. If you make an effort to change the way you travel, it can change the way you see the world.

A local chef from Vamizi Island with the catch of the day; organic fruit and vegetables are grown by the owners and enjoyed by the guests the Black Sheep Inn; the Black Sheep Inn's composting loo-with-a-view

Chapter overview map

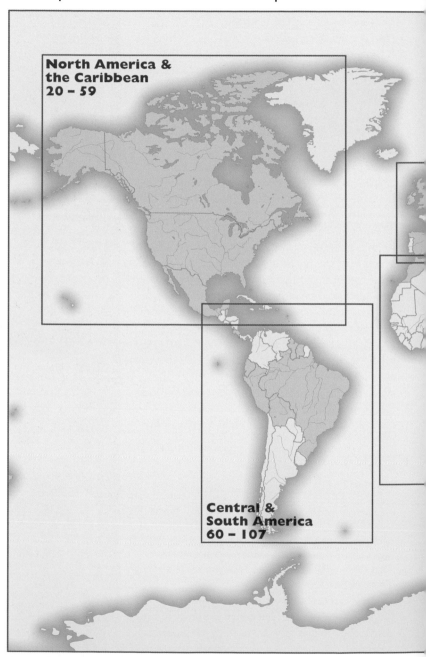

North America &
the Caribbean
20 – 59

Central &
South America
60 – 107

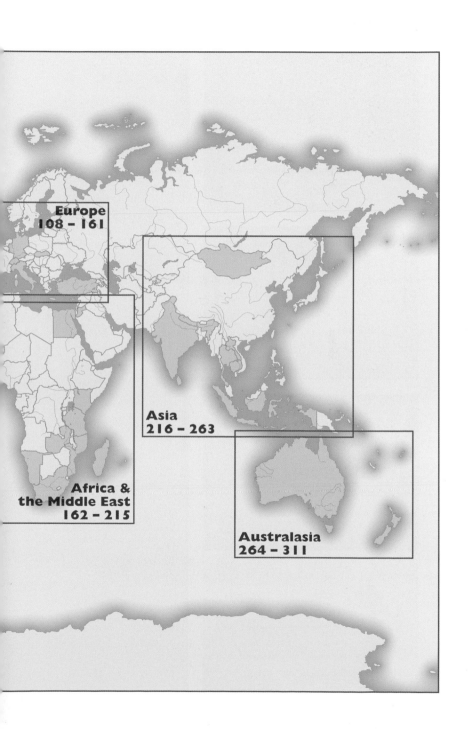

Europe
108 – 161

Asia
216 – 263

Africa &
the Middle East
162 – 215

Australasia
264 – 311

North America & the Caribbean

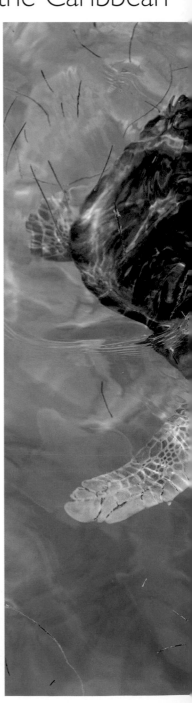

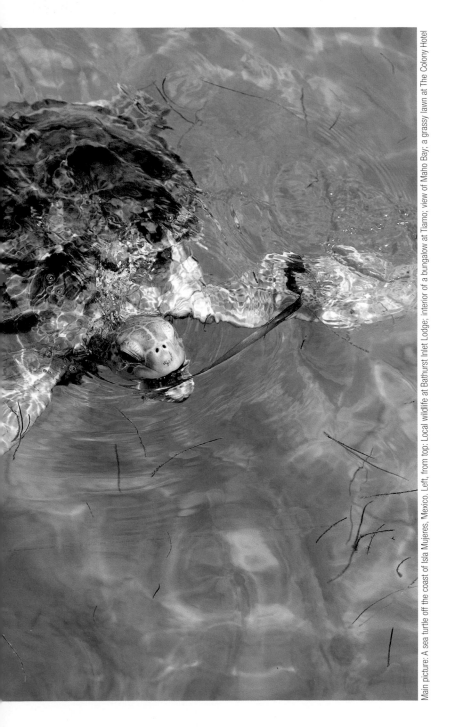

Main picture: A sea turtle off the coast of Isla Mujeres, Mexico. Left, from top: Local wildlife at Bathurst Inlet Lodge; interior of a bungalow at Tiamo; view of Maho Bay; a grassy lawn at The Colony Hotel

Locator map & budget guide

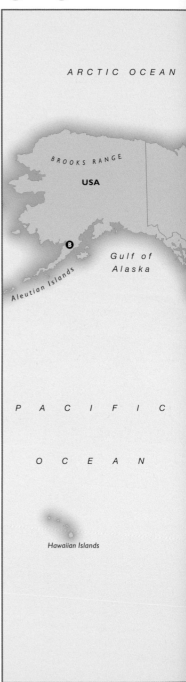

- ● Budget (up to US$100)
- ● Moderate (US$100–250)
- ● Expensive (US$250–500)
- ● Blow out (more than US$500)

Prices are for a double room, or two people, per night

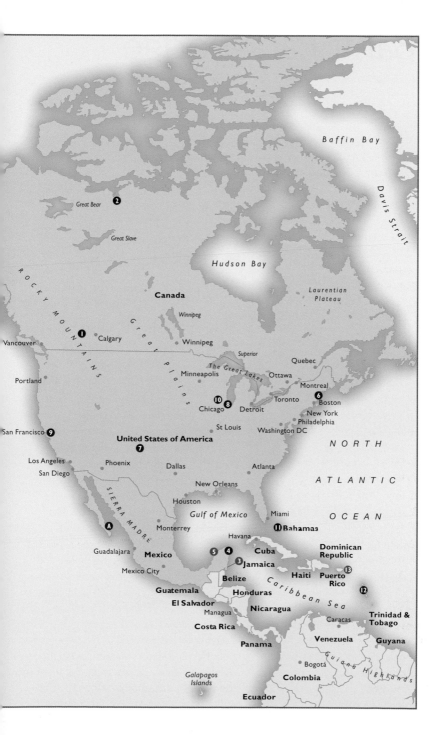

Baffin Bay

Davis Strait

Great Bear ❷

Great Slave

Hudson Bay

Canada

Laurentian
Plateau

Winnipeg

ROCKY MOUNTAINS

Great Plains

❶ Calgary

Winnipeg

Vancouver

Superior

Quebec

Portland

Minneapolis

The Great Lakes

Ottawa

Montreal

San Francisco ❾

❿ ❽
Chicago   Detroit

Toronto

❻ Boston
New York
Philadelphia
Washington DC

Los Angeles

St Louis

United States of America
❼

San Diego

Phoenix

Dallas

Atlanta

NORTH

SIERRA MADRE

New Orleans

ATLANTIC

Houston

Guadalajara

Ⓐ

Monterrey

Gulf of Mexico

Miami

OCEAN

Mexico

Mexico City

Havana

⓫ Bahamas

❺ ❹
❸ Jamaica

Cuba

Dominican
Republic

Belize

Haiti Puerto
Rico ⓭

Guatemala

Honduras

Caribbean Sea

⓬

El Salvador

Managua

Nicaragua

Caracas

Trinidad &
Tobago

Costa Rica

Panama

Venezuela

Guyana

Bogotá

Guiana Highlands

Galapagos
Islands

Colombia

Ecuador

Banff Park Lodge

222 Lynx Street, Banff, Alberta, T1L 1K5, Canada
+1 403/762-4433 / www.banffparklodge.com / info@banffparklodge.com

BANFF is an odd town. Beautiful, undoubtedly. Charming, certainly. But beyond the spectacular setting, and the tourists thronging the main street, and the busy hotels, and the ubiquitous souvenir shops, it is hard to get a handle on the place.

Situated in the Rocky Mountains, this little town of just 6,700 inhabitants is Canada's most popular resort, attracting more than 4 million visitors every year. And that's what makes it odd. At any given moment, locals are vastly outnumbered by outsiders. The town's demographics change from day to day.

Almost from the moment the town was established in the 1880s, efforts have been made to preserve its remarkable environment and to limit human impact. Banff National Park, Canada's first, was set up in 1885, and a century later the area was accorded UNESCO World Heritage Status.

The local council has been proactive in making Banff one of the most eco-friendly places in the country, with a host of environmental initiatives aimed at ensuring that, ultimately, the town has 'no net negative impact' on its natural surroundings.

In a place where the majority of the population is transient, it is crucial for the tourist industry to lead by example. Banff Park Lodge was one of the first hotels to introduce a thorough environmental management system. This involves making real and continuing improvements in key areas such as guest education, responsible purchasing, waste management and recycling, water conservation and energy efficiency.

The hotel has replaced its old, water-cooled industrial refrigerators with air-cooled models, which save water and electricity, and there are also plans to supplant the air conditioning with a system that employs groundwater to cool the building passively.

ECO**FILE**

Rooms: 192 rooms, 19 suites.
Rates: From CAN$137 (US$130) per room per night in low season (Oct–Dec); from CAN$264 (US$250) per room per night in peak season (Jun–Sep).
Location: Close to the centre of Banff, in the Canadian Rockies.
Best time to go: Year-round.
Getting there: From Calgary, travel by coach for 2 hours to Banff.
CO_2 emissions: Rtn flight to Calgary from New York 0.71 tonnes; London 1.98; Sydney 4.09. Rtn transfer 0.04.
Offset cost: $11.25; £15.15; A$77.30.

Responsibility: Banff Park Lodge has received a plethora of awards in recognition of its environmental work. It was the first independent hotel in Canada to be awarded four leaves under the Hotel Association of Canada's Eco-Rating Program, a scheme run in conjunction with Audubon International.
Environmental: ⵌⵌⵌⵌⵌ
Social: ⵌⵌⵌⵌⵌ

As a result of all these measures, Banff Park Lodge was the first hotel in Canada to be awarded the prestigious Environmental Choice Eco-Logo, a certificate introduced by the government agency Environment Canada to help consumers identify products and services with genuine green credentials.

From inside the hotel looking out, it is clear just what is at stake. Every room takes in a vista of pine trees and snow-flecked mountains. Banff National Park encompasses some of the most stunning scenery on the planet, luring more and more visitors – by 2020, it is estimated that annual numbers may rise as high as 19 million.

South of the hotel looms Sulphur Mountain, which is accessible via cable car or by a 90-minute hike. To reach the 2,285m-high (7,495ft) summit on foot is the more satisfying option. From the top, you are rewarded with a 360-degree view.

Banff lies far below, unobtrusive, enfolded by the glacier-blue waters of the Bow River on one side and the monolithic hulk of Tunnel Mountain on the other. From up here you can also see the tarmac ribbon of the Trans-Canada Highway stretching towards Calgary, just 130km (80 miles) away. Each day, the road brings a never-ending stream of new arrivals. Sustainable hotels such as Banff Park Lodge set the tone for their visit, helping to ensure that they leave Banff as they found it.

Bathurst Inlet Lodge

PO Box 820, Yellowknife, NWT, X1A 2N6, Canada
+1 867/873-2595 / www.bathurstinletlodge.com

YOU wake up feeling on top of the world. Literally. Bathurst Inlet Lodge is 50km (30 miles) inside the Arctic Circle, far beyond the reach of any road. The air is clean and clear, and the summer light shimmers with startling intensity. Stepping outside, you feel the rare exhilaration of being somewhere seemingly remote and pristine.

Getting here entails flying by Twin Otter floatplane across 580km (360 miles) of empty tundra. With every passing kilometre it seems that civilization is receding, an impression strengthened further on arrival at the lodge, which is housed in a motley collection of historic buildings that formerly made up a Hudson's Bay Company trading post and a Roman Catholic mission.

And yet, despite its isolation, this tiny outpost is acutely vulnerable to the impact of the modern world. When you gaze out at the inlet from the shore, you are standing on the climate change frontline. In winter, these waters are choked with ice, but in recent years the big freeze has started later and the spring thaw has come sooner.

The local wildlife is especially sensitive to the altering rhythms of the climate. More than 80 bird species nest here, including peregrine falcons and the globe-trotting arctic tern, which migrates from Antarctica.

Resident mammals include caribou, musk ox, grizzly bears, wolverines and arctic wolves. On boat trips and inland hikes, guided by the resident naturalist, you are regularly rewarded with once-in-a-lifetime sightings.

There is also the opportunity to visit the numerous Inuit archaeological sites in the area, some of which date back thousands of years, and to spend time with members of the Kingaunmuit Inuit clan who continue to live here. In economic terms, their existence is made viable by the lodge, which was established in 1969 by Glenn Warner, a retired Canadian Mountie who fell in love with the region and its people during his regular patrols by dogsled. In 1984, the local Inuit residents became full partners in the lodge with the Warner family, and are now actively involved in running it during the short summer.

Climate change could conceivably extend the five-week opening period, but another possible consequence is less welcome. Due to thinning ice in the Arctic Ocean, the Northwest Passage is opening up as a shipping route between the Pacific and the Atlantic. Plans have been tabled to build a port at Bathurst Inlet, together with an all-weather road to Yellowknife, a development that could have a catastrophic effect on the lodge and on the enduring traditional lifestyle of the local Inuit. Sadly, even in this special place we are reminded that nowhere on the planet is truly remote.

ECOFILE

Rooms: Accommodation for up to 20 guests, with traditional 'honey bucket' toilets (permafrost precludes a sewerage system).

Rates: From CAN$3,592 (US$3,395) for 7 nights per person all inclusive, including air charter from Yellowknife.

Location: On the shore of Bathurst Inlet in the Canadian Arctic, 580km (360 miles) from Yellowknife.

Best time to go: The lodge opens 5 weeks from late Jun into Jul.

Getting there: From Edmonton, take a 1.5-hour turboprop flight to Yellowknife, then a 2-hour light aircraft flight to Bathurst Inlet.

CO_2 emissions: Rtn flight to Edmonton from New York 0.71 tonnes; London 1.91; Sydney 4.14. Rtn transfers 0.41.

Offset cost: $16.60; £17.35; A$84.95.

Responsibility: Although the lodge's policy is to buy locally when possible, by necessity most supplies are flown in with the tour groups. However, the lodge's role in the community is absolutely vital, and guests are provided with the chance to interact with the Inuit, trading stories and songs during the regular cultural evenings.

Environmental: ØØØØØ
Social: ØØØØØ

Paddle power

One of the greenest ways to explore a marine environment is by sea-kayak. **Robin Barton** headed to Baja California for four days of paddling around the protected Isla Espíritu Santo.

There are no hotels, restaurants or tour guides on Espíritu Santo island, just 6m-high (20ft) cacti, scorpions and an elusive indigenous species of wild cat. The only way to stay on the island is in a tent, and the best way to see it is by sea-kayak.

This is how I find myself squaring up to a 1.5m (5ft) swell and brisk squalls charging across the surface of the sea, sitting in the cockpit of a kayak just a few inches above the water. It's the first day of a four-day trip up the west coast of Espíritu Santo, a 9,400ha (23,300-acre) island just off Baja California in the Sea of Cortés, and only my second day of sea-kayaking ever. Thankfully, we've already practised 'wet exits' – the knack of banging on the hull of an upturned kayak, then pulling off the sprayskirt to swim out of the cockpit – with our guide, Leah Blok. All the same though, I'm relieved when we eventually make it to the beach where we will camp for the night.

Jacques Cousteau described the Sea of Cortés – the narrow but menacingly deep channel of water between the 1,600km-long (1,000-mile) Baja Peninsula and mainland Mexico – as 'the world's

This page: Kayaking in the Bay of Candelero as the sun sets over the Sea of Cortés

aquarium'. In terms of flora and fauna, it's one of the most diverse seas on the planet, containing 31 marine mammal species (one-third of the world's whale and dolphin species), 500 species of fish and more than 200 bird species. It's also an extremely fragile ecosystem, under pressure from developers on both sides of the sea. This is why Espíritu Santo, 30km (20 miles) offshore from La Paz at the southern end of Baja, was bought by the Nature Conservancy for US$3.3 million in 2003, when it became a protected area.

Our sea-kayaking trip, organized by the La Paz-based Baja Outdoor Activities (run by British expat Ben Gillam and his wife, Alejandra), is as low impact as possible. Apart from the boat trip over to the island and back, we will be powering our own way up the west coast, converting calories into kinetic energy. Everything we pack in, we pack out, and that means everything. We'll even be using a porta-potty – we can't use a composting toilet because the sand contains no bacteria to break down waste – and we've been asked to wash in sea water with biodegradable shampoo.

The west coast of Espíritu Santo, which means 'Island of the Holy Spirit', is a series of sandy coves divided by rocky headlands. When we're not kayaking, we'll be pitching tents on one of the 20 deserted beaches. In our time off we can practise rescues and

Clockwise from top: The calm waters of a cove protected by 'rocky headlands'; an organ pipe cactus overlooking Playa Coralito; pre-kayaking checks

Clockwise from bottom: Landing at Candelero beach; camping on the secluded beach; kayaks pulled onto the sand after a hard day's paddling

Baja. But this is not an entirely benign stretch of water: last year a female decathlete died during a 13km (8-mile) open-water crossing in the Sea of Cortés – the weather turned nasty and she capsized. Although several fishing boats scoured the area, none could spot her kayak's white hull among the whitecaps.

'Sea-kayaking requires that you think about currents and wind, and you need to take much more notice of the weather forecast than if you're going out on the local lake,' says Leah. In light of her words, I find it particularly reassuring that we mastered a large swell that first day – proving that even in inexperienced hands sea-kayaks can cope with quite severe conditions.

At dawn on day two (with no electricity for lighting, time in bed is determined by when the sun sets and rises), pelicans line up in the blue sky for breakfast, plummeting into the bay one after another like a squadron of dive-bombers. Look closely and you can see them turn their heads sideways at the last minute to protect their oesophagus.

rolls, or snorkel among tropical fish, doing our best to avoid the poisonous pufferfish and stingrays. We can also go for hikes into the rocky interior of Espíritu Santo, where towering organ pipe and cardón cacti bring home the importance of conserving water.

With warm water, mild weather and sheltered seas, few winter kayaking destinations can match

Our day begins with a 10km (6-mile) paddle to Candelero beach, which along with Musteno is the most attractive sand strip on the island. With every stroke I appreciate the pleasure of paddling more: it's all I can do to stop myself racing off towards the horizon like a clockwork toy. As we surf into the bay with the tide at the end of the day, I can see stingrays gliding along the sea floor and there's a profound silence apart from the gurgle of water under my bow.

There's an art to kayaking, and stringing a series of perfect strokes together brings the same joy as surfing. Steering is by foot-operated pedals, which turn the kayak's rudder left and right, although better kayakers can control direction solely with their paddles.

We kayak north at about 3kph (2mph), seeking shelter behind Isla Gallina, Isla Gallo and Isla Ballena, and giving the headlands a wide berth: this is where waves rebound off the cliffs to create a choppy area of water. Clapitus is the technical term for this, although 'soup' is our guide's more descriptive word for it. The longer a kayak, the faster and more stable it may be in rough seas: my 5m (17ft) fibreglass Seaward Tyee is a middle-of-the-road model, but enthusiasts will spend thousands on sleeker, carbon-fibre kayaks. Buoyancy comes from two chambers, fore and aft, and so confirming that the neoprene and plastic covers enclosing these are secure is part of the morning's pre-kayaking checks.

Our final day brings the biggest test, a 4km (2.5-mile) open-water crossing between Espíritu Santo and the smaller Isla Partida, where a sea lion colony will provide the afternoon's entertainment. After just three days, I'm confident enough to relish the challenge. The discovery of Baja California in 1536 may have been the last great adventure of conquistador Hernan Cortés but, like me, you'll want to go back for more.

ECO**FILE**

Location: Espíritu Santo island, Sea of Cortés, between Baja California and western Mexico (tours depart from La Paz, Baja California).

Getting there: La Paz can be accessed by plane via Mexico City. National carriers Aeromexico (www.aeromexico.com) and Mexicana (www.mexicana.com), and budget airlines such as Aero California (www.aerocalifornia.com), fly to La Paz from various Mexican cities. You can also drive to La Paz in 2 days from the US border down the Baja Peninsula, or take a ferry across the Sea of Cortés from Los Mochis on the mainland.

CO_2 emissions: Rtn flight to La Paz from New York 1.78 tonnes; London 2.92; Sydney 4.02.

Offset cost: $44; £30.80; A$97.15.

Rates: Booking tours direct through Baja Outdoor Activities costs from MX$4,600 (US$420) per person on a fully supported 4-day trip. Booking through UK operator Journey Latin America (www.journeylatinamerica.co.uk) costs from £344 (US$690) per person.

Best time to go: Dec–Mar.

Further information:
www.kayakinbaja.com
www.vivalapaz.com

Responsibility: Creating no fumes and no noise, kayaking is as low impact as it gets. Once you're on Espíritu Santo, you're responsible for keeping the island's delicate ecosystem pristine: all waste is collected and removed, and washing is done with eco-friendly products.

Balamku

Majahual, Quintana Roo, Mexico
+52 983 839 5332 / www.balamku.com / information@balamku.com

THERE'S something quixotic about Balamku. The double-storeyed circular *palapa* lodgings, dazzling white under the deep blue of the Yucatán sky and topped with jaunty caps of thatch, look like truncated windmills, waiting for someone to put the sails on so the breeze from the Caribbean Sea can give them a turn.

This hospitable little resort of just eight rooms, in a rapidly burgeoning area of the Mayan Riviera, is quietly lifting the bar for beachside tourism in Caribbean Mexico. The resort exists completely independent of the electricity grid, with a self-sufficient system of solar panels and wind turbines that keeps it powered 24 hours a day. Water is largely recycled into a tropical-fruit and vegetable garden, and composting toilets ensure minimal beachside pollution for the beautiful milk-white sand that lies a stroll from every cabana door.

The interiors of the *palapas* combine North American comfort with Mayan colour and décor – the brightly painted walls are offset by saffron bed linens and a carefully chosen smattering of paintings, sculptures and masks. Most rooms can also hook into the resort's wireless Internet connection. The best accommodation is on the upper storey of the *palapas*, with wonderful views out over the beach and the

brilliant aquamarine sea. Lying in the hammocks on the pretty patios, lulled by the gentle zephyrs, is deliciously relaxing. Food is limited to breakfast – a generous spread of assorted tropical fruit, cooked meats, eggs, cheeses, pancakes, crusty bread and coffee served in the bright and breezy dining room.

A few minutes' cruise down the sandy coast road by car or along the shore in one of the resort's free kayaks gets you to the town of Majahual. Less than five years ago this was a small collection of fishermen's huts; now it is a resort in the making, complete with gift shops and travel agencies. These cater for growing numbers of cruise-ship passengers and a host of eager expats, whose hippy-chic dining rooms sit alongside local fish, beans and rice restaurants, the latter producing the best food.

The sea at Majahual is as breathtaking as the white-sand beach. A reef some 100m (110yds) from the shoreline offers decent snorkelling, with a real possibility of seeing at least one species of turtle. And there's good diving too – especially at the wreck-riddled Banco Chinchorro Biosphere Reserve, the second-largest coral atoll in the world. Here, manta rays, reef sharks and large barracuda are a common sight.

Inland are the sinuous bird- and crocodile-rich lagoons of the Sian Ka'an Biosphere Reserve, along with a host of little-visited Mayan sites. These include the largest pre-Colombian city south of Teotihuacán, Calakmul, which covers 60sq km (23sq miles) in the El Petén rainforest; Chicanná and Balamku (after which the resort was named), with some of the most elaborate carving in the Americas; and Chacchoben, which until a few years ago was little more than a series of mossy mounds in a sea of cornfields.

Nights at Balamku are particularly special, with the gentle lap of waves on the shore and the sky lit by a panoply of stars. In spring, nesting turtles are a common sight. For now, both they and Balamku remain undisturbed by jet-skis and bawdy holidaymakers being towed around on huge inflatable bananas. Sadly, less than 20 years ago the same was true of the mega-resort of Playa del Carmen, just a few hours to Balamku's north.

ECOFILE

Rooms: Eight rooms in 3 thatch-roofed *palapas*.
Rates: MX$770–930 (US$70–85) per night per double room, including breakfast and taxes.
Location: 5km (3 miles) south of Majahual in the state of Quintana Roo on Mexico's Caribbean coast. The nearest major airport is Cancún, 400km (250 miles) to the north.
Best time to go: Sep–May.
Getting there: From Cancún, travel 4–5 hours by bus to Majahual, where a pick-up can be arranged.
CO_2 emissions: Rtn flight to Cancún from New York 0.55 tonnes; London 2.28; Sydney 4.48. Rtn transfers 0.07.
Offset cost: $9.25; £17.60; A$85.10.

Responsibility: Balamku's owners maintain sound practices to protect the resort's environment, while at the same time gently encouraging guests to consider and minimize the impact of their stay. Time spent here would be a good first dip of the toes for anyone new to the waters of ecologically responsible tourism. Most of the staff are drawn from the local community, although the latter would benefit more if the lodge introduced additional local training and education programmes.
Environmental: ⊘⊘⊘⊘⊘
Social: ⊘⊘⊘⊘⊘

Hotel Eco Paraíso Xixim

Municipio de Celestún, Yucatán, Mexico
+52 988 916 2100 / www.ecoparaiso.com / info@ecoparaiso.com

ECO**FILE**

Rooms: 15 thatched adobe cabins.
Rates: MX$1,630–2,071 (US$148–188) for a double room, including breakfast and taxes; MX$1,983–2,423 (US$180–220) with dinner included.
Location: 10km (6 miles) north of Celestún village, near the western tip of the Yucatán Peninsula. The nearest airport is Mérida, 90km (56 miles) to the east.
Best time to go: Sep brings migratory birds, baby turtles and an end to the simmering summer.
Getting there: From Cancún, drive 5 hours to Celestún via the ruined Mayan city of Chichén Itzá. Alternatively, fly 50 mins to Mérida, from where you can take a bus or taxi to Celestún. Some American airlines fly direct to Mérida.
CO2 emissions: Rtn flight to Cancún from New York 0.55 tonnes; London 2.28; Sydney 4.48. Rtn transfer by car 0.24; by plane and car 0.09.
Offset cost: $10.40; £18.20; A$86.50.

Responsibility: Eco Paraíso Xixim minimizes waste production, recycles water, employs local people and sponsors environmental education in the local community.
Environmental: ∅∅∅∅∅
Social: ∅∅∅∅∅

THIS little beachside retreat may be only a few hours' drive from the mega-resort of Cancún, but it sits in a Mexican Caribbean as yet unspoilt by freeways, high-rise hotels and the associated trappings of mass tourism. Like the beaches at Cancún, those around Xixim are made up of miles of soft, powdery, white-pepper-fine sand lapped by a turquoise sea. Yet aside from a smattering of ecotourists, the only visitors here are nesting turtles, terns and shore crabs, and all is quiet but for the wind in the palm fronds and the call of the seabirds.

Eco Paraíso is determinedly low key, comprising a cluster of palm-thatched adobe cabanas nestled behind a line of dunes amid a grove of coconut palms. There are no TVs, phones or air conditioning, and furnishings are simple. Every cabana has an en suite bathroom, a separate sitting area with a sofa bed

and writing desk, and a sleeping area decked out with two queen-sized beds. Louvred windows catch the sea breezes and overlook a small terrace furnished with two armchairs and slung with Yucatecan hammocks made of eco-friendly *sisal*. The cabanas share a small swimming pool and the usually deserted beach is just a two-minute stroll away.

The relaxing setting complements both the extensive programme of wildlife-watching tours available at the resort and the light adventure activities on offer here, which ensure some interaction with nature. The principal attraction is the adjacent Ria de Celestún estuary, home to the only mainland colony of flamingos in the northern hemisphere (totalling some 30,000 individuals), together with 320 other bird species, a number of which are endemic to the Yucatán. The resort also offers a range of Mayan cultural tours. Uxmal and other ancient sites along the Ruta Puuc lie within easy access of Eco Paraíso, and are equally as spectacular yet far less tramped than the more famous Chichén Itzá to the east.

Food at Eco Paraíso is decent. Breakfasts are generous, with a range of cereals, cakes and juices complemented by Mexican staples such as *huevos à la mexicana* (scrambled eggs with tomatoes and onions) and wholemeal *pan Xixim* bread. In the evening, the resort offers a four-course candlelit dinner, usually with a seafood or Mexican main course.

Unlike many resorts in the Yucatán, Eco Paraíso is a responsible operator. The swimming pool and hotel water are solar-heated, and the food served in the restaurant is organic and sourced from local villages. Greywater goes through an anthracite filter and is used to irrigate a garden planted entirely with native species, and kitchen waste is composted for use as garden growbags. Local schools come to walk the nature trails, learn about the resort's recycling systems and visit the small museum by the reception.

Villas Ecotucan

Laguna Bacalar, Quintana Roo, Mexico
+52 983 834 2516 / www.villasecotucan.info / ecotucan@yahoo.com

YOU have to get up early to see one of the best sights Villas Ecotucan has to offer. The lodge sits on the shores of one of Central America's most beautiful lakes: Laguna Bacalar. The Mayan word *bacalar* translates as the 'place where the sky is born', for the sun rises spectacularly over the lake's eastern shore, casting a rich golden, tropical light over the lodge, and the ever-changing moods and colours of the water are like those of the sky itself. In bright sunlight the lake is a palette of myriad blues – almost indigo in its deeper reaches, shading through royal blue to brilliant aquamarine and cloudy white in the shallows. Under a stormy sky cover it is gunmetal grey, fading into turquoise and cream. The changes are a consequence of the exceptional clarity of the water and the white lime that covers the lake's bottom and crystallizes into strangely shaped rocks around its edges. The region is a honeycomb of dozens of underground rivers that cut through the porous limestone of the Yucatán Peninsula and emerge into the lake or surrounding natural waterholes, known locally as *cenotes*.

Bacalar's beauty has not gone unnoticed by developers. Large-scale retirement homes and weekend vacation spots have begun to threaten its pristine beauty, while untreated sewage and run-off into the lake have led to periodic algal blooms, damaging the fragile ecosystem and changing the lake's many colours to a uniform dull green. Together with the nearby ecotourism camp at Botadero San Pastor, Villas Ecotucan is doing its best to redress the balance and establish sustainable tourism as a viable alternative to large-scale development. All the staff are locals and the lodge runs environmental education classes with local schools.

Sound ecotourism practice extends to the lodge itself, which is run entirely on solar electricity. Public areas are built from sustainably sourced local wood and palm thatch, and the five thatched cabanas are each built from the trees that were felled to make space for them. The cabanas lie secluded in their own grove of native shrubs within a pretty garden, which is kept in prime condition using harvested rainwater and filtered greywater. The interiors are bright and spacious, rich in colour, and have naturally cool tiled floors and airy high ceilings.

There are plenty of activities on offer, from kayaking and mountain-biking to trips to the various Mayan cities that litter the El Petén rainforest. These are far less frequented than the more famous Chichén Itzá, yet are equally as impressive. Naturalist guides also supervise walks into the surrounding secondary forest, which is home to more than 200 bird species and small mammals such as the ocelot.

With so much development taking place across much of the Yucatán, it is enlightening to watch the sky being born with each new day at Villas Ecotucan.

ECOFILE

Rooms: Five stone and thatch cabins.
Rates: MX$550–715 (US$50–65) per cabin per night, based on double occupancy and including breakfast.
Location: 5km (3 miles) north of Bacalar, just inland from the Mayan Riviera on Mexico's Caribbean coast. Villas Ecotucan is 350km (215 miles) south of the nearest major airport at Cancún.
Best time to go: Oct–May.
Getting there: From Cancún, travel by bus for 5 hours towards Bacalar, from where it's a short taxi-ride to the lodge.
CO2 emissions: Rtn flight to Cancún from New York 0.55 tonnes; London 2.28; Sydney 4.48. Rtn transfer 0.06.
Offset cost: $9.15; £17.55; A$84.95.

Responsibility: Villas Ecotucan takes its 'citizens of the earth' ethic seriously. With a policy of hiring and nurturing local staff, recycling water, focusing on renewable energy and reducing its footprint on the surrounding area, it sets high environmental and social standards in an area where they are sorely needed.
Environmental: ☉☉☉☉☉
Social: ☉☉☉☉☉

The grizzly trail

Alaska's remote Katmai National Park has the world's highest density of grizzy bears. **Richard Newton** joined a guided walking tour through the area for some close-up encounters.

It's the golden rule of bear-watching: don't get yourself eaten. A fatal encounter will be bad news not only for you, but also for the bear. In a human and bear showdown, the animal will be shot, paying the ultimate price for your mistake.

Modern humans don't naturally belong in bear country. For confirmation of that, I need only look at the backpack wedged behind my seat as I fly by floatplane towards Alaska's Katmai National Park. Packed inside it – besides clothes, food, a tent and a sleeping bag – is a generous supply of insect repellent, water purification tablets, maps, a bell and a can of pepper spray. Stripped of these essentials, I would be at the mercy of the wilderness.

From the air, Katmai appears completely alien. Beyond the coastal mudflats, the terrain is a raw mass of volcanoes and glaciers. The desolate Valley of Ten Thousand Smokes at the heart of the park bears testament to the 1912 eruption of Mt Novarupta, which exploded with twice the force of Krakatoa – it was the biggest eruption of the 20th century. The area is still volcanically active, a fact made clear as we fly past an ominously smoking peak.

Returning coastward, we descend over pine forest to a soft touchdown on Kaflia Lake, fracturing its glassy stillness. Tranquillity soon returns. With the engine silenced, we drift to a beach. I leap from one of the floats and stride

This page: A grizzly bear cub tests his claws. Opposite: Relaxing on a sand bar in the river; a mother and her cub. Pages 40–1: Bears fishing for salmon

up the sand. Turning to face the Cessna, I notice that my footprints have crossed another set, larger, deeper, unshod.

'That's one helluva male,' says the pilot, inspecting the tracks. I don't have to take his word for it. A hundred metres (110yds) along the beach, the grizzly bear in question emerges from a thicket and ambles towards us. The pilot motions for me to edge back to within range of the plane. 'We're upwind of him, so he knows we're here. We'll just let him pass.'

We remain on the sand, stock-still. A cloud of mosquitoes swirls around me. Insects known locally as 'no-see-ums' bite through my trousers, undeterred by the coating of repellent. I hardly notice them as the bear closes in, his cinnamon-coloured coat ruffled by a bitter breeze off the nearby Serpent's Tooth Glacier.

At 20m (22yds) the bear halts, snorts cursorily, then alters course to give us a wide berth. In profile, his size is fully appreciable. Much of his bulk is seasonal. It is mid-September, a time of year when bears throughout Alaska are gorging themselves in preparation for winter hibernation.

Grizzly bears are omnivorous, and at the moment there is plenty of food to go round. The undergrowth is full of ripe berries, and in the rivers thousands of salmon are migrating upstream to spawn. At places like Brook Falls, not far from here, congregations of up to two dozen bears galumph through the water in pursuit of the fish. They

39

are wilfully profligate, often taking only a single bite from a successful catch before discarding it.

So when I head off into the bush with two companions, we have no fear of the bears hunting us down – there are easier meals available to them at the moment. Even so, we must be on our guard. Katmai boasts the world's highest density of grizzlies, with 2.25 per sq km (5.77 per sq mile). Our greatest danger is a surprise meeting.

Because we are the interlopers here, it is up to us to announce our presence as we walk along the bear trails. The bells tied to our packs jangle as we walk. We talk loudly, and in dense cover we burst into song. Making a racket is our first line of defence.

If that fails, and we inadvertently blunder into a close encounter, we must suppress our prime instinct: to run. The bear's instinct would be to give chase, and it could easily outrun us. In response to a charge, we must stand our ground, raise our arms to appear bigger, and talk reassuringly to the bear all the while. That's the theory, anyway.

In the event of things getting really serious, we have three more options. The first is to scale a tree: grizzlies are not great climbers. If no such retreat is available, we can aim a blast of pepper spray into the bear's face. The final option is to curl up into the foetal position and play dead.

It is highly unlikely that it will come to that. My companions have spent weeks on end in this environment without incident. Bear encounters are common, but attacks are exceptionally rare. At this time of year they are most likely to involve a female defending her cubs. When we see one such family on a ridge ahead of us, we stop. The mother stands on her hind legs, scenting us. Then she drops back to all fours and guides her two youngsters away.

ECO**FILE**

Location: Katmai National Park, on the Alaska Peninsula, about 470km (290 miles) southwest of the state's largest city, Anchorage.

Getting there: There is no road access to Katmai National Park. From Anchorage, take a 55-min flight to Kodiak Island, then fly 40 mins across the Shelikof Strait by floatplane.

CO_2 emissions: Rtn flight to Kodiak Island via Anchorage from New York 1.62 tonnes; London 2.15; Sydney 3.59. Rtn transfers 0.04.

Offset cost: $31; £16.50; A$67.60.

Staying there: Katmai Wilderness Lodge (www.katmai-wilderness.com) is the only permanent lodge within the park, offering eco-friendly log-cabin accommodation in prime bear habitat.

Rates: A 3-night stay, including flights from Anchorage via Kodiak and guided bear-viewing, costs from US$2,781 per person and can be booked through All Alaska Tours, (see below).

Best time to go: Mid-Jul, Sep.

Further information: The Katmai National Park Service website www.nps.gov/katm provides the latest infomation for visiting the park. Alaska tours www.alaskatours.com

Responsibility: Bear-watching on foot in southwest Alaska enables you to immerse yourself in an unspoilt environment while creating only minimal impact, as you get around on the trails the animals themselves have made. Besides grizzly bears, other species in the park include moose, caribou, wolf, red fox and lynx. Whales can be seen offshore.

By October, food will be scarce, and the few bears still active will be increasingly hungry. Then the rules of engagement change. Humans are potentially on the menu, and any hike here must be conducted with extreme caution. The reality of the threat was dramatically illustrated in 2003, when the controversial environmentalist Timothy Treadwell and his girlfriend, Amie Huguenard, were killed and eaten by a male grizzly beside Kaflia Lake. The tragedy was documented in Werner Herzog's film *Grizzly Man*, which is essential viewing for anyone planning an excursion into bear country.

It is all too easy to romanticize the bears and their environment. During our four short days in Katmai, we come to fall completely under the spell of the ruggedly beautiful landscape, and find ourselves craving the adrenalin rush that comes with each bear encounter. Yet the wilderness can be tough and unforgiving, and we must accept that for the duration of our stay we are more than mere observers; we are an integral part of it. This is a rare privilege, yet it is also a responsibility.

The Colony Hotel

140 Ocean Avenue, PO Box 511, Kennebunkport, ME 04046, USA
+1 207/967-3331 / www.thecolonyhotel.com / sales@thecolonyhotel.com

SINCE 1914, the Colony Hotel, one of the last surviving New England holiday resorts from the golden age, has sat imposingly on a rocky Atlantic promontory at the mouth of the Kennebunk River. The adjectives come easily as you take stock of this great white wooden edifice: venerable, genteel, grand. But you could also add dynamic, revolutionary and innovative. Unlikely as it may seem, this old, family-owned resort is ahead of its time.

ECOFILE

Rooms: 124.
Rates: US$199–624 per room per night.
Location: Kennebunkport, on the southern Maine coast.144km (90 miles) from Boston.
Best time to go: The hotel is open mid-May–late Oct.
Getting there: From Boston, drive north for approximately 1.5 hours to Kennebunkport.
CO_2 emissions: Rtn flight to Boston from New York 0.10 tonnes; London 1.46; Sydney 5.32. Rtn transfer 0.09.
Offset cost: $2.75; £11.60; A$101.

Responsibility: The Colony Hotel was the first environmentally responsible hotel in Maine, adopting the policy long before it was fashionable. The philosophy is deeply rooted, and includes some quirky touches. For instance, old bedspreads from the guest rooms are cut up and sold in the gift shop as dog blankets.
Environmental: ⬤⬤⬤⬤◒
Social: ⬤⬤⬤⬤◒

The hotel has belonged to the Boughton family since 1948, and is currently in the hands of Jestena Boughton, a lifelong environmentalist. She began to apply her personal beliefs to the running of the hotel in 1989, and in 1994 she formally established the Colony Hotel Ecology Group to bring environmental sensitivity to all aspects of the hotel's daily operations.

Styrofoam containers, aerosol sprays and plastic bin liners were outlawed, replaced with greener alternatives that, at the time, were more expensive. Recycling was introduced, and today the wicker wastepaper baskets in the rooms have four compartments to encourage guests to divide their waste into recyclable categories (if they don't, the housekeeping staff will do it anyway). While other luxury resorts try to keep their green practices as unobtrusive as possible for fear of alienating their pampered guests, the Colony has opted for a more participatory approach. Guest and staff education features high on the agenda, with bulletin boards in the hotel bearing the latest environmental news. On Saturdays in July and August, the resident naturalist leads tours on the nearby beach and discusses the problems affecting Maine's coastal ecology.

Native plants have been reintroduced to the hotel's 45ha (112-acre) gardens, chemicals

have been eliminated in favour of biological control methods, and appropriate leftover food from the kitchens is used for a bird-feeding programme. These measures have contributed to the grounds being designated as a Backyard Wildlife Habitat by the National Wildlife Federation.

Far from putting people off, the hotel's green ethos has become a selling point. Since 1994, occupancy has increased by 15 per cent, and many corporate clients arrange meetings here specifically because of the hotel's green credentials.

The small town of Kennebunkport, which can be reached on foot or by sightseeing trolley, is a popular base for whale-watching tours. In a four-hour trip off Maine's coast, several species are regularly seen, including humpback, fin, minke and, if you're lucky, the majestic blue whale.

As you return to port, the Colony Hotel gazes down impassively, a benign landmark that has watched the comings and goings for more than 90 years. Its time-warp ambience is one of its great attractions. Guest rooms in the main building have retained their classic character, with antique furniture and flowery wallpaper. There is neither television nor air conditioning. But while you may be immersed in a bygone era, the realities of the 21st century cannot be held at bay. The Colony Hotel is living proof that it really is possible to go back to the future.

Dobson House

PO Box 1584, El Prado, NM 87529, USA
+1 505/776-5738 / www7.taosnet.com/dobsonhouse / dobhouse@newmex.com

DOBSON House is architectural proof that two problems can make a solution. Garbage is abundant, affordable building materials are scarce. For maverick architect Mike Reynolds, the answer was simple: why not make houses out of garbage? 'We have mountains of car tyres and there's no way of getting rid of them,' he says. 'When you beat earth into them they become the densest thermal mass you could want. Great for building.'

Over the course of 30 years of trial and error, Reynolds has developed what he calls the earthship, a building that resembles a cross between a greenhouse and a bunker. The thick U-shaped outer wall, which provides passive heating and cooling, is constructed using car tyres filled with rammed earth. The interior walls are built with beer cans and covered in adobe. In its purest form, an earthship is self-sufficient in water and electricity, and disposes of its own sewage.

The environs of Taos in New Mexico are at the centre of Reynolds's earthship revolution. Here, these eccentric buildings have become almost mainstream. At the Greater World Community, 19km (12 miles) north of the town, there is an impressive housing development of 130 earthships of all shapes and sizes. When retired Dallas couple Joan and John Dobson arrived in New Mexico in 1996 with the dream of creating a sustainable bed-and-breakfast on a stunning 10ha (25-acre) hilltop plot overlooking the 100m-deep (330ft) Rio Grande Gorge, Mike Reynolds was the natural choice of architect.

The Dobsons not only commissioned the house; they also helped to build it. During the three-year construction, they hauled into place 2,000 discarded car tyres and 20,000 aluminium cans, encasing it all with 34 tonnes of red sandstone. Power is provided by 26 solar panels supplemented by a rarely used back-up generator, and the garden, which is enclosed by walls made from glass bottles, is irrigated with collected rainwater.

From outside, the 550sq m (6,000sq ft) house looks like something out of *Star Wars*. But radical design has not been at the expense of comfort. The two guest suites are spacious and airy, with separate sleeping and sitting areas, and offer spectacular views of the Sangre de Cristo Mountains. Thanks to the building's design, the interior temperature remains at an almost constant 24°C (75°F).

Eco-friendly construction has a long tradition in this part of America. Not far from Dobson House is Taos Pueblo, a village of multi-storied adobe houses continuously inhabited for more than 1,000 years. Up here, at 2,100m (7,000ft) above sea level, the Pueblo Indians learned how to fend off the extremes of summer and winter by utilizing the effects of sun and shade. Many of the principles they pioneered at what is now a UNESCO World Heritage Site have been incorporated into earthship design, proving there really is nothing new under the sun.

ECO**FILE**

Rooms: Two suites.
Rates: From US$118 per room per night; minimum 2-night stay.
Location: El Prado, just north of Taos, New Mexico, 217km (135 miles) from Albuquerque.
Best time to go: Year-round.
Getting there: From Dallas-Fort Worth, take a 110-min flight to Albuquerque, then hire a car and drive 2.5 hours to Taos.
CO_2 emissions: Rtn flight to Dallas-Fort Worth from New York 0.49 tonnes; London 2.17; Sydney 4.34. Rtn transfers 0.35.
Offset cost: $11.65; £18.50; A$86.65.

Responsibility: The Dobsons have proved their environmental commitment with hard labour. As you sit back and enjoy their wonderful, relaxing home, give some thought to the fact that they built 80 per cent of it with their own hands. That dedication has been carried over into the day-to-day running of the B&B.
Environmental: ⊘⊘⊘⊘⊘
Social: ⊘⊘⊘⊘⊘

Fairmont Chicago

200 North Columbus Drive, Chicago, IL 60601, USA
+1 312/565-8000 / www.fairmont.com/chicago / chicago@fairmont.com

THE skyline of Chicago, viewed from the Lake Michigan shore, is testament to unbridled competition. Companies and individuals have vied for more than a century to build ever higher into the Illinois sky. The surrounding prairies have been swallowed by urban sprawl, and the lake has endured decades of industrial pollution, leaving a legacy of bacteria, pesticides, heavy metals and other toxins locked in the sediment. Several times each year, wave action stirs the release of dangerous levels of pollutants, forcing the temporary closure of the city's beaches.

The lakeside rooms of the Fairmont Chicago provide a vista of this ailing body of water; every time you look out, you are reminded of the city's impact on its fragile natural surroundings. Fortunately, the tide has turned, and a new competition has gripped the city's businesses: everyone is now eager to prove their green credentials.

Leading the way is the Fairmont. At first glimpse, it appears to be an unlikely environmental pace-setter.

It is a glitzy 37-storey five-star hotel located close to the upmarket stretch of Michigan Avenue known as the 'Magnificent Mile'. Conspicuous consumption is what five-star hotels are invariably all about, and the Fairmont's challenge has been to adhere to its green ideals without compromising on luxury.

In 1990, the hotel's parent company, Toronto-based Fairmont Hotels and Resorts, introduced the Green Partnership Program, a radical initiative to bring genuine sustainability to all of its hotels. At the Chicago property, more than 200 environmental initiatives have been introduced, from comprehensive recycling, to the introduction of low-energy light bulbs, to the donation of old uniforms (minus the badges) to the underprivileged. Every employee is encouraged to submit fresh ideas to improve the hotel's sustainability, with each hotel in the Fairmont group competing to be the 'Environmental Hotel of the Year'.

At the start of the Green Partnership Program, the company conducted a comprehensive environmental audit. Some of the findings were shocking. It was discovered that the average guests throws away 1kg (2.2lb) of waste each night (mainly paper products and beverages), and that the average occupied room uses 825 litres (180 gal) of water each day. Now, the majority of the Fairmount Chicago's waste is recycled (there is a dedicated recycling centre in the basement), and water consumption has been cut by a third.

In a hotel of this size, seemingly small initiatives can have a dramatic impact, and they represent a way of operating that any hotel could easily implement. A scheme to recycle used bars of soap for donation to a homeless shelter, for example, adds up to nearly a tonne (2,200lb) of soap being given away each year. And the donation of minibar items close to their sell-by date to a shelter for victims of domestic violence amounts to 4,000 cans of Coke and 1,000 bags of popcorn annually.

A dedicated 'green team', consisting of ten employees from different departments, ensures that there is no let-up in the efforts to maintain and improve sustainability. Rival hotels in the city have taken notice, and many have introduced similar schemes. The Windy City thrives on competition, and now, at last, that competitive spirit is helping to change Chicago's environment for the better.

ECOFILE

Rooms: 692.
Rates: City view rooms from US$169 per room per night; lake view rooms from US$259.
Location: Downtown Chicago, 29km (18 miles) from the airport.
Best time to go: Year-round.
Getting there: Fly to Chicago O'Hare Airport, then take a taxi.
CO_2 emissions: Rtn flight to Chicago from New York 0.27 tonnes; London 1.78; Sydney 4.76. Rtn transfer 0.005.
Offset cost: $4.05; £13.35; A$89.

Responsibility: In 2006, Fairmont's Green Partnership Program received the prestigious Tourism for Tomorrow Award. New innovations continue to be introduced. From 2007, all computers at the check-in desks are wind-powered, which across all the company's North American properties equates to an annual greenhouse gas reduction of almost 100 tonnes.

| Environmental: | ∅∅∅∅∅ |
| Social: | ∅∅∅∅∅ |

Hotel Triton

342 Grant Avenue, San Francisco, CA 94108, USA
+1 415/394-0500 / www.hoteltriton.com

SAN Francisco can always be relied upon to subvert the rulebook. So, eco-friendly design should have an earthy, back-to-nature aesthetic, should it? Step into the lobby of Hotel Triton and think again.

Brace yourself for a blizzard of gaudy colour. First impressions are vital. While you size up the hotel, you can't help thinking that it is making its own judgement about you. Do you blend in with the vivid purple and gold décor, the jazzy furnishings and the eye-popping flower power mural on the wall behind the reception desk? Your environmental credentials may be impeccable, but are you hip enough?

Opposite the gate to Chinatown, and within a five-minute walk of Union Square, the Triton is right at the heart of trendy San Francisco and is a favourite home-from-home for style-conscious, eco-conscious celebrities. Several famous names have even put their personal stamp on the place by designing their own eco-suites.

Anthony Kiedis of the Red Hot Chili Peppers is the guiding hand behind one such suite, the 'Red Hot Love Nest'. The room is decorated with photos of the band and uses recycled touring cases for bedside tables. Other celebrity designers include the actor Woody Harrelson (whose 'Woody's Oasis' suite includes personal memorabilia, hemp curtains and furniture made from fallen trees), the late Jerry Garcia of the Grateful Dead,

ECOFILE

Rooms: 140 rooms. Standard rooms are very small, so it's worth splashing out to stay in one of the celebrity-designed eco-suites.
Rates: Standard rooms from US$150 per room per night; celebrity eco-suites from US$190.
Location: Downtown San Francisco, close to Chinatown and the Theatre District, and 25km (15 miles) from the airport.
Best time to go: Year-round.
Getting there: Fly to San Francisco Airport, then take a taxi.
CO2 emissions: Rtn flight to San Francisco from New York 1.14 tonnes; London 2.43; Sydney 3.63. Rtn transfer 0.004.
Offset cost: $17.10; £18.65; A$68.

Responsibility: The Hotel Triton is the model for Kimpton Hotels' award-winning EarthCare initiative, which has been extended to all of the chain's properties throughout the US. For the average guest, the environmental initiatives are non-intrusive, but every aspect of the hotel's daily operations has been overhauled in the past decade.
Environmental:
Social:

and guitarist Carlos Santana. Ten per cent of the nightly room rate for the eco-suites goes to the celebrity's chosen environmental charity.

The Collage Eco-Suite, created by model Angela Lindvell and designer Alexandra Spadea, and boasting a collage made by fashion icon John Galliano, typifies the hotel's stylish reinvention of sustainable design. In this case, pink is the new green, with unrelentingly rosy walls and fittings. Says Alexandra: 'Since we are trying to bring green to the mainstream we have to beware of the typical green design look. Not only do I want people to fall in love with the room, but I hope that there will be a lot of good love vibe going on in there!'

Yes, this is unmistakably San Francisco, vibes and all. This city, perhaps more than any other in the United States, is receptive to radical thinking, and so, in the 1990s, it was the obvious choice when the Triton's owners, Kimpton Hotels, decided to launch an Eco-Floor in one of their properties. By 2003, the environmental practices that had been introduced on the Triton's seventh floor were extended to every floor of the hotel. These include an initiative to recycle 60 per cent of the hotel's waste (there are recycling baskets in every room), energy-saving light bulbs and appliances (which coincidentally cut energy costs by 75 per cent), low-flow and other water-saving devices, and a responsible purchasing policy.

The Triton is not the first urban hotel to dedicate itself to sustainability. But from the moment you step through the door, and for the duration of your stay, you discover that it is possible for a hotel to deliver genuine environmental commitment while retaining a zany dash of panache.

Inn Serendipity

7843 County P, Browntown, WI 53522, USA
+1 608/329-7056 / www.innserendipity.com / info@innserendipity.com

WHEN it comes to living sustainably, Lisa Kivirist and John Ivanko, the owners of Inn Serendipity, wrote the book. In 2004, they published *Rural Renaissance: Renewing the Quest for the Good Life*, an engaging how-to guide that tells the story of their escape from the stresses of the Chicago advertising industry to their current idyllic existence in rural southern Wisconsin.

From the start, they aimed to forge 'a life simple in design yet rich in meaning'. Inn Serendipity is more than just a charming bed-and-breakfast: for many visitors, it is a watershed experience, providing a first-hand taste of a different, more rewarding lifestyle.

In 1996, Lisa and John bought a 2.2ha (5.5-acre) property near the town of Monroe in Green County, an area that proudly claims to be the 'Swiss Cheese Capital of the USA'. Here, amid beautiful rolling farmland, the couple set about retro-fitting the century-old farmstead with solar and wind power. It now uses 100 per cent renewable energy.

In the gardens they grow organic produce, and they have recently built a solar and biodiesel greenhouse, incorporating straw-bale walls and windows salvaged from a demolished school, to enable them to harvest food year-round, including bananas, papayas and other tropical plants. The vegetarian and vegan breakfasts served to guests are largely home-grown and incorporate ingredients that are often picked that morning. Leftovers are composted to help grow future breakfasts.

Lisa and John offer every guest a tour of the property. If you aren't already interested in the intricacies of organic farming and green energy, you soon will be — their enthusiasm is contagious. Among the many quirky touches is a solar recharging station for their 1974-vintage all-electric CitiCar, which, despite being

ECO**FILE**

Rooms: Two. The Writing Room has an en suite; the Music Room has a bathroom across the hall.
Rates: Writing Room US$120 per night; Music Room US$105 per night.
Location: Browntown, near Monroe in southern Wisconsin. 240km (150 miles) from Chicago.
Best time to go: Year-round.
Getting there: From Chicago O'Hare Airport, drive 3 hours to Browntown, Wisconsin.
CO2 emissions: Rtn flight to Chicago from New York 0.27 tonnes; London 1.78; Sydney 4.76. Rtn transfer 0.09. Offset cost: $5.30, £14, A$92.55.

Responsibility: 'It's tough to teach what you don't know or do,' say Lisa and John. Their commitment to a sustainable lifestyle is evangelical. Everyone who comes into contact with them, either as a reader of their books or as a guest at the inn, is likely to be altered by the experience.
Environmental: ⊘⊘⊘⊘⊘
Social: ⊘⊘⊘⊘⊘

oddly shaped like a piece of cheese, is an ideal solution for minimizing the environmental impact of local commuting.

Owing to Inn Serendipity's rural location, most guests have no option other than to drive here in standard gas-guzzlers. To offset the carbon dioxide emissions of the journey, the room rate includes a donation to Trees for the Future.

In recent years, Lisa and John have purchased their own 12ha (30-acre) tract of forest – Inn Serendipity Woods – in Vernon County, two hours northwest of the bed-and-breakfast. An A-frame cabin is available to rent there, overlooking a spring-fed pond that is apparently perfect for skinny-dipping.

Things are a little more formal at Inn Serendipity itself, but the place does retain the odd bohemian touch. The two guest rooms, for instance, reflect Lisa and John's innate creativity. The Music Room is decorated with musical memorabilia, while in the Writing Room guests are invited to contribute to an ongoing manuscript, *Serendipity – A Novel in Many Parts*.

The connection you are able to establish with past and future guests is in keeping with Lisa and John's overriding philosophy. They may be largely self-sufficient, but they remain passionately committed to developing a sense of community. While you are a guest here, you are welcomed into that community. It is all part and parcel of being in serendipity.

Should I hire a car?

THE basic choice is made for you. If you intend to venture beyond the major cities during your stay in the United States, car hire is a necessity. The country is truly vast, and much of it is out of reach of regular public transport.

But can you justify adding to an already mammoth environmental problem? Vehicles in the United States account for two-thirds of the nation's petroleum consumption and contribute 7 per cent of the world's total greenhouse gas emissions. How can you stand in line at the car-rental counter without betraying your green ideals?

Fortunately, it is no longer simply a question of whether to drive or not to drive. Some cars are greener than others, and an increasing number of rental companies offer reduced-emission vehicles. It's not a perfect solution, but at least it's a start.

One such company is Bio-Beetle Eco Rental Cars, established by green activist Shaun Stenshol (www.bio-beetle.com). His vehicles, which are available for hire in Maui and Los Angeles, run on 100 per

cent biodiesel, one of the most eco-friendly fuels available. The bad news is that there is only one biodiesel filling station in Maui (closed at weekends), and just three in Los Angeles.

A more mainstream option is EV Rental Cars (www.evrental.com), which offers hybrid electric/gasoline vehicles at eight US airports, including Los Angeles, San Francisco and Las Vegas. On average, hybrid cars achieve 1,000km (600 miles) on a single tank of petrol, and can be topped up at any filling station.

The demand for greener hire cars is growing rapidly, and the big players are beginning to take note. In 2006, Hertz (www.hertz.com) introduced its 'Green Collection' of 35,000 fuel-efficient cars, available across the US. Purists may quibble with Hertz's definition of 'green' (no hybrid vehicles have been included initially), but it is a positive indication that America's car-rental industry is on the road to a more eco-conscious future.

Tiamo

South Andros Island, Bahamas
+1242 357 2489 / www.tiamoresorts.com / info@tiamoresorts.com

THE kayak is there for the taking. You haul it across the width of the white-sand beach into the clear, lapping waters of the South Bight, a broad inlet that cuts an azure swathe across Andros, the largest of the 700 islands of the Bahamas. You paddle away from shore, then look back. Something is missing. How did you lose an entire resort?

The answer is, by design. Indiana-born Mike Hartman and his wife, Petagay, first arrived here in 1995 with dreams to create a luxury hotel with a difference. They set foot on a beautiful beach fringed by palm trees planted years ago when there was a village here. Only the mildewed stone foundations remain of that settlement, long since overwhelmed by the virulent tropical vegetation.

'The fact that people used to live here set our minds at ease about building a resort in what appeared to be a pristine location,' Mike recalls. 'We kept as much of the original vegetation as possible, built all the bungalows out of pine from sustainable forests, and designed them on stilts to prevent erosion and maintain natural airflow.'

Tiamo opened for business in 2001. On the surface, it functions like any other small beach hotel, but Mike and Petagay's environmental ethos underpins all aspects of its design and operation. High-pitched reflective roofs and wrap-around verandas maximize passive cooling. The showers are solar-heated and the soap is phosphorus-free. Power

is supplied by the largest privately owned solar electricity-generating system in the Caribbean. Guests are asked to take all of their non-biodegradable rubbish away with them, and natural waste is dealt with by composting toilets installed in every bungalow. The toilets are efficient and don't smell, and they transform the most mundane of human activities into a mission with a purpose – to help make the garden grow. In the treatment tanks under each of the 11 guest bungalows, the waste breaks down into organic peat within six weeks. You find yourself flushing with pride.

The inherent fragility of this island is plain to see when you take a guided nature walk into the interior. The limestone terrain is flat and jagged underfoot, and the landscape is punctured by caves and sinkholes. There is abundant birdlife, and the chance to glimpse an endemic and highly endangered lizard, the Andros Island iguana (Tiamo helps fund research and conservation for the species).

Offshore, you can dive and snorkel on the world's third-largest barrier reef, extending 225km (140 miles) down the eastern side of the island, or explore some of the numerous blue holes of the South Bight. The waters above these holes team with marine life.

In the evening, guests gather in the main lodge and dine together at a long table. Proof of Tiamo's success is in the small talk. Where else do guests chat about solar power and composting toilets? Tiamo has more impact on its guests than they have on it.

ECO**FILE**

Rooms: Eleven passively cooled, solar-powered, wooden-framed beachfront bungalows.

Rates: From BS$295 (US$295) per person per night, including transfers by boat from Congo Town.

Location: On the southern shore of the South Bight, Andros Island, a 30-min boat trip from Congo Town. 106km (66 miles) from Nassau.

Best time to go: Nov–May, when risk of hurricanes is minimal.

Getting there: From Nassau, take a 20-min turboprop flight to Congo Town. Half-hour transfers by boat from there are arranged by the lodge.

CO_2 emissions: Rtn flight to Nassau from New York 0.40 tonnes; London 1.97; Sydney 4.91. Rtn transfer 0.03. **Offset cost:** $6.35; £15; A$92.30.

Responsibility: From conception to operation, Tiamo's environmental credentials are impeccable. By educating local staff and international guests, the resort's ethos is spread near and far. Owners Mike and Petagay Hartman have established the South Andros Island Preservation Initiative in association with local community leaders to promote conservation on the island.

Environmental: ⵁⵁⵁⵁⵁ
Social: ⵁⵁⵁⵁⵁ

Papillote Wilderness Retreat

PO Box 2287, Roseau, Commonwealth of Dominica
+1767 448 2287 / www.papillote.dm / papillote@cwdom.dm

DOMINICA has an identity problem. The island's promotional literature invariably includes the forlorn refrain: 'Pronounced Dom-en-EE-ka – not to be confused with the Dominican Republic'. But confusion is a daily reality, and Dominicans are resigned to having much of their mail end up in the Spanish-speaking republic some 800km (500 miles) away.

Scenically, however, Dominica is unmistakable. Just 26km (16 miles) wide, it rises sheer from the sea, with four peaks reaching up more than 1,200m (4,000ft). The interior is among the wettest places on earth, blanketed in thick rainforest that grows with triffid-like virulence. Hemmed in by unremitting greenery, and lacking tourist beaches, this is the 'Nature Island of the Caribbean'.

Anne Jno Baptiste arrived here from the United States more than 45 years ago, and in 1969 she opened Papillote Wilderness Retreat on a forested hillside in the Roseau Valley, within a short walk of Trafalgar Falls (just one of 14 major waterfalls on the island). Over the decades, her small hotel has taken root in the landscape, blending seamlessly with it.

From the veranda of your room you look out into 1.6ha (4 acres) of dense tropical gardens, a lovingly cultivated chaos of rich greenery and vibrant blooms. Butterflies and hummingbirds flit between the flowers, and the sounds of the surrounding rainforest mingle with the frequent patter of rain. You don't come to Dominica primarily to sunbathe.

Papillote defines what this island is all about. It is like stepping into one of Henri Rousseau's famous jungle paintings. Your immersion can be literal: within the grounds there are three hot pools, fed by the natural mineral springs that bubble up from Dominica's volcanic underworld. After a trek into the mountains, a lazy wallow in one of these spas is the perfect way to unwind.

The most popular hike takes you up steep trails within the nearby Morne Trois Pitons National Park to Boiling Lake, a scorching volcanic spring in the appropriately named Valley of Desolation. Alternatively, you can spend time in the highland orange groves in the north of the island, where two colourful endemic parrot species are often glimpsed, the jaco and the sisserou (proudly depicted on the national flag).

It is best to be away from Papillote during the day if a group of cruise-ship passengers is expected; they tend to overwhelm the place. But at all other times the hotel's drowsy charm is seductive. The restaurant, with windows open to the elements, serves local specialities. At breakfast, you enjoy an outstanding view of the forest canopy in the valley below, and at dinner exotic sounds fracture the velvet darkness while you eat.

Most people who stay at Papillote fall under its spell. Its lush gardens, friendly staff and the indelible stamp of Anne Jno Baptiste's personality are part of the magic, but what is most unique is the sense of connection it gives you with Dominica. Here, you don't just visit the Nature Island; you become part of it.

ECOFILE

Rooms: Seven rooms, including 4 suites, each individually designed and furnished.
Rates: EC$267–347 (US$100–130) per room per night.
Location: Southwest Dominica. Most flights arrive at Melville Hall Airport, 38km (24 miles) from Papillote, on the northeast coast.
Best time to go: Nov–May, when the risk of hurricanes is minimal.
Getting there: From Antigua, take a 40-min turboprop flight to Dominica's Melville Hall Airport, from where it's a 1-hour taxi ride to Papillote.
CO2 emissions: Rtn flight to Antigua from New York 0.63 tonnes; London 1.84; Sydney 5.31. Rtn transfers 0.08.
Offset cost: $10.65; £14.45; A$101.

Responsibility: Electricity comes from Dominica's regular system; more than half the country's supply is hydroelectric (on a still day, you'll hear the hum of the hydro plant at Trafalgar Falls). Papillote has an enduring commitment to local produce, arts and crafts. The gardens are a showcase of local flora.

Environmental:	⌀⌀⌀⌀⌀
Social:	⌀⌀⌀⌀⌀

Unknown crops

Maho Bay Camps & Concordia Estate

PO Box 310, Cruz Bay, St John, US Virgin Islands
+1340 715 0501 / www.maho.org / mahobay@maho.org

THE island of St John in the US Virgin Islands is an unlikely place for a revolution, and an oil billionaire and a civil engineer would appear to be unlikely revolutionaries. But what happened on a hillside here in 1976 helped change the face of global tourism.

The billionaire was Laurance Rockefeller, who bought up most of the island in the 1950s and then turned it over to the US National Parks Service for safekeeping. More than 60 per cent of the total area is consequently cloaked in tropical forest and cacti-studded scrub, spared the rampant development of neighbouring islands. Stanley Selengut was the civil engineer who had the dream to build a few unobtrusive tourist cottages within the national park, which from the start he envisaged as a low-impact resort consisting of environmentally friendly tent-cottages.

Maho Bay Camp invented many of the best practices followed by ecolodges today. The original 18 cottages were solar- and wind-powered, and linked by raised walkways to protect the vegetation and prevent erosion. Roof scoops catch and circulate the sea breeze, providing natural air conditioning. Composting toilets and a proactive recycling programme deal with the waste.

Over the past three decades, Maho Bay Camp has grown to 114 cottages. At the same time, concerted ecological regeneration has improved the natural surroundings. 'We've controlled feral animals and done native landscaping,' says Selengut. 'After well over a million visitors, our 14 acres (5.6 ha) are much healthier as a balanced ecosystem than the park around us. People can actually make it better rather than destroy it.'

The lease for those 5.6ha runs out in 2012, but Selengut is already engaged in a US$20 million project to expand a similar camp on land he owns on the other side of the island. Estate Concordia embraces 21ha (51 acres) of a beautiful peninsula fringed by the Caribbean Sea. Ultimately, it will consist of 40 tents, with a yoga centre, restaurant and 'Trash to Treasures' studio, where some of the resort's waste will be turned into artworks.

Many of the ideas pioneered at Maho Bay have been refined at Concordia. The secluded tent-cottages at the new resort, which sleep up to six, are more comfortable, equipped with private bathrooms and kitchenettes. As at Maho Bay, guests are responsible for their own housekeeping, including making the beds and sweeping the floors. It's not the typical pampered Caribbean idyll, but you soon become house-proud, forging a proprietorial bond with your tent-cottage.

Within easy access of the two properties is a network of more than 20 trails criss-crossing the national park. Some lead to deserted bays, where you can lounge on the sand or snorkel over coral reefs. Or you can head for the hills, with only the birds and scuttling lizards for company. From the crest of each summit, you are rewarded with a panorama of St John, a stunningly beautiful island that is, in more ways than one, fundamentally green.

ECOFILE

Rooms: State-of-the-art eco-tents, each with a private deck overlooking the sea. For a touch more luxury, there are also 9 studio apartments.

Rates: Tent-cottages at Maho Bay Camp are from US$80 per night, for 2 people. Tent-cottages or studio apartments at Estate Concordia are from US$95 per night, for 2 people.

Location: Maho Bay is on the north coast of the island of St John; Estate Concordia is on the island's south coast.

Best time to go: Nov–May.

Getting there: From Cyril E King Airport on the island of St Thomas, take a 30-min taxi ride to Red Hook, from where there is a 20-min ferry service to Cruz Bay on St John. From Cruz Bay, it is a short taxi ride to Maho Bay or Concordia.

CO_2 emissions: Rtn flight to St Thomas from New York 0.58 tonnes; London via New York 2.12; Sydney via New York 5.79. Rtn transfers 0.02. **Offset cost:** $8.75; £16; A$108.45.

Responsibility: After more than 30 years, there is no hiding place for Selengut and his resorts. They can be judged not by their well-meaning aspirations, but on their record. And it is impressive. The green ethos is no mere marketing tool; it has always underpinned everything the resorts are and everything they do.

Environmental:	⌀⌀⌀⌀⌀
Social:	⌀⌀⌀⌀⌀

Central & South America

Main picture: The Amazon River snakes through the rainforest. Left, from top: A monkey at Yachana Lodge; the Bunkhouse and local children at the Black Sheep Inn; a shady veranda, La Quinta Sarapiquí

Locator map & budget guide

● Budget (up to US$100)
● Moderate (US$100–250)
● Expensive (US$250–500)
● Blow out (more than US$500)
Prices are for a double room, or two people, per night

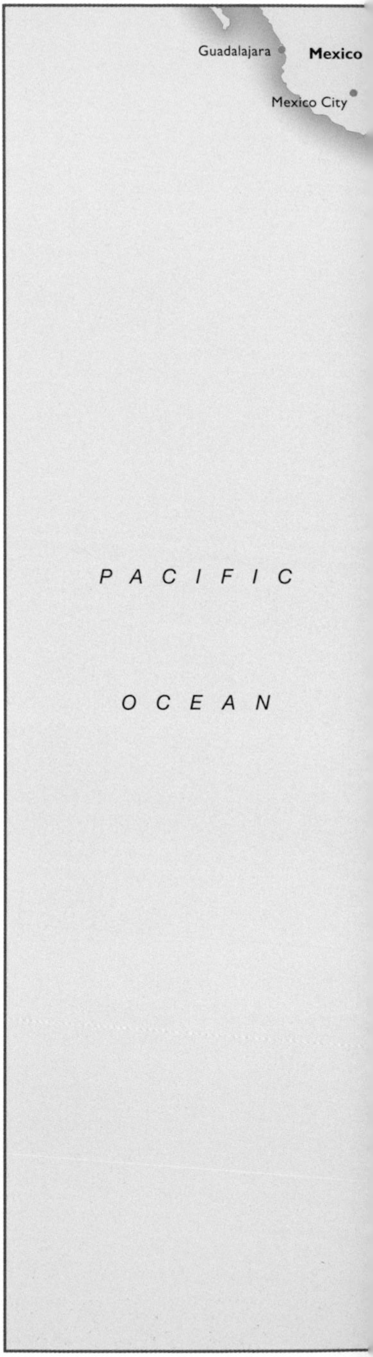

Guadalajara
Mexico
Mexico City
PACIFIC
OCEAN

Accommodation

Features

Ethical travel dilemma

West Indies

ATLANTIC

OCEAN

Caribbean Sea

① Belize
② Honduras
Guatemala
El Salvador ③ **Nicaragua**
Managua ③
④ ⑥
Costa Rica ⑤
Panama

Medellin ·
Bogotá ·
Cali ·
Colombia

Caracas ·
Venezuela **Guyana**
Suriname
Guiana ⑭ ⑰ **French Guiana**
Highlands

Ecuador
⑪ ⑬
⑫

Galapagos
Islands

⑩
Amazon Basin

Belém ·

Peru

ANDES

Lima ·

Brazil

⑧

Recife ·

⑮⑯
⑦
La Paz ·
Bolivia

Ⓐ

Brasília ·

Salvador ·

Brazilian Highlands

⑨

Paraguay

Ⓑ Rio de Janeiro
São Paulo ·

Chile

ANDES

Cordoba ·

Uruguay
Santiago · Montevideo ·
Buenos Aires ·

SOUTH

Pampas

ATLANTIC

Argentina

OCEAN

Falkland/
Malvinas Islands

Cape Horn

South Georgia

Chaa Creek

PO Box 53, San Ignacio, Cayo District, Belize
+501 824 2037 / www.chaacreek.com / reservations@chaacreek.com

ENSCONCED within a majestic 148ha (365-acre) nature reserve along the steep, jungle-swathed banks of Belize's Macal River is Chaa Creek, which has grown organically over more than 25 years into the country's plushest ecolodge.

The lodge comprises 18 palm-thatched cottage rooms and six individually designed luxury suites surrounded by lush tropical gardens. The top-of-the-range suites are hyper-indulgent 'treetop' villas, whose soaring thatched roofs cascade down the hill in a sequence of stepped living areas, culminating in a deck where you can gaze out at the leafy heights from your private Jacuzzi. The garden villas are only slightly more modest, also managing to include four-poster beds and their own Jacuzzis. The simplest rooms on offer are the solar-powered *casitas* (small bungalows) at the Macal River Camp in the thick of the forest.

ECO**FILE**

Rooms: 24 luxurious palm-thatched cottages and villas, plus 10 timber *casitas* (small bungalows).
Rates: BZ$590–880 (US$300–450) per night for a double room; *Casitas* BZ$107 (US$55) per person per night.
Location: 15km (9 miles) from San Ignacio, in the Belizean interior near the Guatemala border.
Best time to go: Oct–May.
Getting there: From Belize City, hire a car and drive for approximately 2 hours to San Ignacio along the Western Highway. The lodge can arrange transfers for an extra fee.
CO2 emissions: Rtn flight to Belize City from New York 0.63 tonnes; London 2.38; Sydney 4.34. Rtn transfer 0.06.
Offset cost: $10.35; £18.30; A$82.20.

Responsibility: Chaa Creek belongs to a bold breed of eco-lodges that take environmentally conscious tourism out of the mosquito net and into the four-poster. The lodge has a total commitment to local employment, forest rehabilitation and organic farming.
Environmental: ∅∅∅∅∅
Social: ∅∅∅∅∅

The lodge runs one of the best spas in Central America, offering a menu of therapeutic massages, seaweed wraps, Vichy showers and even a five-course feast of treatments utilizing the healing properties of chocolate. You can take maximum advantage of the wild setting by opting for a massage on the veranda of your cabin, surrounded by the songs of the forest. And those who like to be pampered in private can even choose to stay in the newly built Spa Villa, set in gardens blooming with hibiscus and bougainvillea, and furnished with its own beautifully appointed therapy room.

Aside from showering you with sybaritic pleasures, Chaa Creek ensures that there is also plenty of opportunity to get active in the surrounding rainforest. Trips usually begin with a visit to the on-site Blue Morpho Butterfly Farm and Natural History Centre, which offers an educational prelude to rainforest fauna, flora and ecology. After this, the forest itself can be explored on foot, in a kayak or on horseback. The guiding is excellent, and there is also a range of self-guided walks around the lodge, including the Rainforest Medicine Trail, which showcases and documents the medicinal plants found in the jungle.

The lodge also runs a broad range of educational and environmental projects. These include repopulating the surrounding forest with howler monkeys, sponsoring environmental education programmes in local schools, and the Maya Farm, which uses traditional Mayan and modern agricultural techniques to produce much of the resort's organic food.

With a 100-strong staff drawn entirely from local villages and a best-practice policy that encompasses recycling, water management and renewable energy, Chaa Creek proves that, just as sustainable doesn't have to mean ascetic, luxury doesn't have to be rapacious. You can indulge yourself here with a clear conscience.

Steppingstones

Englishtown, Toledo, Belize
www.steppingstonesbelize.com / info@steppingstonesbelize.com

WHETHER sports fishing and ecotourism are compatible is debatable. Advocates claim that, by its very nature, angling is low key and low impact, and that its popularity has led to populations of catch-and-release species being protected from commercial overfishing. Critics, on the hand, claim that it is cruel, and that even when fish are put back into the wild their mouthparts are often so badly damaged that they cannot feed effectively. Chris and Sue Harris, the English couple who built and run Steppingstones, stand firmly in the camp of the former.

But there is more to Steppingstones than just fishing. The lodge has been built using mostly locally sourced material (including driftwood) on a caye, or small island, in the turquoise waters of the Belizean Caribbean. There are just two cabana apartments, together with the owners' house and a staff cottage. The entire resort uses collected rainwater and greywater run-off, and is run on solar power, with occasional generator back-up when the weather is cloudy. Despite this, each of the cabanas has round-the-clock electricity, with fridge, satellite TV and power points. In fact, a stay at Steppingstones is a bit like housesitting a friend's beach retreat: you get the run of an entire floor, with open-plan kitchen, living room, two double beds and a bathroom. All are furnished and decorated to feel homey, and there are thoughtful flourishes like shelves full of decent novels and rainy-day board games. The second-floor veranda commands a dreamy view of the Caribbean, shades the room and keeps it cool – so much so that even on the hottest days there is little need for fans or air conditioning.

The Harrises are committed and knowledgeable anglers. They generously share tips on how the local bonefish and permit fish

ECOFILE

Rooms: Two self-contained apartments in a two-storey cabana.
Rates: BZ$215–320 (US$110–165) per night per double room, including return boat transfers from Placencia.
Location: On an island an hour's boat ride from Placencia in southern Belize. The nearest international airport is Belize City.
Best time to go: Apr–Jun is the best season for fishing.
Getting there: From Belize City, fly to Placencia. Boats for the 1-hour trip to the resort leave from the airfield.
CO2 emissions: Rtn flight to Belize City from New York 0.63 tonnes; London 2.38; Sydney 4.34. Rtn transfer to Placencia 0.06.
Offset cost: $10.35; £18.35; A$82.25.

Responsibility: Steppingstones earns kudos for being virtually self-contained in terms of water and energy, and for minimizing its impact on the surrounding land. All staff and guides employed at the lodge are local.
Environmental: ⌀⌀⌀⌀⌀
Social: ⌀⌀⌀⌀⌀

react to various different types of kit, and they're also members of the local fishermen's cooperative (with whom they run projects on marine conservation). There are plenty of activities for non-anglers, too. There's a reef just offshore with great snorkelling (kayaks and snorkelling gear are available at the resort), 1.5km (1 mile) or so of unspoiled beaches for sunbathing, and boat trips that go in search of manatees or cruising whale sharks. One of the best locations for primates in Belize – the community-run Monkey River Village – is nearby, and Steppingstones organizes trips there and into the Belizean rainforest. The lodge is therefore an ideal choice for a combination holiday comprising beach time and relaxation with wildlife-spotting, and – if you feel it's genuinely eco-friendly – some angling.

Finca Rosa Blanca Country Inn

Santa Bárbara de Heredia, Costa Rica
+506 269 9392 / www.fincarosablanca.com / info@fincarosablanca.com

FINCA Rosa Blanca is nestled in a tiered garden filled with tropical flowers and trees, and is surrounded by lush secondary-growth wood-land. Views of Costa Rica's central valley are magical, especially at dawn, when the rich Central American sun turns fields of coffee and corn deep golden and silhouettes the cones of distant misty volcanoes. The lodge combines one of the highest levels of sustainability of any of the green rooms in the Americas with the luxury, intimacy and chic design of an urban boutique hotel.

The best of the hotel's rooms are the master and junior suites housed in the main building. These are clustered around an airy atrium that functions as a split-level communal living area and library. Each room is individually styled. The Rosa Blanca Suite – a two-tiered circular room at the top of the inn – is extraordinary. Stairs lead from a lower room decorated with rainforest murals to an upper chamber with a bed at its centre, windows for walls and magnificent 360-degree views of the valley. Organic shapes and Gaudíesque fittings curl throughout the suite, while in the bathroom an aquamarine tub is surrounded by lush plants and filled by mineral water from an artificial rocky spring.

Other suites are decorated with beautiful tropical art, mock Audubon paintings of forest birds, and indigenous masks. Another popular suite, El Guarumo — an intimate but bright little hobbit hole of curves and arches tucked away along a corridor — is a perfect love-nest for discreet couples.

Despite its beautiful setting, Rosa Blanca is more of a base than a location in its own right. Although the inn's horses can be hired for rides to the nearby Barva volcano, there's no really wild country in the immediate environs, and cars or organized tour buses are a necessity here. Both can be booked through Rosa Blanca or an agency like Camino Travel, as can guided tours of the various national parks, private reserves and cloud forests that lie within a day-trip. Highlights include the smoking volcanoes of Poás and Irazú and the elfin cloud forests around their craters; Braulio Carillo National Park; and tours of some of the best coffee farms in Central America. Adventure activities like whitewater rafting are also easily organized, as are bird-watching trips. Like the standard of service in the hotel in general, the guiding is excellent, and wildlife experts are available on request.

ECO**FILE**

Rooms: 15 rooms (2 master suites, 2 villas and 11 junior suites) in both the main house (these are best) and smaller houses in the garden.

Rates: C140,000–220,000 (US$270–425) per double room per night, including breakfast. Dinner is C18,000 (US$35) extra.

Location: 15 minutes' drive from San José International Airport in the Costa Rican capital.

Best time to go: Dec–Apr is the driest season.

Getting there: From San José airport, Rosa Blanca can arrange transfers to the hotel. Alternatively, transport and tours can be organized through Camino Travel (www.caminotravel.com), a well-regarded sustainable travel operator.

CO_2 emissions: Rtn flight to San José via Miami from New York 0.79 tonnes; London 2.04; Sydney 5.19. Rtn transfer 0.01.

Offset cost: $11.85; £18.05; A$97.20.

Responsibility: The Rosa Blanca is one of only three locations in Costa Rica to have received five Certificate of Sustainable Tourism leaves under the stringent *turismo sostenible* scheme and is a model of eco-tourism best practice. Its recycling, energy conservation and community work are textbook, and ingredients for almost all the dishes on the delicious menu are drawn from its own permaculture garden or local sources. Trees can be planted at the lodge to offset carbon emissions.

Environmental: ⌀⌀⌀⌀⌀
Social: ⌀⌀⌀⌀⌀

Should I stay or should I go?

MANY tourists arriving in Central or South America wonder whether they should even have got on the plane. A return flight from London to Costa Rica, for example, produces 2.5 tonnes of CO_2 per passenger, and from Sydney it's a whopping 4.32 tonnes. Even a flight from relatively nearby New York produces 0.78 tonnes of CO_2. To put this in perspective, scientists claim we need to reduce our individual carbon footprints to about 3–4 tonnes per year (including all household and other personal emissions) in order to avoid dangerous climate change. When you take this into consideration, it's easy to see that your eco-travels may not be as green as you think. On the other hand, the cost of losing tourism in Central and South America would be a disaster for the local environment and, most ironically, for global carbon emissions.

Costa Rica has gained a reputation for its incredible biodiversity: 5 per cent of the world's species are found here, within only 0.1 per cent of its land mass. Less than a generation ago, hunting and deforestation were rife. Yet scientific tourism led to the establishment of the first national parks, and subsequent ecotourism has resulted in more than a quarter of the country being given over to reserves. Costa Rica is now the only nation on earth where reafforestation exceeds deforestation.

The Costa Rican pattern is spreading in this part of the world. Pressure from scientific visitors and ecotourists has led to the establishment of numerous national and private reserves throughout Central and South America, including Manu National Park in Peru, Mamirauá Sustainable Development Reserve in Brazil, Noel Kempff Mercado National Park in Bolivia, and Iwokrama Wilderness Reserve in Guyana. It has also provided a source of income for local people, many of whom would otherwise be cutting down trees to create slash-and-burn smallholdings and hunting wildlife. Even in Costa Rica, jungle lodge guides are almost invariably ex-poachers who have become gamekeepers.

In addition to choosing a green place to stay, there are ways to ensure that a visit to Central and South America is of maximum possible benefit to the locals and therefore to the forest and the planet as a whole. Try to visit projects that rely on tourism for their survival and preserve areas where deforestation would be a real danger without ecotourism – like Cristalino in Brazil (see pages 84–5), or Sarapiquí in Costa Rica (see pages 76–7). Using local guides, eating in local restaurants (not international chains) and buying local products harvested by local producers boosts the local economy and shows local people that sustainable tourism is a real economic alternative to hunting and logging. In many Central and South American countries, wildlife is seldom noticed by the majority of people, let alone valued. Showing genuine, heartfelt appreciation of wild animals and plants, and taking pleasure in the local culture and language, can change values, as it has done in Costa Rica.

Hotel Punta Islita

Península de Nicoya, Guanacaste, Costa Rica
+506 231 6122 / www.hotelpuntaislita.com / info@hotelpuntaislita.com

THERE'S a delightfully secluded, end-of-the-road feel to Hotel Punta Islita. Wrapped around a high bluff overlooking a half-moon bay of tawny sand, the hotel is hemmed in by rocky headlands and encircled by hills cloaked in dry tropical forest. The drive in enhances the sense of romantic isolation, as it has to be coordinated with tidal rhythms in order to cross the two saltwater rivers that cut Punta Islita off from the outside world for half the day.

With its 47 rooms and cottage-like *casitas* occupying every strata from the top of the bluff to the fringe of the bay, plus a nine-hole golf course and a beach club complete with children's pool and playground, Punta Islita is on a more ambitious scale than the average eco-retreat. Yet through sensitive landscaping and design – the rooms are built in an unobtrusive style and hunker down into the

hillside, with screens of vegetation creating a sense of intimacy – it manages to feel uncluttered and in keeping with the natural surroundings.

Elegant rusticity is the hallmark of the rooms, which come with locally hewn teak four-poster beds, plenty of quirky local art, and water – water everywhere! Pacific Ocean views are a feature of nearly all the rooms. The suites include an additional private deck with Jacuzzi, while the *casitas* and two-bedroom villas add an individual plunge pool.

Islita beach, reached by shuttle service from the ridge top, is maintained by the resort to Blue Flag standards. A similar ethic has been applied to its 20ha (50-acre) private forest reserve, maintained under the watch of a full-time biologist to encourage the propagation and preservation of endemic flora and fauna, including howler monkeys and scarlet macaws. The hotel also sponsors a turtle patrol at the nearby Camaronal beach, helping to revive a population under threat from poaching.

True to its green leanings, Punta Islita keenly fosters a positive impact in the local community too. The ever-helpful staff are almost all drawn from nearby villages, and everything from room furnishings to ocean-fresh seafood is sourced from local suppliers.

Most intriguing of all, the resort has harnessed the revitalizing power of self-expression, commissioning local artists and craftspeople to create paintings and sculptures for the hotel, and establishing an open-air art gallery. As well as being beautiful, colourful artworks in their own right, each piece is a representation of an individual's pride, and a symbol of a community that has found renewed purpose with the help of sensitively managed tourism.

When you are not doing your bit to save local culture, chill out beside the swim-up bar in the stunning infinity pool. Here you can plan a day of activities, which may range from an adrenalin-pumping exploration of the jungle canopy by zipline to a soothing hot-stone massage in the resort's Casa Spa. Could there be a better place to discover the pleasures of social responsibility?

ECO**FILE**

Rooms: 47 thatch-roofed rooms, in cottage-style *casitas* and villas.

Rates: C93,000–285,000 (US$180–550) per double room per night, including breakfast but excluding taxes.

Location: On the Pacific coast of the Nicoya Peninsula in northwestern Costa Rica. The nearest major airport is San José, though some international flights serve Liberia, 80km (50 miles) from the hotel.

Best time to go: Early Dec, for perfect weather and low rates.

Getting there: From San José, drive or take a connecting flight to Liberia. From there, charter aircraft transport guests to Islita's tiny airfield, or you can drive down the peninsula along a rugged but scenic road (hire a 4WD).

CO_2 emissions: Rtn flight to San José via Miami from New York 0.79 tonnes; London 2.04; Sydney 5.19. Rtn transfers 0.11.

Offset cost: $13.35; £18.80; A$99.05.

Responsibility: Hotel Punta Islita works hard to achieve a significant positive impact on local villages, with innovative programmes to encourage vital communities by fostering education and creativity. It also takes a leading role in environmental stewardship to make sure surrounding beaches and forests are kept in prime condition.

Environmental:	∅∅∅∅∅
Social:	∅∅∅∅∅

Lapa Rios

Puerto Jiménez, Costa Rica
+506 735 5130 / http://laparios.com / info@laparios.com

ECO**FILE**

Rooms: 16 private bungalows.
Rates: C114,000–176,000 (US$220–340) per person per night, based on double occupancy and including 3 meals, transport to and from Puerto Jiménez, a guided tour, taxes and service charges.
Location: 332km (206 miles) southeast of San José.
Best time to go: The dry season (Dec–Apr), although there are far fewer visitors at other times.
Getting there: From San José, fly 50 mins to Puerto Jiménez.
CO2 emissions: Rtn flight to San José via Miami from New York 0.79 tonnes; London 2.04; Sydney 5.19. Rtn transfer 0.07.
Offset cost: $12.85; £18.55; A$98.45.

Responsibility: Lapa Rios is one of the few tourist facilities in Costa Rica to have been awarded five Certificate of Sustainable Tourism leaves. The kitchen even runs on methane generated by the lodge's pigs, water is solar-heated, and the conservation of resources, energy and water are second to none. Staff are drawn almost exclusively from the local community and trained by Lapa Rios. Their children can attend a special school funded by the lodge.

Environmental:	∅∅∅∅∅
Social:	∅∅∅∅∅

LAPA Rios is living proof that it is possible to run an ecologically and socially responsible operation in the rainforest while at the same time providing luxurious accommodation, excellent food and first-rate service.

The lodge is set in the private Lapa Rios Reserve, made up of secondary-growth jungle, on the Osa Peninsula in the remote south-eastern corner of Costa Rica. The reserve abuts onto the primary growth of the Corcovado National Park, one of the country's wilder corners. And while the landscape in the park cannot compare in expanse and

grandeur with the Amazon to the south, it is fringed by pretty beaches and overflows with wildlife: ecotourism has been so successful in the region that hunting has been almost entirely marginalized.

The lodge is made up of a series of palm-thatched buildings set in forested gardens on a hillside and linked by pretty gravel paths. Views from the bungalow terraces and the restaurant are wonderful – over heliconias and banana palms busy with visiting toucans and capuchin monkeys, and out across recovering jungle to *Carbonera* beach and the sea. Virgin wilderness, cut with fast-flowing clear-water streams and busy with millions of tanagers, trogons and manakins, rises up behind the lodge and ascends into the *Corcovado* National Park. The air here is thick with the call of tree frogs and cicadas, and heavy with the fragrance of rainforest and Pacific surf.

The bungalows themselves are among the most comfortable and spacious in any rainforest, anywhere. Each has two lush, queen-sized beds draped with mosquito nets and set on polished hardwood floors under an 8m-high (25ft) palm-thatched ceiling. Behind is a beautiful hardwood commode with a porcelain basin set below a large mirror. This leads to a large, powerful, hot shower. There's a sofa and a generous desk, and windows as large as a double bedsheet, which bring the natural light streaming in. Despite their huge windows, the bungalows are as private as a locked bedroom – overlooked by only their own veranda, the garden and that magnificent view.

The food at Lapa Rios is excellent, and is served in a vast open-sided thatched *palapa* with an exterior terrace overlooking the forest and the Pacific. If you can drag yourself away from the view, you can indulge in a range of activities, from guided walks and overnight camping in the national park, to dolphin-watching, sustainability tours and even football matches with the lodge employees.

La Quinta Sarapiquí Country Inn

PO Box 43-3069, Sarapiquí, Costa Rica
+506 761 1300 / www.laquintasarapiqui.com / info@laquintasarapiqui.com

WITH a visit to La Quinta you can be sure that you are giving your money to a venture that is 100 per cent Costa Rican. While many lodges in Central America are US- or European-owned and run, La Quinta is the product of the dedication and charisma of a Costa Rican couple – Leo and Beatriz Jenkins.

The Jenkins family have been Costa Rican for generations, and they're imbued with the mix of energy and optimism that characterizes many Central Americans. Leo and Beatriz built La Quinta from modest means, without the generous grants or ample savings invested in many of the US-owned ecolodges in Costa Rica. And while the owners of those establishments are often notable by their absence, Leo and Beatriz are always at La Quinta, taking tours in the forest or waxing lyrical about the endangered great green macaw.

The country inn is set on a former farm in Sarapiquí just north of the famous turtle-nesting beaches at Tortuguero on Costa Rica's Caribbean coast. It makes an easy stop-off on a trip between there and the country's most visited attractions – the permanently erupting Arenal volcano and the cloud forests of Monteverde.

The Sarapiquí region needs ecotourists – this is one of the Costa Rica's poorest areas and has its highest levels of environmental degradation. Here, environmental protection is in the hands of responsible private operators like the Jenkins.

The lowland forests that once proliferated in Sarapiquí are home to one of the world's largest, rarest and most beautiful parrots, the great green macaw, which nests only in mature almendro (mountain almond) trees. Almendros are much sought after for their fine timber, so to protect both the trees and the parrots La Quinta has established the Lapa Verde project, named after the macaw (see Ecofile).

Rooms at La Quinta are simple. Double or twin beds with mosquito nets, terraces and en suites are housed in concrete huts connected by causeways set in a little heliconia-filled garden. Visitors are invited to plant trees here to offset the carbon from their flights, and Leo and Beatriz have introduced shrubs, flowers and ponds that attract numerous tree frogs, butterflies and brilliantly coloured hummingbirds. Much of La Quinta's food is grown in the garden; it is wholesome, varied and plentiful, and served in the large communal dining room. The lodge also has a bar, and there is a swimming pool and small river for cooling off from the tropical heat.

La Quinta is an ideal destination for families with small children. It's not set in the rainforest itself but in a self-contained campus, so it provides a safe base for visiting nearby wildlife sanctuaries and reserves. La Quinta also organizes whitewater rafting, pony treks and forest walks, as well as community-based classes like paper-making and cooking.

ECOFILE

Rooms: 28 rooms in bungalows, either standard or superior (with air conditioning).

Rates: From C34,000 (US$65) per room per night, excluding taxes and food (around C6,000/US$12 per meal).

Location: 90km (55 miles) northwest of San José, the capital.

Best time to go: Dec–Apr is the driest season.

Getting there: Fly to San José, from where the lodge can arrange car transfers. Alternatively, transport to the lodge and tours in the area can be organized through Camino Travel (www.caminotravel.com).

CO_2 emissions: Rtn flight to San José from New York 0.79 tonnes; London 2.04; Sydney 5.19. Rtn transfer 0.06.
Offset cost: $12.60; £18.40; A$98.15.

Responsibility: The inn has established a project to boost the population of the endangered great green macaw by protecting the alemandro trees the birds depend on. The project has two goals: to replant almendro trees, and to buy mature trees (many of which are green macaw nesting sites) from local farmers. La Quinta also actively supports other local conservation projects, which receive less attention than many elsewhere in Costa Rica, and it works with local schools and farming communities. In addition, trees can be planted at the lodge to offset carbon emissions.

Environmental: ⌀⌀⌀⌀⌀
Social: ⌀⌀⌀⌀⌀

Chalalán Ecolodge

189 Sagarnage Street, 2nd floor, Office #35, La Paz, Bolivia
+591 2 231 1451 / www.chalalan.com / info@chalalan.com

CHALALÁN Ecolodge – which sits between the Andes and the low-land Amazon in the heart of one of the largest tracts of wilderness in the Americas – is a testament to the power of ecotourism. In 1992, the *Tacana* people of San José de Uchupiamonas decided to put a stop to illegal logging in their ancestral forests. With help from Conservation International and a loan from the Inter-American Development Bank, they planned and implemented a sustainable tourism project that would protect both their forests and their traditional way of life. The result is a beautiful lodge that pioneered the mix of nature-based eco-tourism and cultural interaction that characterizes the best green rooms in the Amazon.

The lodge is built around Chalalán lagoon, where a fleet of dugout canoes is on hand for exploring the gallery forest and a jetty doubles up as a diving board for early morning swims. The six cabins beside it – three shared and three private – are built to resemble traditional *Tacana* houses, making use of inherently sustainable materials gathered from the secondary forest. Their roofs and walls are made of palm thatch and the floors have been constructed from locally sourced hard-wood. A spacious, shady terrace overlooking the lagoon is slung with a

traditional Amazonian cloth hammock. The only material concessions to the outside world are the tiles in the bathrooms, the flush toilets and the mosquito nets.

Chalalán is entirely staffed and administered by residents from the *Tacana* village of San José, 25km (15 miles) away, up the Tuichi River. It is also solar-powered, and all waste is recycled, filtered or composted. The food is wholesome throughout, with a strong emphasis on river fish. The culinary highlight is *dunuquavi*, a local dish of river catfish cooked in a leaf parcel and served on the last night of the trip as a prelude to an evening of traditional Tacana dancing and storytelling.

Activities include river trips and a range of hikes – self-guided or supervised by *Tacana* staff – on the 30km (20 miles) of trails that surround the lodge. Each of these trails is themed to reveal aspects of the forest, such as the usage of medicinal plants, rainforest animal behaviour, fungi and birdlife. The five-hour trek to the Rayamayo and Eslabon rivers normally results in sightings of both howler and spider monkeys, peccaries and, possibly, Madidi's newest species, the GoldenPalace.com titi monkey (*Callicebus avrei palatti*). The primate's bizarre name, bid for at auction, contributed US$650,000 to conservation funds for Madidi National Park. Between canoe trips and hikes, you can swim in the lagoon or learn to make *Tacana* crafts.

ECO**FILE**

Rooms: Three private cabins and 3 shared Tacana-style bungalows.
Rates: $b2,930–3,500 (US$379–449) per person for 5 days/4 nights, including all meals and transfers.
Location: Madidi National Park, 5 hours by canoe from Rurrena-baque in northwest Bolivia.
Best time to go: The dry season, between Jun and Nov.
Getting there: Fly to La Paz, then take an 18-hour bus ride or fly by turboprop to Rurrenabaque (410km/255 miles) the starting point of a 5-hour motorized canoe ride to the lodge. Rurrenabaque is on the back-packer circuit, with plenty of accom-modation and restaurant choices if you want to break the long journey.
CO2 emissions: Rtn flight to La Paz from New York 1.78 tonnes; London 2.92; Sydney 1.02. Rtn transfer to Rurrenabaque by plane 0.09; by bus 0.07.
Offset cost: $27.70; £22.55; A$76.65.

Responsibility: Chalalán is a model for indigenous communities who want to reclaim their territory from exploitation, and is living proof that ecotourism can benefit both the environment and local people.
Environmental: ⬤⬤⬤⬤◐
Social: ⬤⬤⬤⬤⬤

Spotting jaguars

Noel Kempff Mercado National Park is one corner of the
Amazon where jaguars still lurk in their natural wild habitat.
Alex Robinson went in search of them and was rewarded
with sights few people have ever witnessed.

The first thing I saw as I climbed out of the tiny plane was an old man
in a tattered pink shirt running towards us at some speed from the
jungle camp. He was clearly distraught. 'Get me out of here!' he splut-
tered. 'There's a big jaguar in the camp every night…right outside my
room! I know he's going to come in through my window and take me!
I can't sleep here anymore! Take me back to Santa Cruz!'

I looked at Tim, who'd be our guide for the next ten days. 'Oh,
don't worry,' he said to me, 'jaguars don't eat people,' then turned to
reassure the old man likewise in gringo Spanish. But he didn't look
convinced and he was a local – so I wasn't so sure either.

The day before I had seen my first jaguar, safe behind the walls of a
sunken enclosure in Santa Cruz zoo – and it was no pussy cat. Staring
back at me with a regal self-assurance was 20 stone of rippling muscle,

This page: The tabletop of Huanchaca at the centre of the park. Opposite: 'El Encanto'

claws and teeth. Here in the jungle I was sure they'd be larger and fiercer, and I looked at Los Fierros – the cluster of little huts that was to be home for the next two nights – with some trepidation.

For years I'd cherished a David Attenborough-induced dream of getting into the heart of the living rainforest. It had taken me on treks in leech-infested Sumatra, through Australia's Daintree and to the Mayan temples of El Petén in southern Mexico. But even within the first few minutes spent at Los Fierros I could see that these had been mere walks in the woods compared to the Amazon. There was wildlife everywhere. Big cat footprints covered the dust runway, which from the air had looked like a tiny red gash scratched out of a vast green sea of trees and savannah. Chestnut-fronted macaws cackled in the trees, and a family of coatis scurried through the undergrowth.

Noel Kempff Mercado National Park is one of the most spectacular rainforest destinations in the world – a pristine 1.5 million ha (3.7 million-acre) expanse of forest, savannah and wetlands centred on Huanchaca, a 250sq km (100sq mile) tabletop mountain rising sheer from the surrounding plains. Such mountains stretch north into Brazil and right across the great central plains of South America, but it is only here, and in the Jalapão region and around the Río Negro in northern Brazil, that they are still close to a primordial state. Huanchaca was discovered by a pilot and biologist Noel Kempff Mercado, who

This page: Taking only pictures and leaving only footprints; the park's thick undergrowth is the perfect hiding spot for jaguars

across a 1sq m (10sq ft) window. The noise in the dark beyond was unearthly, with all manner of coughs, barks, scuffles and snarls. Something sniffed and snorted a few feet away from the door. In the end, I slept in the shower.

Adrenalin must have kept me from feeling groggy the next day, because we were up at dawn, racing through dry *cerrado* (savannah) forest towards the edge of Huanchaca. Along the way, the Jeep kept breaking thick cobwebs draped between the trees, and when we climbed out of the car the bull bar and cab were covered in spindly green spiders.

'We walk from here,' said Tim, pointing to a little trail that cut into the dark forest. I felt like we were about to enter Tolkien's Mirkwood. We climbed up a low incline under the towering trees. Black spider monkeys frolicked above us in the canopy and every now and again an electric-blue morpho butterfly glided gently across the path. Yellow sunlight dappled the ground and the air was thick with strange scents — heavy perfume from occasional flowers, damp leaves and the pungent, porky musk of a passing herd of peccaries. They were some way off, but Tim still got nervous and forced us to stop near a cluster of tall trees and keep quiet until the pig grunts and clatter of teeth had faded into the background whirr of cicadas.

The path steepened and became more rocky, and after about three hours I began to hear the far-off rumble of a giant waterfall. Eventually it became distant thunder and then a roar,

became entranced by its beauty and unique biodiversity. He championed the mountain in the Bolivian parliament and his work led to it becoming a national park. It also led to his death, as he was shot on the mountain by cocaine traffickers in 1986. Today, the traffickers are long gone and the park is a UNESCO World Heritage Site. Even so, it is still in peril and desperately underfunded.

But it is wild — so much so that I didn't sleep at all well that first night. We were allocated a cabin on the edge of Los Fierros, right next to the forest itself. All that separated us from the Amazon was a millimetre of plastic gauze which drowned out even the shrill calls of the screaming piha birds. As we rounded a corner, the forest cleared like a stage curtain to reveal the most beautiful waterfall I've ever seen.

'El Encanto,' said Tim, 'the Enchanted One. Besides yourselves, only a few thousand people have ever seen it.' Water poured from a cleft carved out of the towering sunburned rock face of Huanchaca some 100m (300ft) above. The stream fell, then seemingly paused and fell again, eventually plunging into a deep, clear pool of cool water. The rocks behind were covered in layers of dripping moss, and as we arrived a flock of brilliant scarlet macaws floated in front, contrasting perfectly with the velvety green.

After several hours of swimming and soaking up the sun, it was hard to say our goodbyes to El Encanto and we left it far too late. We arrived back at camp well into the night, after weaving through the *cerrado* and leaving startled anteaters, crab-eating foxes and racoons in our wake. Following a late supper we walked back to the runway with halogen lamps, and Tim shone the beam along the red dust. At the far end, a pair of deep green cat eyes stared back at us before blinking and disappearing into the trees.

On the flight back to Santa Cruz I looked out of the little Cessna at the carpet of green that stretched around Huanchaca. What first appeared as an infinite horizon was transformed after only half an hour into a patchwork of soybean and cattle land. I reflected that it was only because of the curiosity of a tourist – Noel Kempff Mercado himself – that there was forest around Huanchaca at all. No doubt he would have been pleased that the money from ecotourists like me is helping to ensure that the park's jaguars and trees remain safe from poachers and loggers.

ECO**FILE**

Location: 600km (372 miles) from Santa Cruz in northeastern Bolivia, on the Río Iténez/Guaporé, which forms the border with Brazil.

Getting there: By plane with the Fundación Amigos de la Naturaleza (FAN; see 'Further information'), or on a tour organized by a South American operator such as Neblina Forest (www.neblinaforest.com) or a local operator such as Ruta Verde (www.rutaverdebolivia.com).

CO_2 emissions: Rtn flight to La Paz from New York 1.78 tonnes; London 2.92; Sydney 4.02. Rtn transfer 2.23.

Offset cost: $44; £30.80; A$97.15.

Staying there: There are 2 jungle camps in the park: Los Fierros, in the heart of the forest (best for wildlife); and Flor de Oro, on the Iténez. Guests at Los Fierros stay in simple fan-cooled cabins with en suites and queen-sized beds. Flor de Oro is a bit more comfortable – some rooms have terraces and air conditioning.

Rates: Vary depending on the transport chosen and the operator, but generally around $b1,160 (US$150) per day, including meals.

Best time to go: Mar–Sep.

Further information:
Noel Kempff Mercado NP +591 3 355 3835, www.noelkempff.com
FAN +591 3 329 717, www.fan-bo.org

Responsibility: FAN works with the Bolivian government, NGOs and ecotourism operators. Its efforts ensure the ongoing survival of this unique South American biome, and it also supports villages within the park. All tour operators work through the organization, so you can be sure any visit is helping to protect the park.

Cristalino Jungle Lodge

Alta Floresta, Mato Grosso, Brazil
+55 66 3512 7100 / www.cristalinolodge.com.br / info@www.cristalinolodge.com.br

BIRDWATCHERS, hang on to your hats. This amazing wildlife lodge is the best place in South America to see lowland Amazon species. Among the 550 bird species recorded here, spectaculars like the harpy eagle and zigzag heron are common sights. Aside from Iwokrama in Guyana (see pages 100–1), there's nowhere in the Amazon where visitors stand a better chance of seeing tapirs, jaguars and other big mammals.

The Fundação Ecológico Cristalino (Cristalino Ecological Foundation) private reserve, which is owned by the lodge, and the adjacent Cristalino State Park, which extends northward into the state of Pará, are a refuge for Amazonian wildlife fleeing from the ravages of the central Brazilian soybean, cattle and logging industries. The region was included as one of the 'highest priority areas for conservation of biodiversity' in the Brazilian Amazon, as defined by the seminal *Biodiversidade Amazônia* workshop held at *Macapá* in 1999. Up until the mid-1970s, this area formed the heart of an enormous stretch of lowland rainforest that extended not only north to the distant Amazon River, but also nearly 1,000km (600 miles) south towards the Pantanal wetland region. Today, however, fields extend almost all the way to the Pantanal, and even Cristalino State Park is threatened by the powerful farming lobby that dominates local politics. As Cristalino relies largely on tourism for its existence, and for its conservation campaigning (through the Cristalino Ecological Foundation) and scientific and community work, there can be few lodges anywhere better suited to a visit from conscientious travellers, and nowhere in South America more deserving of ecotourist dollars.

The lodge has a range of rooms. The VIP cabins are the most comfortable rainforest rooms south of Costa Rica: stylish tile-roofed wooden chalets with windows for walls, double beds, en suite bathrooms with solar-powered hot-water showers, separate living areas with sofas and hammock-slung terraces. Standard rooms are simpler, in concrete cabins with tiled floors, double or twin beds and en suites. The cabins are set in a forest glade dotted with fruit trees, and are connected to one another and the restaurant area by pathways. There are also more Spartan dorm rooms in the main restaurant and complex.

Wildlife is the focus of activities at Cristalino, but there are also options for adventure activities like rappelling and camping in the forest, which involves sleeping in hammocks. Facilities are excellent and the guiding is the best in the Amazon. The bird list was compiled by legendary ornithologists like Robert Ridgley and Kevin Zimmer, and is thick with endemics. Specialist birding guides can be organized on request to up your species count, but the lodge guides generally know where to find even the most elusive animals. The 50m-high (160ft) viewing tower is the best in the neotropics and offers the chance to see numerous canopy species as well as rare *saki* and *titi* monkeys. There is also a hide next to a clay lick for viewing tapirs, peccaries and, occasionally, big cats. Telescopes, binoculars and tape recorders are available, and there is an excellent small library of field guides. Self-guided and guided walks and canoe and launch trips give guests the chance to spot more wildlife, and there are optional trips to riverine communities and the harpy eagle nest at the lodge's twin hotel in Alta Floresta town, two hours away.

ECOFILE

Rooms: Four VIP bungalows, 8 standard bungalows, 5 dorms with 2 beds per room and shared bathrooms.

Rates: R$240–340 (US$125–175) per person per night, including all meals, local and naturalist guides and transfers from Alta Floresta.

Location: 819km (508 miles) north of Cuiabá, capital of Mato Grosso state in central Brazil.

Best time to go: Year-round.

Getting there: Fly to Cuiabá via São Paulo, then take a 2-hour flight or 12-hour overnight bus to Alta Floresta, where you will be met for the final 1.5-hour van and powerboat trip to the lodge.

CO_2 emissions: Rtn flight to Cuiabá via São Paulo from New York 2.49 tonnes; London 3.08; Sydney 4.46. Rtn transfer to Alta Floresta by plane 0.19; by bus 0.15.

Offset cost: $39.80; £24.45; A$86.90.

Responsibility: Cristalino gets a full five leaves for having a private rainforest reserve that is one of the most important bastions against rainforest destruction in the region. It practises recyling, treats wastewater and blends in well with the forest.

Environmental:	ØØØØØ
Social:	ØØØØØ

Fazenda San Francisco

Estrada Miranda-Corumba, Pantanal, Mato Grosso do Sul, Brazil
+55 67 325 6606 / www.fazendasanfrancisco.tur.br / sanfco@terra.com.br

IT is advisable to watch where you're going in the Pantanal. The place swarms with spectacled cayman (a kind of crocodile), herds of capybara (the world's largest rodent), anaconda (no introduction required) and, as if that wasn't quite enough, big cats. This mix of wilderness and cattle country covers an area of swamp, forest, savannah and scrubland almost as large as France, preserving 3 per cent of all the wetlands on earth. It is thick with birds, including the ostrich-like rhea and the 1.5m-tall (5ft) jabiru stork. Sharp-taloned beady-eyed raptors are as abundant as crows in a cornfield, and the bawdy yell of parrots and macaws ricochets through the burning sky. The best place of all in the Pantanal to see these creatures is at the Fazenda San Francisco.

The lodge has a long way to go before it reaches the high ecotourism standards attained by its fellow countrymen at Cristalino (see pages 84–5) and Uakari (see pages 88–9). Recycling is scant, energy conservation lax and the environmental education of staff minimal. Yet despite this, Fazenda San Francisco plays a crucial ecotourism role. It is

a pioneer in the heart of southern Mato Grosso do Sul's macho cattle-ranching country, and runs a unique programme of big cat protection that allows for the survival of jaguar, puma and ocelot alongside herds of cattle.

Since the turn of the millennium, the lodge has been managing the *Gadonça* project, investigating whether it is possible to run a profitable cattle ranch without culling big cats. Its research clearly demonstrates that when ranchers preserve healthy populations of deer, capybara and peccary, big cats kill them in preference to domestic cattle. *Gadonça* has also proved that the tourist revenue earned from spotting jaguars in the wild far exceeds the money saved (in heads of cattle) by killing them.

Nowadays, San Francisco all but guarantees a sighting of at least one species of big cat during an overnight stay. Guests also always see plentiful cayman, capybara, rhea and marsh deer, and can enjoy birdwatching second to none outside the Amazon.

Accommodation at the lodge is in simple concrete huts set in a bougainvillea garden visited by hundreds of red-capped cardinals, busy flocks of parakeets and families of rhea. The double or twin air-conditioned rooms have tiled floors, en suites and fridges. Paths connect the huts to a swimming pool, terraced public lounge and a cavernous open-sided refectory that serves huge portions of meaty fare – complemented by local staples of red beans, rice, squash and assorted vegetables – to feed hungry wildlife-spotters.

ECO**FILE**

Rooms: Nine apartments in concrete cabins, sleeping 28 people.
Rates: R$249 (US$128) per person, based on double occupancy in an apartment with air conditioning, a fan and a fridge, and including 2 diurnal tours and a night tour or night activity, breakfast, lunch and dinner, a local guide and insurance.
Location: 36km (22 miles) from Miranda and 232km (144 miles) from Campo Grande.
Best time to go: Aug–Sep is the best season for wildlife. Nov–Mar is wet and the Pantanal floods; the rest of the year is dry. Temperatures can reach 40°C (104°F) in Jul–Aug.
Getting there: From São Paulo or Rio de Janeiro, fly to Campo Grande. Buses run from there to Miranda, or the lodge can arrange transfers.
CO2 emissions: Rtn flight to São Paulo from New York 2.17 tonnes; London 2.75; Sydney 4.14. Rtn transfers by plane and bus 2.88.
Offset cost: $74.45 £41.90; A$130.45.

Responsibility: It is against Brazilian environmental law to kill big cats. Yet despite this, jaguars, pumas and ocelots are perceived as threats to livestock and are often shot on sight. Their pelts are openly displayed on walls and floors, even in many self-proclaimed 'ecolodges'. In contrast, at San Francisco they not only buck this trend but also provide a business model that could be crucial for the survival of the largest big cat populations in the Americas.
Environmental: ∅∅∅∅∅
Social: ∅∅∅∅∅

Mamirauá Reserve & Uakari Lodge

Tefé, Amazonas, Brazil
+55 97 3343 4160 / www.uakarilodge.com.br

MAMIRAUÁ Sustainable Development Reserve lies in the heart of the Amazon rainforest between two great arteries of water – the Amazon and its black-water tributary, the Río Negro. Together with the adjacent Amanã Reserve and contiguous Jaú National Park, Mamirauá forms the largest tract of protected tropical rainforest on the planet – an area larger than most European countries. That it exists at all is largely because of the work carried out here, and a visit to the reserve will help to ensure that this work continues.

In the rainy season, the Negro and Amazon are connected by a network of waterways that teem with life. Birds and fish are so abundant that the area is one of a handful protected under the international Convention on Wetlands treaty as invaluable to the future of the planet's biodiversity. Among the thousands of rare, threatened and endangered species are numerous large riverine mammals, and reptiles including two species of dolphin, as well as manatee and rare black cayman. There is an abundance of primates unrivalled anywhere in the world. And this is to say nothing of the scenery, with its seemingly endless labyrinths of fresh water, its vast skies and unbroken expanses of rainforest.

Visitors to Mamirauá are accommodated in the Uakari Lodge, named in honour of the red-faced monkey whose protection was ultimately the raison d'être for the establishment of Mamirauá. There can be nowhere more integrated with the Amazon itself than a lodge that rises and falls with its waters, staffed by the descendants of people who have lived with the river for thousands of years. Wildlife is everywhere. The calls of the frogs, cicadas, monkeys and birds in the surrounding trees are an ever-present soundtrack. Dolphins fish and blow in the river's waters, and an enormous black cayman lives like a troll below the lodge's restaurant.

Rooms are spacious but simple wooden affairs, with en suites, double beds with mosquito nets, and enormous windows with fly screens. The food here focuses on river fish, rice and beans, served with green salads, and to drink there are juices made from a bewildering variety of fruits unfamiliar to non-Amazonians – like pungent cupuaçu, refreshing tapereba or camu camu, with more vitamin C than any other fruit so far discovered.

Mamirauá is dominated by water – the Amazon heartland feels more like a series of ever-entwining giant lakes broken by causeways of terra firma forest than a collection of rivers. As a result, days in the reserve are spent largely on the river, either in motorized launches or dugouts, with short walks through the forests and visits to caboclo villages. Guiding is first class, and the lodge also has a small library of helpful field guides.

Although the reserve was created to protect and sustain the forests and their people and wildlife (largely through the sheer determination of a group of Brazilian and European scientists), ecotourism is crucial to its survival. Mamirauá receives both governmental and non-governmental funding (through organizations like the Wildlife Conservation Society), but tourist income supports many of the community projects run within the reserve. Tourists also provide one of a range of sources of sustainable income for an increasing proportion of the 10,000 caboclo people living in the reserve, and they are encouraged to visit local villages.

ECOFILE

Rooms: Ten floating wooden cabins, twin or double, all with en suites.

Rates: R$290 (US$150) per person per night, including all meals and transfers from Tefé; reductions for longer stays.

Location: Mamirauá Sustainable Development Reserve, a 2-hour launch ride from Tefé town. Tefé sits on the banks of the Amazon River, 663km (411 miles) upstream of Manaus, the capital of Amazonas.

Best time to go: Year-round. The rivers are highest Apr–Aug.

Getting there: From Manaus, take a connecting 40-min flight to Tefé or a 2-day Amazon River boat journey (food is included in the ticket price and you sleep in hammocks on the deck – supply your own hammock and rope to tie it to the beams). From Tefé, take a 1-hour motor canoe to the Uakari Lodge.

CO_2 emissions: Rtn flight to Manaus via Miami from New York 1.47 tonnes; London 3.09; Sydney 5.89. Rtn transfer to Tefé by plane 0.15.

Offset cost: $24.10; £24.30; A$113.

Responsibility: Mamirauá has been instrumental in creating the largest area of protected tropical forest in the world. Recycling, energy conservation and extensive work with local communities make this a model of Amazonian ecotourism.

Environmental:	ⵁⵁⵁⵁⵁ
Social:	ⵁⵁⵁⵁⵁ

Favela chic?

The *favelas*, or slums, of Rio may be better known for their high crime rates than as visitor destinations, but **Alex Robinson** found that these communities are welcoming organized tours.

Left to right: The sprawling favelas of Rio; tourism creates a source of income for this local artist; a crèche for orphans funded by tourism; local children in the favelas

Perhaps it's because of Seu Jorge or the Favela Chic clubs and CDs. Perhaps it's because of the music videos and grainy TV adverts inspired by the Brazilian film *City of God*. But Rio de Janeiro's *favelas*, or slums, are, it seems, cool. At least five new companies have started *favela* tours in the last few years, while others offer trips to *favela* dance parties. Since 2005, it has even been possible to stay in a *favela* hotel. Some Brazilians are merely perplexed: why do gringos want to visit a *favela*? Do they know how dangerous it is there? Others are insulted: are the world's rich descending on Rio to go on safari in the urban jungles of the world's poor? Do they want to see 'the exotic other'? I'd resisted the temptation to visit the *favelas*, but on a trip to Rio in the spring of 2007 I decided it was time to investigate.

I started with some reading, then wished I hadn't. In 2005, UNESCO Brazil published a report on violence in the country, most of which takes place in *favelas*. Among other things it states the following: 'More people have died of gunfire in Brazil than in conflicts such as the Gulf War, the First and the Second Intifadas, the dispute between Israel and Palestine and the conflicts in Northern Ireland, both in terms of absolute figures and in annual averages.' Gunfire, the report claims, is the most common form of death for Brazilians under 25, and more people of any age are killed by guns in Brazil than on the roads. I remembered a Rio friend of mine telling me how she had gone to visit a schoolfriend in a *favela* the day after a police

shoot-out and witnessed 'blood trickling out of one little alley into the open gutter'.

The Irish and English who went with me to Rocinha – Rio's largest slum – seemed less than aware of the facts. 'When you hear a firework go off,' said Luís, the guide on our walking tour, 'that's the drug runners letting each other know that the police have arrived.' Everyone grinned. We'd seen a patrol car pass up the little road winding into Rocinha a few minutes before – tanned arms out of the windows, AK47s propped against the wing mirrors. It was like a cartoon. Luís didn't think it was funny. 'I'm telling you this to warn you,' he went on earnestly. 'The community welcome us here, but be careful with picture-taking after you hear a firework.' The community meant the traffickers: many of Rio's *favelas* are run by organized crime. I once interviewed Anderson Sá, the lead singer of Grupo AfroReggae, who grew up in Rio's most notorious *favela*, Vigario Geral. He'd told me that

This page: Locals and tourists come together on the dance floor at a *baile funk*, a party held in Rio's poverty-ridden *favelas*

tacit supporter like for a football team. Every kid has his idols and ours were the traffickers. They had the power and the respect. They had the best clothes and the best-looking girls. And I knew no different.'

We tourists, it seemed, were in Rocinha because the traffickers wanted us to be there. But why?

Luís led us through a honeycomb of pedestrian alleys lined with little bars and shopfronts. One was a hairdresser, complete with an enormous woman in curlers. An old man was lazily reading a paper in another, a dog lying asleep in the corner. Young girls giggled. Then we veered down a steep alley barely wide enough for two and up a narrow flight of steps into a graffiti artist's studio. Naive paintings of Rio's views and a smattering of conceptual art covered the walls. The artist gently touted his work and I asked him what he thought of tourists coming here. '*Muito legal.* Great,' he said. 'I sell paintings,

for as long as he could remember he and his friends had played cops and robbers, and the robbers were always the good guys. 'As we grew up it was natural to gravitate towards the gangs, as a

other people run a crèche for orphans with tourist money.' Then he turned to me and added, 'You know…there are people who leave Rocinha every morning wearing suits and ties on their way to jobs behind a desk in a bank. I want outsiders to know that we are normal people.'

Later that night I went to a *baile funk*. These are weekend parties held in warehouse-sized buildings in *favelas* throughout Rio. Enormous bouncers on the door searched us for guns and we went nervously with our guide straight to the VIP area. But before long I and the other tourists were on the dance floor, writhing and wriggling with the Brazilians. Everyone was welcoming and friendly. 'My best freernd livin in Clap Ham, Lawndon,' one enormous shirt-less guy told me in grinning broken English. 'You speak Português? An you from Brighton!' a girl exclaimed. 'My cousin live there! You know the Honey Club?' I knew it well. I'd been there only a few weeks before. I smiled at her and looked around me at the *baile funk*. Half-drunk men were trying to attract the attention of uninterested groups of girls. Couples were snogging in the corner. Well-groomed muscled types in tight shirts were leaning against the walls trying hard to look aloof and cool. Suddenly it all looked very like the Honey Club: suburban and totally normal; a long way from the exotic other, but not so very far from home.

The tour and the dance party changed my perspective. Companies like Be a Local, Rio Hiking and Marcelo Armstrong's Favela Tour are responsible operators, helping to support projects within the *favelas* they visit. And in the decade they've been operating, no tourist has ever met with trouble – a sure sign that in the eyes of the *favelas* they are friends who are helping to show the world their dignity.

In his famous song *Eu Sou Favela (I am the Favela)*, the great samba singer Bezerra da Silva sang that Rio's slums are not a refuge for bandits but a social problem. And whilst Brazil's politicians fail to address this problem it is left to private citizens like Luís and Marcelo to make a difference. Visiting a *favela* with a responsible operator is a resoundingly good thing.

ECOFILE

Location: Rio de Janeiro.

Getting there: Staying in a *favela* is not advised and on no account attempt a self-guided tour; instead, go with a local tour operator. The best of these are Be a Local and Favela Tour, both run by excellent English-speaking operators. If the prospect of visiting a *favela* is too daunting, the Santa Teresa Tour run by Rio Hiking is a fascinating insight into Rio's prettiest neighbourhood, with guides from the local *favelas*.

CO_2 emissions: Rtn flight to Rio de Janeiro from New York 2.20 tonnes; London 2.68; Sydney 4.20.

Offset cost: $32.65; £20.10; A$78.55.

Staying there: Accommodation can be arranged through Be a Local.

Rates: Vary; usually R$60–100 (US$30–50) per person per day.

Best time to go: Year-round.

Further information:
Be a Local +55 (0)21 9643 0366, www.bealocal.com
Favela Tour +55 (0)21 3322 2727, www.favelatour.com.br
Rio Hiking +55 (0)21 2552 9204, www.riohiking.com

Responsibility: Be a Local, Favela Tour and Rio Hiking all contribute considerable percentages of their profits to *favela* community projects.

Black Sheep Inn

Chugchilán Village, Cotopaxi, Ecuador
+593 3 281 4587 / www.blacksheepinn.com / info@blacksheepinn.com

SET just north of the Equator on the little-travelled Quilotoa Circuit – a dirt-track traverse encircling the jewel-like volcanic-crater lake of Quilotoa – Black Sheep Inn is not only a model of a low-impact lifestyle, it is also comfortable and welcoming. The nine private cabins and bunkhouse are built of traditional straw, adobe and tile, whitewashed in classic Ecuadorian style and heated by wood-burning stoves. A recently completed renovation has added private bathrooms to three of the rooms, while hot showers are standard, thanks to the effective solar-power system.

The food dished up at Black Sheep is excellent, and is exclusively vegetarian and almost entirely home-grown. Meals are served communally in the snug kitchen, and can be washed down with ozone-purified water or a bottle of Chilean wine.

The lodge's eco-credentials are first class. Owners Andres Hammerman and Michelle Kirby are hard-core permaculturalists. They also recycle all their greywater, build sauna walls out of empty bottles and feed their veggie scraps to their flock of curly-horned sheep. Reducing, reusing and recycling is so thorough that the inn produces just 30g (1oz) of waste per guest per day. In addition, the Black Sheep also educates staff, local people and guests in ecotourism practice.

Not satisfied with just being environmentally friendly, the inn is heavily involved in community-based projects as well. Michelle teaches English and computing at the local school, while Andreas is Chugchilán's elected 'King of Garbage', having helped the village initiate a separation and recycling scheme in 2005. Both have taught permaculture design courses to village residents, set up a 'library' of

ECOFILE

Rooms: Nine comfortable private rooms and a shared bunkhouse.
Rates: US$25–70 per person per night, including dinner and breakfast.
Location: In Chugchilán village, on the north Ecuadorean altiplano. The nearest airport is Quito, 180km (110 miles) to the south.
Best time to go: The high Andes of Ecuador have a year-round temperate climate.
Getting there: From Quito, either take a 4-hour taxi ride to Chugchilán, or a 6-hour bus ride (change at Latacunga).
CO_2 emissions: Rtn flight to Quito from New York 1.26 tonnes; London 2.66; Sydney 4.23. Rtn transfer by taxi 0.11; by bus 0.03.
Offset cost: $20.30; £20.80; A$81.15.

Responsibility: Black Sheep's owners live and breathe the permaculture and ecotourism ethos, with a practical approach that benefits the local community. This ever-evolving place also provides ample inspiration to guests, plenty of whom stay on as volunteers and leave as dyed-in-the-wool conservationists.

Environmental:	ØØØØØ
Social:	ØØØØØ

Andean musical instruments to support folk traditions, and helped young locals to train as interpreters and guides to the threatened Iliniza Ecological Reserve that surrounds the property.

The location is so beautiful that it would be easy enough to just slip into the slow pace of farm life and watch the Andean clouds roll by. But that would be to miss out on the (carefully mapped) range of hikes Black Sheep Inn offers around Quilotoa Lake. The best of these includes a rugged return trek through the stupendous ashen gorge of the Río Toachi. Other activities include a visit to the indigenous market in Saquisili, where Quichua farmers in bowler hats haggle over livestock and vegetables, and local craftsmen sell beautiful knitwear and carvings.

Kapawi Lodge

Urbanizacion Santa Leonor, Manzana 5, Solar #10, Guayaquil, Ecuador
+593 4 251 4750 / www.canodros.com / canodros@canodros.com

LYING in an extraordinary off-the-map setting in southeastern Ecuador, ten days' hard trek from the nearest town or road, Kapawi has carved itself a place at the forefront of indigenous eco-tourism. The lodge has been established as a joint project between the forest-dwelling Achuar people and the for-profit Canodros company, and aims to go where no business plan has gone before: to create a lodge from nothing, then give it away, all in the name of preserving an ancient forest culture and the forest itself.

The lodge is nestled in deep forest near the foothills of the Andes, which are washed by frequent tropical rains. As you lie back in your hammock under a palm-thatched veranda, a raging thunderstorm lashes the lagoon below with lightning crashes and gobs of rain. Then, within five minutes, the storm rumbles off into the distance and the blue sky is filled with the chirrups of tanagers and the loud cries of howler monkeys.

Kapawi hits the target of looking chic and feeling comfortable without passing on huge costs to the local ecosystem. The 20 spacious palm-thatched cabanas are built using traditional materials and local technology (the staff eagerly point out the ingenious wooden 'nails' used to pin the door frames into place), and they are raised on stilts above a small lagoon rich with bird and reptile life. Sixty per cent of power is solar-generated, all biodegradable waste is buried in the jungle or filtered and converted to forest fertilizer, and everything non-organic is packed off to the capital, Quito.

The cabana interiors are minimally adorned – comfortable beds with mosquito nets, a deckchair or two, a tiled bathroom equipped with biodegradeable soap and shampoo, and a solar-heated shower. Outside is a little veranda with a view and a hammock – the perfect vantage point for watching not just the dramatic weather, but also the misty lagoon as it comes alive at first light.

Kapawi is not just about getting in touch with nature; it's about understanding it. There are plenty of activities on offer. All excursions are led by an *Achuar* guide and accompanied by an English-speaking naturalist, who between them can locate and identify any of the 540 species of birds that have been spotted in Kapawi's environs. Days typically begin with a self-guided nature hike on the paths around the lodge – great for small bird and primate life. Breakfast is followed by a canoe ride on the tranquil Capahuari River in search of macaws, and afternoons can be spent relaxing or squelching through the forest to an indigenous *Achuar* village.

In addition to the guides, anywhere between 70 and 90 per cent of the lodge's staff come from local villages. The aim is to ensure that a suitable skills pool exists by 2011, when the *Achuar will* assume full control of Kapawi. By that time the lodge will already have contributed US$600,000 to the Achuar, enabling them to preserve primary forest in their 5,000sq km (1,950sq mile) reserve by foregoing their only previous economic activity – cattle ranching – which required them to cut down trees.

ECOFILE

Rooms: 20 thatched houses built in traditional Achuar style, set on stilts above a tranquil lagoon.

Rates: From US$670 per person, based on double occupancy, for 3 nights/4 days to US$1,405 for 7 nights, plus US$224 for return transfers from Quito.

Location: On the Río Pastaza, 240km (150 miles) southeast of Quito near the Peru–Ecuador border.

Best time to go: Feb–May are wettest and best for wildlife.

Getting there: Fly to Quito, then take a 45-min turboprop flight over the Andes to Coca, and transfer to a motorized canoe for the final 1-hour journey up the Río Pastaza.

CO2 emissions: Rtn flight to Quito from New York 1.26 tonnes; London 2.66; Sydney 4.23. Rtn transfer 0.07. **Offset cost:** $19.75; £20.50; A$80.50.

Responsibility: Kapawi's ground-breaking company-community partnership is a model for others to follow. Although Kapawi is accessible only by plane, its long-term impact on ranching and forest destruction could far outweigh the emissions of the small 19-seater turboprops.

Environmental: ✓✓✓✓✓
Social: ✓✓✓✓✓

Yachana Lodge

Mondaña, Oriente, Ecuador
+593 2 252 3777 / www.yachana.com / info@yachana.com

YACHANA translates from Quichua as 'a Place for Learning', and the lodge certainly lives up to its name, whether you're a short-stay guest, a volunteer on one of its many community projects or one of the local Quichua children. Alongside the trips into the rainforest common to most South American ecolodges, Yachana offers the opportunity to master all sorts of skills and to explore all manner of academic disciplines, from discovering how to make poison arrows from dart frogs, chocolate from cacao or flour from manioc, to attending seminars on sustainable agriculture, forest ecology or neotropical biology.

The lodge sits on the fast-flowing Río Napo, a tributary of the Amazon that spills out of the high Andes. It is three hours upstream from the oil town of Coca and is set in a 1,200ha (3,000-acre) reserve made up of a mix of primary and secondary forest. The lodge was founded by FUNEDESIN, a non-profit foundation dedicated to protecting Ecuador's rainforest by educating and empowering its native peoples.

Accommodation is in a main lodge building and in a row of private hardwood cabins set behind a bank of vegetation overlooking the river and shaded by ample trees. Each is bright and airy, and is decorated with colourful indigenous art. The showers are solar-heated and

verandas overlook trees filled with pygmy marmosets. Food is served communally around a long dining table and is largely vegetarian, with many of the ingredients grown in the lodge's permaculture garden.

Yachana forms one element of a rustic riverside campus that includes a permaculture school, a community health centre and a computing technical college with wireless Internet. There's also a chocolate factory – a fair-trade enterprise in which organically grown cacao is purchased from local farmers at an above-market price, processed at Yachana, and sold both abroad and in the lodge shop. Profit is largely ploughed back into local community and environmental projects.

Learning and cultural exchange are weaved together with trips into the forest to see flora and fauna. The lodge's main guide, Juan, who occasionally travels to the UK to tell schools about the wonders of the Amazon, has eyes sharp enough to spot the most elusive animal high up in the canopy, a fascinating knowledge of rainforest plants and their uses, and the ability to split a plum from 35m (40yds) with a dart from his blowgun.

At Yachana, visitors are exposed to the knowledge gleaned by local Quichua people from thousands of years of living with the Amazon. But they give plenty back too – the Quichua learn that their culture, which is often underrated in Ecuador, is valuable to foreign tourists. And they also acquire practical skills that will help to ensure the survival of their culture in a market-driven world from which they can no longer isolate themselves.

ECO**FILE**

Rooms: 17 modern rooms with river views, some in the main lodge, others in separate hardwood cabins.

Rates: From US$405 per person for 3 nights to US$540 for 4 nights, including all meals and transfers from Coca.

Location: 50km (30 miles) west of Coca, which has the nearest airfield.

Best time to go: Sep–Dec is the driest season.

Getting there: From Quito, take a 10-hour bus trip or 35-min flight to Coca (260km/160 miles), where you will be met by your guide.

CO2 emissions: Rtn flight to Quito from New York 1.26 tonnes; London 2.66; Sydney 4.23. Rtn transfer to Coca by plane 0.07; by bus 0.05. **Offset cost:** $19.80; £20.50; A$80.50.

Responsibility: The lodge practises recycling and energy conservation, grows its own food and provides vital support for indigenous communities, making it an excellent model for responsible tourism.

Environmental:	ⵁⵁⵁⵁⵁ
Social:	ⵁⵁⵁⵁⵁ

Iwokrama Field Station & Canopy Walkway

PO Box 10630, 77 High Street, Kingston, Georgetown, Guyana
+592 225 1504 / www.iwokrama.org / iwokrama-general@iwokrama.org

GUYANA is off the tourist map for most visitors to South America, although it's hard to see why. It boasts the largest percentage of national territory covered in primary forest of any country in the continent, if not the world. It is replete with astonishingly beautiful landscapes – including the 300m-high (1,000ft) Kaieteur Falls, which rival Iguaçú as the most spectacular on earth. It has a fascinating mix of cultures, from African-Caribbean and East Indian to Native American. And last but by no means least, there is nowhere better to see neotropical wild animals.

The Iwokrama Forest Field Station forms part of a complex of sights and lodges in the Guyanese interior. These include Dadanawa and Karanambo lodges in the expansive Amazonian Rupununi wetland savannah, Rock View ecolodge on the edge of the Pakaraima mountains, and the Macushi Indian village of Surama. The field station itself lies in the heart of primary rainforest protected by the Iwokrama Wilderness Preserve, on the banks of the Essequibo, Guyana's longest river.

The Iwokrama Canopy Walkway, also in the preserve, lies two hours south of the field station near the village of Surama. Unlike almost all accessible forest in the Latin American Amazon, this preserve has never been hunted or logged – even selectively – and the variety and abundance of its wildlife is astonishing. Jaguar and puma are common sights, particularly on the road between Surama village and the canopy walkway. And in terms of lowland rainforest species, the birdwatching is

simply second to none in the neotropics. With the exception of Cristalino Jungle Lodge in Brazil (see pages 84–5), there is nowhere better in the world for seeing the spectacular harpy eagle.

Accommodation at the field station is rustic but comfortable. Rooms are housed either in communal wooden hostels, connected by an external covered veranda, or in separate thatch-roofed cabanas. The latter have private en suites and both come with netting on the windows and the beds. They sit in a large glade in the forest, together with the research centre itself and a huge restaurant building where comfort food is served with a stunning view out over the Essequibo.

ECO**FILE**

Rooms: Three thatch-roofed cabins, each sleeping 6, plus spill-over into the main building, which is also used for scientific researchers. Six satellite camps, dotted throughout the forest, can be used by hikers.

Rates: G$27,000 (US$135) per cabin per day, including all meals but excluding transfers.

Location: 331km (206 miles) south of the capital, Georgetown.

Best time to go: Anytime except the rainy season (May–Jul).

Getting there: From Georgetown, drive by 4WD or take a bus 6–7 hours to the camp. Alternatively, take a 1-hour flight with Trans Guyana Airways.

CO_2 emissions: Rtn flight to Georgetown from New York 1.14 tonnes; London 2.04; Sydney 5.07. Rtn transfer by car 0.19; by bus 0.05; by plane 0.09.

Offset cost: $19.85; £16.80; A$98.55.

Responsibility: Iwokrama protects 371,000ha (917,000 acres) of virgin rainforest. This has the highest species range for fish and bats of any area this size in the world. It also has an extraordinarily high diversity of birds for a lowland area, with more than 500 species. Ecotourism is integral to Iwokrama's business plan, which aims to make the reserve financially self-sufficient. The NGO actively supports 14 local indigenous communities, including Macushi Indian villages, providing them with training, employment and education.

Environmental: ∅∅∅∅∅
Social: ∅∅∅∅∅

Pantiacolla Lodge

Calle Saphy 554, Cusco, Peru
+51 84 238323 / www.pantiacolla.com / pantiac@terra.com.pe

THIS simple, rustic lodge sits on the edge of Manu National Park, where the Andes meet the Amazon to create some of the most spectacular wilderness scenery in South America. Manu's manifold forest types also make it one of the world's biodiversity hotspots, with more recorded bird species than any location, with the exception of Madidi National Park in Bolivia (see pages 78–9). More than 500 different species have been recorded around Pantiacolla, and there are 1,000-plus within the 18,811sq km (7,336sq mile) Manu Biosphere Reserve. In addition, there are healthy populations of rare reptiles and mammals here, including tapirs and jaguars.

The lodge's 14 palm-thatched double bungalows are built in an

unobtrusive indigenous style and arranged in a small forest encampment. They are as comfortable as virgin rainforest will allow. Furnishings
include a simple table and chair and a large double bed with mosquito
net; the windows look out over a small veranda
into the bungalow complex. Paths lead from
each bungalow to a separate block with
showers and toilets, and to a communal dining room and bar, which has a small library of
wildlife and birding books. Trips to the toilet
at night can be daunting – there's no electricity, the forest around is a cacophony of
insect and frog song, and the green eyeshine
of visiting ocelots and other forest cats flash
in one's torch beam.

Every morning the numerous trails radiating out from the lodge are covered with the
fresh spoor of resident peccaries, anteaters,
tapirs and big cats. Visitors invariably see
monkeys in the surrounding trees, as well as
brightly coloured manakins, cotingas and
other spectacular birds flitting quietly in and
out of the branches. Hides and viewing towers around the lodge offer the chance to see
more elusive species. Pantiacolla's guiding is
excellent, with the staff trained by Dutch
biologist owner, Marianne van Vlaardingen.
Specialist birding guides are also available
on request.

Pantiacolla is more than just a lodge. Trips
here are usually combined with a choice of
camping expeditions into the Manu Reserved
Zone, which begins some two hours downstream by canoe at the junction of the
Madre de Dios and Manu rivers. These
include nine-night excursions along the river
to the famous Blanquillo clay lick (where
thousands of parrots and macaws gather
every morning), and to the Otorongo and
Salvador oxbow lakes, which are renowned
for their giant otters and jaguars. Each is a
real adventure, with treks and canoe rides by
day, and evenings spent around the campfire
listening to tales from the guides of adventures searching for the lost Inca gold of Paititi
in the surrounding Pantiacolla Mountains.
Camping in the rainforest may be sweaty
and uncomfortable, but it is also incredible.

ECOFILE

Rooms: 14 rustic bungalows, each
with separate bath, in a forest camp.
Rates: From S/2,500 (US$795) per
person for a 5-day trip, to S/2,600
(US$825) for 9-day trip, including
transfers from Cusco, all meals and
guide fee, but excluding the S/160
(US$50) park entry fee.
Location: At the base of the
Andes, 200km (125 miles) northeast of Cusco.
Best time to go: Apr–Oct.
Getting there: From Lima, either
fly 1 hour or take a 20-hour bus
trip to Cusco (1,165km/724 miles).
From Cusco, a 2-day (11-hour)
drive through Andean cloud forests,
staying in basic huts en route,
takes you to Atalaya. Alternatively,
you can fly there in 45–60 mins.
From Atalaya, guests travel for
5–7 hours by motorized canoe
to the lodge.
CO2 emissions: Rtn flight to
Lima from New York 1.71 tonnes;
London 2.56; Sydney 4.43. Rtn
transfer to Atalaya via Cusco by
plane 0.42; by bus and car 0.32.
Offset cost: $31.75; £22.40; A$90.85.

Responsibility: Former logger
Gustavo Moscoso and biologist
Marianne van Vlaardingen have
devoted their property to conservation, research and education. They
are also working with the local Yiné
people to set up a self-sustaining
indigenous tourism project.
Environmental: ⬤⬤⬤⬤◯
Social: ⬤⬤⬤⬤◯

Tambopata Research Centre & Posada Amazonas

Reserva Nacional Tambopata, Peru
+51 14 218347 / www.perunature.com / sales@perunature.com

TAMBOPATA Research Centre (TRC) offers very basic accommodation in an unforgettable location. Doors and windows may be flimsy, walls mere partitions and furnishings Spartan, but TRC is the remotest lodge in the Tambopata-Candamo Reserved Zone, one of the most biodiverse regions on earth. It also sits next to one of the most spectacular and most photographed sights in the Amazon – the Tambopata clay lick, which is truly the stuff of wildlife films. Every day, just before dawn, the greatest number of parrot and macaw species and individuals ever recorded gathers here in a rainbow-hued cacophony.

TRC's basic facilities reflect its history. The lodge was originally set up as a scientific station for research into the surrounding forests, which are among the best places in the Amazon to see more elusive indicator species such as the tapir, jaguar and harpy eagle. Tourism to the area began in the 1990s through Rainforest Expeditions, which now runs TRC and continues to sponsor research. There are often scientists in residence and volunteer biologists on hand to offer expert guiding during their time off from doctoral research, and many of the Rainforest Expeditions guides (all of whom are Peruvian) are also biologists.

Rainforest Expeditions also runs the Posada Amazonas, which is far closer to Puerto Maldonado and hence less costly to stay at. The lodge is run in conjunction with the *Ese-Eja* indigenous people, who work at the lodge, receive 60 per cent of its operating profits, and benefit from a programme of schooling and practical training. Donations from guests support the fascinating ethno-botanical centre, a kind of walk-in community pharmacy where all ailments are treated with medicinal plants free of charge.

While it is not in such pristine surroundings as TRC, Posada Amazonas also sits within the Tambopata-Candamo Reserved Zone and has plenty of natural attractions that can be explored with an English-speaking Ese-Eja guide or a birdwatching expert. Rooms here are grouped in three simple palm-thatched hardwood lodges connected by boardwalks and built in traditional *Ese-Eja* style, with open walls allowing for the circulation of air. No electric light (or water heating) intrudes on the jungle setting (although a generator is switched on briefly every day for charging batteries), but kerosene lanterns light the paths at night and provide an intimate camp-fire atmosphere around the large communal dining table.

ECOFILE

Rooms: Tambopata Research Centre (TRC) has 18 Spartan rooms in a remote lodge; Posada Amazonas has 30 lantern-lit rooms with cane walls in indigenous-style lodges.

Rates: From S/700 (US$225) per person for 2 nights at Posada Amazonas, to S/3,000 (US$945) per person for 7 nights at TRC, including all meals and transfers.

Location: On the Tambopata River in southeastern Peru. The nearest airport is Puerto Maldonado.

Best time to go: May–Sep for relatively cool and dry weather.

Getting there: From Lima or Cusco, fly to Puerto Maldonado, where transfers can be arranged. The trip to Posada Amazonas by motorized canoe takes 90 mins, while that to TRC requires an overnight stop at the company's Refugio Amazonas.

CO2 emissions: Rtn flight to Lima from New York 1.71 tonnes; London 2.56; Sydney 4.43. Rtn transfer to Puerto Maldonado 0.21.

Offset cost: $28.50; £20.75; A$86.75.

Responsibility: Tambopata Research Centre remains one of the principal biological research centres in the Amazon and relies on tourism for its existence. Posada Amazonas has dealt with delicate cultural issues to show local communities that are reliant on logging and hunting the economic value of conservation, and the worth of their own culture.

Environmental: ⦸⦸⦸⦸⦸
Social: ⦸⦸⦸⦸⦸

Awarradam

Dr J F Nassylaan 2, Paramaribo, Suriname
+597 477088 / www.surinamevacations.com / mets@surinamevacations.com

FEW visitors make it to Suriname, tucked away in the northeast of South America. Yet like its neighbours it is a travel treasure waiting to be discovered – especially for lovers of nature. But for a narrow strip

of beach and coastal hinterland, the country consists entirely of Amazon forest, broken by the towering ancient boulder mountains of the Guiana Shield, cut by magnificent rivers and replete with animal and plant life. Lost deep in towering virgin forest on an island in the middle of Gran Rio – the prettiest river of them all – is the Awarradam ecolodge.

The lodge lies not only in the heart of the Amazon, but also of a complex of Saramaccan Maroon villages. These were founded in the 17th and 18th centuries by groups of escaped West African slaves, and to this day preserve their unique African culture. Tourists are warmly invited to learn about and participate in Saramaccan rituals and dances, performed in the ancient African language of Kromanti, which has almost died out in its native Ghana. In addition, many of the Saramaccan hunting and agricultural practices are either African or have been learned from indigenous American neighbours.

Awarradam is run by the Saramaccans in combination with the Movement for Ecotourism in Suriname (METS), and provides a much-needed income for a people who are increasingly losing their way of life to the lure of the country's capital city, Paramaribo.

The lodge itself comprises a series of identical thatch-roofed hardwood huts, furnished with simple beds (thankfully covered with mosquito nets) and a plain table and chair. The absence of electricity makes Awarradam all the more magical. But for the lively chatter of the Saramaccan people, the only noises that can be heard are the calls of toucans and macaws in the trees and the rush of the clear water over the stones in the river.

Despite the tranquillity, there's plenty to do, including canoe rides along the Gran Rio's tributaries and walks with English- and Dutch-speaking Saramaccan guides into the rainforest. When it comes to restocking energy levels, the food is simple yet delicious, including river fish supplemented with chicken and beef and accompanied by an assortment of vegetables. A small bar sells beer.

The Saramaccan staff at Awarradam are always friendly and provide efficient service. Tropical flowers decorate the sprucely made-up beds, and oil lamps are lit at dusk and left along the paths and outside every room. But then it never feels truly dark in Awarradam – it is so far from city lights that a thick tapestry of stars brightens the night and twinkles like a million candles in the rushing river.

ECO**FILE**

Rooms: Seven double cabins and 1 quadruple cabin, all with a view of the river and providing sleeping facilities for 18 people in single beds with mosquito nets.

Rates: S$1,500 (US$545) per person for 3 nights/4 days, including transfers, meals and guided day-trips.

Location: 225km (140 miles) south of Paramaribo on the Gran Rio river.

Best time to go: Aug–Nov.

Getting there: Fly to Paramaribo via Quito (Ecuador). Access to Awarradam is only through METS on a 40-min turboprop flight from Paramaribo, followed by a 2-hour motorized canoe ride – a wonderful journey that takes you along the Suriname River, across Brokopondo Lake and into the Amazon forest.

CO_2 emissions: Rtn flight to Paramaribo from New York 1.19 tonnes; London 2.02; Sydney 5.16. Rtn transfer by plane 0.08.

Offset cost: $18.90; £15.70; A$98.

Responsibility: The Awarradam ecotourism project is the only one the author knows of that preserves the way of life of South American-African communities that escaped slavery. Income from ecotourism is integral to the survival of these communities, helping to reduce migration to the cities. The lodge itself is beautifully integrated with its natural surroundings and practises recycling, energy conservation and responsible water usage.

Environmental: ⌀⌀⌀⌀⌀

Social: ⌀⌀⌀⌀⌀

Europe

Main picture: The Yorkshire Dales National Park, England. Left, from top: A poppy at Locanda della Valle Nuova; Hoopoe Yurt Hotel; Anna's House; ready for winter, Casa del Grivo

Locator map & budget guide

- Budget (up to US$100)
- Moderate (US$100–250)
- Expensive (US$250–500)
- Blow out (more than US$500)

Prices are for a double room, or two people, per night

Accommodation

Features

Ethical travel dilemma

Bedruthan Steps Hotel

Mawgan Porth, Cornwall, TR8 4BU, UK
+44 (0)1637 860860 / www.bedruthanstepshotel.co.uk / office@bedruthan.com

ECOFILE

Rooms: 101 doubles and suites.
Rates: £80–124 (US$160–250) per person per night, including breakfast and dinner.
Location: Between Newquay and Padstow on Cornwall's north coast. 415km (258 miles) from London.
Best time to go: Anytime you need some R&R.
Getting there: From London, take a train for 4 hours from Paddington to Bodmin Parkway, followed by a 45-min taxi ride to the hotel, or take the train to Par and change for the branch line to Newquay (5 hours in total), from where it's a 15-min taxi ride to the hotel. It is also possible to fly to Newquay from London.
CO_2 emissions: Rtn flight to London from New York 1.55 tonnes; Sydney 5.63. Rtn transfers by train and car 0.06; by plane and car 0.12.
Offset cost: $24.70; £0.85; A$107.50.

Responsibility: Bedruthan Steps has thought carefully about every aspect of its business and its impact on the environment. Everything from 'big things', like reducing power and water use, to purchasing biodegradable straws has been addressed – and the hotel continually reassesses its initiatives and actions.

Environmental: ∅∅∅∅∅
Social: ∅∅∅∅∅

THE peerless views over Mawgan Porth beach would be reason enough to stay at the Bedruthan Steps Hotel, which takes its name from a perilously steep stairway cut into a nearby cliff face, now owned by the National Trust. Add this scenic splendour to the hotel's spa, tennis courts, excellent restaurant and family-friendly facilities, and you start to understand why people come here year after year.

Perched on Cornwall's wild north coast, Bedruthan Steps is a large and rather ungainly 1960s building that can cater for more than 300 guests – which makes its award-winning green credentials all the more impressive. The rooms are bright, square and spacious, with plasma-screen TVs and broadband Internet access. The majority also have sea views. Comfort is the key, and you immediately feel 'on holiday'. You can find yourself sitting by the window for ages, just watching the surfers below ploughing through the waves like ungainly seals; or snoozing after an indulgent facial or massage, still smelling of fragrant oils and essences.

These comforts come at a surprisingly low environmental cost. Run by a family committed to making every aspect of its business eco-friendly, Bedruthan Steps has gone far further than simply installing energy-efficient light bulbs, providing hand-made toiletries and using new condensing boilers. The outdoor pool is heated with solar panels, a rather wacky grass roof provides efficient insulation, and everything from cardboard to cans is recycled. All the housekeeping products are environmentally friendly, and keycard readers mean that guests can't leave the lights on

when they're not in the room.

The chefs are enthusiastic about using local, seasonal, and ideally organic, produce, and will visit suppliers to ensure production is not just environmentally friendly but also ethical. Fish is local and sustainable, like line-caught sea bass; beef comes from a nearby farm; and turkeys – and eggs – are free-range. Then there are the Cornish cheeses, jams and dairy products, and the salads that are supplemented by leaves from the hotel's herb garden. Great efforts are also made to cater for vegetarians and people on special diets.

The staff are all fully involved in the hotel's green initiatives, which extend to twice-yearly clean-ups of Mawgan Porth beach, and car-sharing schemes operate from nearby Newquay, where many live. Guests are asked to donate £10 (US$20) towards a carbon-offsetting scheme, the proceeds of which are used to plant trees locally, and in low season they receive a discount if they arrive by public transport. The hotel also sponsors local charities, including the Cornwall Wildlife Trust, and encourages guests to purchase eco-friendly nappies from its shop, rather than the conventional type.

Bedruthan Steps is a great base for both surfers and hikers. It's also just a short drive from some of Cornwall's prettiest villages – like Padstow, that fishy mecca for fans of renowned UK chef, Rick Stein. There's loads to do – if you can just tear yourself away from the view.

Bloomfield House

146 Bloomfield Road, Bath, BA2 2AS, UK
+ 44 (0)1225 420105 / www.ecobloomfield.com / info@ecobloomfield.com

GENTEEL and conservative, Bath is not the sort of place where you try to buck convention. You can easily imagine that not conforming in this sedate spa town simply means not raising your little finger when you sip your cup of tea. It's certainly an unlikely place to choose to establish an eco-hotel – especially one that you hope will set a trend across Britain. But that's what Robert and Karen Barnard-Weston have done, using a softly-softly approach to make both guests and local people more aware of environmental issues.

Their elegant and secluded Georgian house, once the home of the town's Lord Mayor, is set on a hill on the outskirts of Bath. It's around five minutes in a taxi from attractions like the superb Roman Baths and Thermae Bath Spa. Bloomfield is a relaxed and lived-in family home – the couple have five children, five cats and a dog. Guests can even bring their own well-behaved dogs if they wish. Go up the honey-coloured steps and through the front door and you're in an unusual oval hallway,

its walls decorated with flamboyant peacocks and lush foliage. The house once belonged to a stage-set designer, who painted lavish *trompe l'oeil* throughout, giving the hotel a wonderfully theatrical air – it's all shabby chic with chandeliers. The Barnard-Westons have played on this theme, furnishing the rooms with antiques and fine old furniture: 'the best form of recycling,' according to Robert. Each room is different, but all are light and clean with large beds, and some have views of Bath and the surrounding countryside. The breakfast room is similarly furnished, comfortable and cluttered, with doors opening onto the tranquil garden. This is filled with rescued plants that were destined for the council dump and that are now partly nourished with greywater from the house.

As Bloomfield House is a listed building, the Barnard-Westons have been unable to install some of the eco-friendly features they would have liked. However, they recycle everything from cardboard to cans – and ensure that it doesn't go to landfill; they use as many low-energy light bulbs as the chandeliers allow; and they use eco-friendly cleaning products wherever possible. They've also installed separate electric radiators in each room, rather than heating the whole house unnecessarily, and use electricity from renewable sources. Their car runs on a biofuel made from rapeseed oil, and guests who arrive by public transport receive a ten per cent reduction on their room rate.

Robert is an environmental consultant and often lectures on sustainable tourism. He was co-founder of Bath's farmer's market and sets great store by providing guests with the same locally sourced food that the family eat. He'll proudly point from the window to show you the proximity of the farm that provides the organic bacon and free-range eggs they serve for breakfast. You'll also have bread from a nearby bakery, and locally produced milk and honey. Breakfast tea and coffee is from fairtrade sources, and vegetarians are catered for as a matter of course.

ECO**FILE**

Rooms: Six doubles.
Rates: £70–140 (US$140–280) per room per night, including breakfast.
Location: On the outskirts of Bath, Somerset. 185km (115 miles) from London.
Best time to go: In spring or autumn to avoid the crowds.
Getting there: From London, take a train for 1.5 hours from Paddington to Bath Spa, then take a taxi for the 5-min transfer to the hotel.
CO_2 emissions: Rtn flight to London from New York 1.55 tonnes; Sydney 5.63. Rtn transfers 0.02.
Offset cost: $23.30; £0.15; A$105.70.

Responsibility: Bloomfield House takes great pride in its organic and locally sourced food. They carry out recycling, composting, and keep energy consumption to a minimum. Hotel rooms are also offered to local charities for fundraising.

Environmental: ∅∅∅∅∅
Social: ∅∅∅∅∅

The Eco-lodge

Rose Cottage, Station Road, Old Leake, Boston, Lincolnshire, PE22, 9RF, UK
+44 (0)1205 871396 / www.internationalbusinessschool.net/eco-lodge.htm /
gclarke@internationalbusinessschool.net

IF you thought you couldn't get away from it all in the heart of
England, think again. This wooden cabin, set in 3.2ha (8 acres) of
unspoilt countryside with woodland, meadow and a large pond, offers
a real 'back-to-nature' experience – but with plenty of home comforts
too. It's a self-catering lodge, with room for four people, and makes
minimal impact on the environment through a variety of measures. Your
electricity comes from a wind generator and your heating from a
wood-burning stove – although there's also gas for cooking if you don't
want to use the range. While your drinking water comes from the
town's main supply, you take your daily shower in filtered rainwater. The
toilet operates in eco-friendly fashion by flushing to a septic tank, and
then on to a reedbed where it is filtered naturally.

The cabin itself was built from wood that was grown nearby in
Lincolnshire. Inside, you have an uncluttered, open-plan living space with
polished wooden floors and comfy seats. There are also two bedrooms, a shower room, and a veranda where you can sit on summer
evenings. There's no television, so you'll have plenty of time to catch up
on all the books you keep meaning to read.

The Eco-lodge is self-catering, so food, of course, is up to you. However, if you want to be really green you won't turn up with a carload of supermarket carrier bags. Instead, you can order lots of organic produce in advance, so you've got things like milk, meat, free-range eggs and bread waiting for you. It's also possible to place an order for organic fruit and vegetable boxes, filled with a selection of seasonal local produce. In addition, there are lots of country pubs and restaurants in the area, as well as shops in nearby Old Leake village and in Boston.

This area is well off the tourist trail, with visitors generally bypassing it in favour of Cambridge and East Anglia to the south, and Yorkshire to the north. However, there is plenty to see. Boston, a market town and port, has historic links to the United States. In the 17th century, migrants from this little town set sail for the New World and founded a settlement on the east coast of America: Boston, Massachusetts.

The lodge is situated in the flat fenland of Lincolnshire, an area that is so close to sea-level that flooding is prevented only by a complex series of sea defences. These low-lying lands, with their huge cloudy skies, are great for birdwatching, and the lodge is just a short drive from a number of bird reserves on the seaside marshes. You've got plenty of choice of walks and cycle rides, too – and it's all so flat you can easily keep going for miles. Then you can get back to your cosy cabin for a hearty meal, before snuggling up with a good book.

ECO**FILE**

Rooms: Self-contained cottage with 2 twin rooms.

Rates: Mon–Fri or Fri–Mon £170 (US$340) plus £5 (US$10) per person per stay; Fri–Fri £340 (US$680) plus £5 (US$10) per person per stay.

Location: About 2.5km (1.5 miles) from Old Leake, Lincolnshire. 208km (130 miles) from London.

Best time to go: Summer.

Getting there: From London, travel by train for 2 hours from Kings Cross to Boston (change at Grantham). Transfers can be arranged from Boston, or it's 20 mins by taxi.

CO_2 emissions: Rtn flight to London from New York 1.55 tonnes; Sydney 5.63. Rtn transfers 0.03.

Offset cost: $23.45; £0.25; A$105.90.

Responsibility: The Eco-lodge is a great way of experiencing a much greener lifestyle, with its low-impact wind power and wood-burning stove. Offering guests the chance to pre-order organic produce for their stay also helps local suppliers.

Environmental: ∅∅∅∅∅
Social: ∅∅∅∅∅

117

The Hen House

Tregarne, Manaccan, Helston, Cornwall, TR12 6EW, UK
+44 (0)1326 280236 / www.thehenhouse-cornwall.co.uk / henhouseuk@aol.com

HEDGES bursting with wildflowers line your way to Tregarne, a tiny hamlet tucked away in the green heart of the Lizard peninsula. This is a corner of Cornwall that seems hardly touched by time: a land etched with narrow lanes, sleepy villages, and coves so secret that you half expect to come upon smugglers hiding tobacco and brandy from the customs men. This is where you'll find the Hen House, an immaculate eco-hideaway that doesn't stint on contemporary comforts. The welcoming owners, Sandy and Gary Pulfrey, created this small bed-and-breakfast by sympathetically converting farmhouse barns that once housed cows, pigs and – as the name suggests – hens. Now there are two double rooms and a self-catering cottage arranged around a pretty courtyard garden, where guests relax on warm summer evenings.

The spacious rooms all have king-sized beds, crisp white linen, TVs, Wi-Fi and en suite bathrooms – so far so conventional. But some of the furniture has been imaginatively created from recycled wood, light bulbs are low energy, toiletries are phosphate-free and toilet cisterns are set to use minimal amounts of water. Electricity comes from renewable sources, and water is collected from the roofs and used on the vegetable plot. Rooms are supplied with bags that make it easy for guests to separate items such as newspapers and cans, so they can be recycled along with waste from the main house. Sandy and Gary seem to have thought of everything – from using eco-friendly laundry and cleaning products, to providing self-catering guests with biodegradable dog-poo bags. Social responsibility is as much a part of their philosophy as is being green, and the Hen House is very integrated into the local community: Sandy's in the choir and Gary's a local coastguard. But it's all done in a non-preachy fashion.

As you might expect at a thoroughly green B&B, virtually everything for breakfast is locally produced and mainly organic, from the bacon and sausages to the apple juice and milk. Eggs come from the couple's own free-range hens, and the bread and jams are home-made.

There's plenty of information to help guests explore the local area, including books of walks and cycle routes. However, it's tempting to spend much of your time just sitting reading in the wildflower meadow behind the house, watching the birds that flock to the garden, or practising some of the t'ai chi moves Gary has taught you in one of his daily pre-breakfast sessions. If you really want to de-stress, opt for some reflexology or Reiki healing in the cosy treatment room, although just soaking up the Hen House's tranquil atmosphere will probably be therapy enough.

ECO**FILE**

Rooms: Two doubles and a self-catering barn (sleeps 3).

Rates: £75 (US$150) per night for a double, including breakfast (£65/US$130 for stays longer than 3 nights); £200–350 (US$400–700) per week for the self-catering barn.

Location: Tregarne, near St Keverne on the east coast of the Lizard peninsula in Cornwall. 467km (290 miles) from London. The nearest mainline railway station is Redruth, 25km (15 miles) away.

Best time to go: Spring.

Getting there: From London, travel by train for 5 hours from Paddington to Redruth, then take a connecting bus 1.5 hours to Helston. The Hen House will do a pick-up from there. It is also possible to fly 1 hour from to Newquay and drive 70 mins to Tregarne.

CO_2 emissions: Rtn flight to London from New York 1.55 tonnes; Sydney 5.63. Rtn transfers by train and bus 0.05; by plane and car 0.15.

Offset cost: $24; £1.15; A$108.15.

Responsibility: Hen House takes its social and environmental responsibilities seriously, from supporting local suppliers to keeping its carbon footprint as small as possible. Waste is recycled, rooms are kept sparkling clean with eco-friendly products, and wildlife is encouraged to thrive in the garden. The owners are continually looking at ways to improve, and have plans for their own wind generator.

Environmental: ∅∅∅∅∅

Social: ∅∅∅∅∅

Slow and steady

On a slow food trail through the countryside of England and Wales, **Rebecca Ford** sipped wines and nibbled on cheeses, discovering along the way that good things take time.

This page: Sparkling wine at Ridge View Estate, Sussex; the Three Choirs Vineyard, Gloucestershire

The scene was ravishing. From the vineyard I could see fields, farms and hedgerows stretched out to the horizon, like a rumpled quilt all patched in green. The grapes were almost ripe, plump with juice and heavy on the vines. The vintner handed me a glass of wine – chilled and crisp and fruity, and I sipped it as the evening sun turned mellow gold. Conditions had been perfect, he told me. It looked as if it would be a vintage year.

No, I wasn't in France, or Spain, or Italy. I was in southern England. For here, on the chalky downlands of Kent and Sussex, vineyards are flourishing – and an increasing number of these English winemakers are winning international awards for the quality of their products. Gone are the days when English wines meant something murky made from parsnips or rhubarb. Now, they even win acclaim in France – especially the 'champagnes'.

This success isn't just down to climate change heating up the country – although that certainly seems to be a factor. It's also due to the fact that the downlands of the south of England have much the same geology as the Champagne region of France, just a short distance away on the other side of the Channel. And it's also because, in recent years, growers have realized that conditions here are ideal for growing acidic grape varieties – the type that are necessary to make a perfect sparkling wine.

Wine-making isn't limited to the southeast, and vineyards are now thriving in Cornwall, the Cotswolds and even Yorkshire.

named vineyard beside a former shepherd's cottage.

This interest in wine-making revives an ancient tradition. The Romans introduced the vine to Britain, and the Normans produced wine here on a large scale. It died out only after the dissolution of the monasteries.

Today, a whole range of traditional British foods and beverages

Many offer tours and tastings, and some provide accommodation as well. The industry's grown so much that there's now an annual English Wine Week, a celebration held at the end of May. With a little help from the Internet and local tourist boards, you can easily put together your own wine tour – and you'll discover lovely parts of the country in the process. I sipped rosé at Chapel Down, a winery perched picturesquely on a hillside in Kent; had some excellent fizz at Ridge View, hidden away among bluebell woods in deepest Sussex; and drank kir royale in a gloriously tranquil valley near Lewes – where Peter Hall makes both wines and kir at Breaky Bottom, his evocatively

are at last receiving the attention they deserve, as both chefs and shoppers start to realize the benefits of using local, seasonal – and, ideally, organic – produce. It's not just healthier and better tasting; it's also much kinder to the environment. You can now find farmers' markets and food festivals from Abergavenny to Aberdeen, all celebrating high-quality food produced with only a small carbon footprint. Included on the menu are Scottish beef, Welsh lamb and Cornish seafood – not to mention real ales, traditional cider, hearty home-baking and delicate honeys.

An increasing number of producers and artisan suppliers are selling directly to the public, and

some also offer guided tours or tastings. As a result, it's now possible to put together all sorts of 'slow food' trails throughout Britain, which won't just introduce you to great local foods, but will also take you to parts of the countryside you might otherwise miss. You can watch chocolates being made on the Isle of Arran, stroke inquisitive goats at a dairy in Yorkshire and walk by rivers rich in watercress near Winchester. You can even visit darkened rhubarb sheds in Wakefield, where the forced crops are picked by candlelight so as to lose none of their sweetness – every so often you'll hear a 'pop' as a shoot bursts open in the blackness. There are some surprises, too, like the tea plantation hidden away on the south coast of Cornwall. The tea is grown on the secluded Tregothnan Estate near St Mawes, where conditions are surprisingly similar to those in Darjeeling. It's light and delicate – the champagne of cuppas.

Wherever you go, you're sure to find a good cheesemaker or two. There's the Northumberland Cheese Company in Blagdon, for instance, where they produce wedges of cheese wrapped in nettles; and the famous Hawes Creamery in the Yorkshire Dales, where you can watch them make classic crumbly Wensleydale – Wallace and Gromit's favourite.

Wales has plenty of cheese producers worth checking out. On a food tour of Pembrokeshire, in the southwest of the principality, I found farmers making everything from delicate white goat's cheeses to firm and pungent blues. At Caerfai Farm, just outside St Davids, there's a little shop at the gate where the family sells its unpasteurized organic cheese. It's an admirably environmentally friendly operation: the cows are mainly fed on pasture, the farm's water is heated by solar power, the farm uses bio-gas made from the cows' manure, and the milking machine is powered by a wind turbine.

I found another farm shop tucked away at Rosebush, a tiny settlement by the wild Preseli Hills, where early Britons found the mighty bluestones for Stonehenge. I went inside and discovered the Jennings family busily wrapping their Pant Mawr cheeses, made of goat's and cow's milk. They gave me generous chunks to taste, some light and crumbly, others rich and smoky.

The most stunning setting, however, must go to Caws Cenarth (*caws* is Welsh for cheese), another family farm tucked away on the border of Carmarthenshire. You reach it down a seemingly endless country lane, laced with thick hedges and cow parsley, and the farmyard itself has stunning views over the gentle Welsh landscape. The family makes several types of organic cheese here, and has set up a little viewing gallery where you can watch the mysterious process in action. There is also a small shop where you can taste the products. These include that most Welsh of cheeses, Caerphilly, as well as a rich buttery blue and creamy rounds of Brie. All you need to go with them is a large chilled glass of that award-winning English wine.

ECO**FILE**

Location: Throughout Britain -- most wines in Kent and Sussex; several cheesemakers in Pembrokeshire.
Getting there: From London, you can catch trains to stations in Kent, Sussex and Pembrokeshire. However, most suppliers are in out-of-the-way places, so a car is usually necessary.
Staying there:
Wines Ockenden Manor, Cuckfield, West Sussex, +44 (0)1444 416111, www.hshotels.co.uk (from £165/US$330 per room per night).
Cheeses St Brides Hotel, Saundersfoot +44 (0)1834 812304, www.stbrideshotel.com (from £140/US$280 per room per night); and Llysmeddyg, Newport, +44 (0)1239 820008, www.llysmeddyg.com (from £90/US$180 per room per night). All rates above include breakfast.
Further information:
Wines www.ridgeview.co.uk
www.breakybottom.co.uk
Cheeses www.wensleydale.co.uk
www.northumberlandcheese.co.uk
www.cawscaerfai.co.uk
www.pantmawrcheeses.co.uk
www.cawscenarth.co.uk
Other www.taste-of-arran.co.uk
www.lownadairy.com
www.yorkshirerhubarb.co.uk
www.tregothnan.co.uk

Responsibility: Going on a slow food trail in Britain isn't just a great way of seeing hidden corners of the countryside; it's also a socially and environmentally friendly holiday option. By supporting small local food producers, you're helping to reduce food miles – and if the producers are organic, it's even better.

Primrose Valley Hotel

Porthminster Beach, St Ives, Cornwall, TR26 2ED, UK
+44 (0)1736 794939 / www.primroseonline.co.uk / info@primroseonline.co.uk

IT'S city chic all the way at this boutique hotel in trendy St Ives, proving that being green doesn't mean that you have to bid farewell to style. A white-painted Edwardian villa, with large windows that make the most of the crisp natural light, the Primrose Valley Hotel sits hidden away in a funny little cul-de-sac just a minute's walk from the pristine powdery sands of Porthminster Beach.

Inside, the building has been given a contemporary makeover by owners Andrew and Sue Biss, who have created sleek and simple interiors that cleverly complement the original architecture. There are lots of polished wooden floors (Forest Stewardship Council-approved), funky bespoke furnishings and sculptural arrangements of fresh flowers. They've also got a small bar where you can get everything from Italian Illy coffee to a selection of Cornish cider, beers and even wines.

Each of the ten bedrooms is different, but Rooms 2 and 3 are particularly sought after, as they've got stunning sea views and private balconies. For an indulgent treat there's a suite with a separate sitting room, and a bathroom with a large walk-in shower, bath and romantic floor-level lighting.

Yet despite this air of understated indulgence, Primrose Valley is a hotel with a surprisingly small carbon footprint. The age of the building means there are limitations

to the measures that can be introduced, but electricity comes from renewable sources, light bulbs are low energy and about 60 per cent of all waste is recycled. The owners use a some eco-friendly cleaning products, encourage guests to request new towels only when necessary, and provide hand-made Cornish soaps in the bathrooms.

Breakfasts here are a real treat, and Andrew and Sue have made great efforts to find the best local suppliers. Their sausages, eggs, smoked goat's cheese, yogurt, butter and milk are all produced nearby. Smart guests also save room for a slice or two of home-made bread and superb Cornish preserves. The morning's meal certainly sets you up for a day on the beach or exploring the picturesque nooks and crannies of St Ives. The town is the artistic hub of Cornwall, home to several contemporary galleries, including Tate St Ives and the Barbara Hepworth Museum. There are also plenty of walks and cycle tracks practically on the hotel's doorstep, as well as one of the most picturesque rail journeys in Britain – the branch line between St Ives and St Erth.

Sustainability goes with social responsibility here, and the hotel operates an opt-out visitor payback scheme, adding £1 (US$2) per room per night to bills, with all proceeds going to the Marine Conservation Society. They're also corporate sponsors of the Cornwall Wildlife Trust and personally give time and commitment to the local community as well as money: Andrew is a member of the St Ives lifeboat crew – a handy fact to know if you're heading into the sea for a dip.

ECO**FILE**

Rooms: Nine doubles, 1 suite.
Rates: £85–145 (US$170–290) per room per night (£160–225/ US$320–450 for the suite), including breakfast. Minimum bookings of 1 week in Jul and Aug.
Location: St Ives, on the north coast of Cornwall. 456km (283 miles) from London.
Best time to go: Summer for sun-seekers, anytime for nature lovers. Closed Dec and Jan.
Getting there: From London, travel by train for 5.5 hours from Paddington to St Ives (change at St Erth). It is also possible to fly 1 hour to Newquay and then hire a car for the 45-min drive to the hotel.
CO2 emissions: Rtn flight to London from New York 1.55 tonnes; Sydney 5.63. Rtn transfer by train 0.05; by plane and car 0.13.
Offset cost: $25.05; £1.05; A$106.30.

Responsibility: Primrose Valley is genuinely committed to being as eco-friendly as possible, without denying guests the little luxuries they crave. It supports a range of local suppliers, recycles waste, uses fair-trade and ethically sourced produce, and encourages visitors to think about their environmental impact.
Environmental: ∅∅∅∅∅
Social: ∅∅∅∅∅

Strattons

4 Ash Close, Swaffham, Norfolk, PE37 7NH, UK
+44 (0)1760 723845 / www.strattonshotel.com / enquiries@strattonshotel.com

AN elegant Queen Anne house with four-poster beds, antique furnishings and chickens contentedly scratching on the lawn hardly sounds like a place that would be at the forefront of a revolution. Yet that's exactly what it is – for Strattons, tucked away quietly in the pretty Norfolk village of Swaffham, was green long before it was fashionable to be so. The owners, Les and Vanessa Scott, came here in 1990 when the house was rather run down, and transformed it into a seductive small hotel with an impressively dainty carbon footprint.

The style is eclectic and theatrical, antiques rubbing shoulders with contemporary artworks – many of which were specially commissioned from local artists. The reception room has a marble fireplace in which a fire is lit with home-made newspaper bricks on cold days, a cowhide rug, a jumble of ornaments and an enormous creamy-coloured chandelier that looks as if it has come from the set of *Swan Lake*. There are lots of books and glossy magazines, and an air of cluttered comfort, the homey appeal enhanced by the couple's affectionate Siamese cats.

The ten bedrooms are individually designed and equally striking. They range in style from the cool comfort of the low-allergen room to the full-blown flamboyance of the Boudoir room, whose specially commissioned mural wallpaper features flying cherubs. The Scotts met at art

school and have used their talents to show that recycling can be creative, as well environmentally considerate: they made a mosaic mermaid for the Portico bathroom using broken crockery and shells.

Swaffham is in the Brecklands, a part of Norfolk noted for its fragile heaths, which support birds like the secretive stone curlew and rare nightjar. During the day you can go walking and cycling, following one of the many routes leading directly from the hotel. In the evening you can sit in the garden and watch the wildlife that the Scotts actively encourage by providing boxes for birds, bats and even frogs. Dine in the restaurant and you'll be served locally sourced and seasonal food, much of it organic. The staff are knowledgeable – they're often taken to see how the produce is made – and you could find anything from Norfolk pigeon to Bingham blue cheese on the menu, as well as a selection of Suffolk wines. Even the oil is from home-grown rapeseed.

Strattons has an impressively comprehensive approach to reducing its environmental impact. This covers everything from how the fabric of the building is treated, to everyday activities such as recycling, using eco-friendly cleaning products and feeding the chickens mash made from vegetable peelings. Measures have also included fitting master switches, so cleaners can ensure all electricity is switched off, installing low-energy light bulbs, and collecting greywater for the vegetable plot. It's the art of green living.

ECO**FILE**

Rooms: Five doubles and 5 suites, some with private terraces.
Rates: £150–225 (US$300–450) per room per night, including breakfast.
Location: Swaffham, in the Breckland region of Norfolk. 160km (99.5 miles) from London.
Best time to go: Summer for the big skies, winter for the birdlife.
Getting there: From London, take a train from Kings Cross to Downham Market and a taxi to the hotel (2 hours in total), or stay on the train till Kings Lynn Bus Station, where a bus runs to Swaffham (3 hours in total). Alternatively, take a coach from London Victoria to Swaffham.
CO2 emissions: Rtn flight to London from New York 1.55 tonnes; Sydney 5.63. Rtn transfer by train and taxi, or by coach 0.03; by train and bus 0.02. **Offset cost:** $23.45; £0.25; A$105.90.

Responsibility: Strattons sets an example for other hotels, with a comprehensive and well-thought-out green policy that's embraced by all the staff. The owners continually look for new ways to reduce the hotel's carbon footprint, recording energy usage and waste levels to set reduction targets.
Environmental: ⦸⦸⦸⦸⦸
Social: ⦸⦸⦸⦸⦸

L'Auberge les Liards

63490 Égliseneuve des Liards, Auvergne, France
+33 (0)4 73 96 89 44 / www.lesliards.com / info@lesliards.com

IF you weren't looking for it, you might never find this cosy guesthouse, nestled in a largely unexplored corner of the Auvergne. The property – part of a smallholding – sits on the slopes of Puy de Liards, an extinct volcano on the outskirts of the sleepy village of Égliseneuve des Liards. The owners, Dutch couple Astrid Ursem and Walter Verhoeve, have created the guesthouse from two ruined farm buildings. There's the main house, which has two guest rooms, and a nearby building, which contains two 'ecological' rooms.

The couple have carried out their renovations carefully, and the ecological rooms in particular have been constructed with natural and traditional materials like wood, clay and straw. Insulation is provided by a mix of hemp, chalk, loam and hay – as well as soil collected from molehills, which they've discovered works well for helping to insulate the floor. The rooms are simply decorated, with natural colours and wooden furniture. The private bathrooms currently have conventional toilets, but Astrid and Walter hope to convert them to flush with rainwater eventually. Guests are provided with eco-friendly soap, there are low-energy lights and household cleaning products are biodegradable.

The guesthouse serves evening meals as well as breakfast, and much of the food is organic and locally produced. The couple will also happily

cater for vegetarians. Bread comes from the local baker, eggs from their own hens, jams are home-made – often from brambles collected on their land – and lentils and cereals are grown nearby.

The Auvergne is a geologist's dream, famed for its mineral springs and landscapes dominated by brooding volcanoes. From l'Auberge les Liards, which is in the fertile Livradois-Forez Regional Park, you can see the volcanoes spread out before you – including the famous peak known as Puy-de-Dôme. The area is home to all sorts of creatures, from birds to badgers, and Astrid and Walter encourage wildlife by allowing plants like nettles to grow around the place. They keep a range of animals, including sheep, geese, rabbits and chickens, as well as a billy goat, a couple of donkeys and some peacocks, which kids will love.

But the guesthouse offers more than clean air and tranquillity: it's also a good base for getting out and doing some exercise. You can get directly onto several waymarked walking trails, which vary in length from one to five hours, there are plenty of cycling and mountain-biking routes, and there are also horseback-riding centres nearby. If you want to explore more widely, the *auberge* can book you on a guided walk with a local English-speaking mountain guide. After all that exertion, you'll feel you've earned your glass of kir, sipped as you sit on the terrace and watch the sun set behind brooding Puy-de-Dôme.

ECO**FILE**

Rooms: Two twins and 2 doubles.
Rates: €38–69 (US$52–94) per room per night, excluding breakfast. Price increases for stays of only 1 night in Jul–Aug.
Location: 40km (25 miles) south of Clermont-Ferrand, in Livradois-Forez Regional Natural Park, Auvergne.
Best time to go: Midsummer – for the sunsets. Closed Nov–Apr.
Getting there: Fly or travel by Eurostar to Paris, then travel by train for 3 hours 50 mins to Clermont-Ferrand and drive 40 mins to the guesthouse. Alternatively, fly 1 hour from Paris to Clermont-Ferrand.
CO2 emissions: Rtn flight to Paris from New York 1.62 tonnes; Sydney 5.62. Rtn Eurostar to Paris from London 0.01. Rtn transfer to Égliseneuve des Liards by plane and car 0.21; by train and car 0.11.
Offset cost: $27.25; £1.65; A$108.90.

Responsibility: L'Auberge les Liards takes green issues seriously. Great efforts have been made to restore traditional buildings sympathetically, and all waste is recycled or composted where possible. With its plans to install solar panels and make better use of greywater, this is a distinctly eco-friendly *auberge*.
Environmental: ⊘⊘⊘⊘⊘
Social: ⊘⊘⊘⊘⊘

Perché dans le Perche

La Renardière, 61130 Bellou-le-Trichard, Orne, Normandy, France
+33 (0)2 33 25 57 96 / www.perchedansleperche.com / perchedansleperche@gmail.com

IT'S dusk. Sitting on your terrace, perched high in the branches of a magnificent chestnut tree, you look over to the pond and watch carefully for a fox or a badger, or maybe a deer slipping silently down to the water for a drink. When the darkness has drawn in, you lean back, breathe in the soft evening air and see if you can pick out any constellations in the velvet sky. The city seems a thousand miles away.

However, this arboreal hideaway in the Perche – part of the lush Orne district of Normandy – is just a couple of hours from Paris. It's a sort of posh treehouse – 'perched in the Perche' – a comfy cabin that's been built into a 200-year-old chestnut tree by British woman Claire Stickland and her French husband, Ivan Payonne. The tree sits on La Renardière (the Foxery), a 10ha (25-acre) estate the couple bought a few years ago, and which they're carefully managing as a natural haven. The flinty land, once used for pasture, sustains all sorts of plants,

including delicate orchids, and attracts a variety of wildlife, especially birds. With sharp eyes you might spot anything from a wild boar to a buzzard. Claire and Ivan have involved local environmental organizations to help them maximize the site's biodiversity, as they want La Renardière to serve as an example of eco-friendly land management. 'We want to share it,' says Claire. The local school, which the couple's two children attend, often comes here to work on nature projects.

The cabin is sleek and simple, with polished wooden floors and plenty of windows for lots of natural light. There's a bedroom, a sitting area with a little kitchen, and a bathroom. Greywater from the cabin, and from Claire and Ivan's house (a renovated 18th-century cottage), is purified through a succession of troughs containing volcanic rock, reeds and plants, before finally being channelled into a wetland area. Cleaning products are bio-friendly, and there are also eco-friendly toiletries in the bathroom. Waste is either recycled or put on the compost heap.

In the morning, someone will pop over with a basket of fresh local food for your breakfast. You'll find organic butter and yogurt, apple juice, Claire's home-made jam and some fresh seasonal fruit – perhaps from the Renardière's garden. There'll also be organic bread from a Perche farm, and fair-trade tea and coffee. In the evening, you can eat at a local restaurant, or feast on Camembert and cider from one of the region's pretty towns.

Le Renardière is within the Perche Regional Nature Park and there's plenty of rolling countryside to explore. You can walk, cycle or canoe – or attend a vegetarian cookery course at a nearby organic farm. And at night you can climb the steps and snuggle into bed in your very peaceful perch.

ECO**FILE**

Rooms: One double in the main cabin and another downstairs.
Rates: €150 (US$205) per couple per night, including breakfast; €250 (US$340) for 2 nights.
Location: 36km (22 miles) from Nogent-le-Rotrou, Orne, Normandy.
Best time to go: Summer.
Getting there: Fly or travel by Eurostar to Paris, then hire a car to drive the 2 hours to Bellou-le-Trichard, from where it's 2–3km (1.5 miles) to La Renardière. Or travel by train for 1.5 hours from Paris to Nogent-le-Rotrou, and drive 30 mins to the guesthouse. Alternatively, from England, take the ferry 3.5 hours from Portsmouth to Caen, then drive another 1.5 hours to the guesthouse.
CO2 emissions: Rtn flight to Paris from New York 1.62 tonnes; Sydney 5.61. Rtn Eurostar to Paris from London 0.01. Rtn transfer by car 0.11; by train and car 0.02. Ferry and car from Portsmouth 0.09.
Offset cost: $25.60; £1.60; A$107.

Responsibility: This is part of an imaginative project that aims to offer comfort in the countryside while introducing people to the needs for, and benefits of, eco-friendly land management. It's a programme that's continually developing, and benefits flora, fauna and the local community.
Environmental: ⵁⵁⵁⵁⵁ
Social: ⵁⵁⵁⵁⵁ

Green footprints

A walking holiday is not just a green option, but also allows you to explore a region in depth, as **Rebecca Ford** discovered on a wander through the Greek island of Samos.

It was early summer on Samos and the wild pomegranates were in bloom. We wandered along tracks lined with plump peaches and figs, stopped to drink in the welcome shade of leafy carob trees, and explored shrines hidden deep in the hills. Some days we found tranquil temples where ancient gods were worshipped, or picnicked in sleepy olive groves that offered distant views of the Aegean. At other times we strolled around tiny villages, far from the tourist trail, and stopped for cups of thick sweet coffee in little cafés. It was slow travel at its best – a walking holiday.

It wasn't so many years ago that putting the words 'walking' and 'holiday' together conjured up images of a sodden week of rugged route marches and basic hostels, probably in the company of hearty hikers with heavy backpacks and a penchant for unflattering outdoor apparel. But this is no longer the case. These days you can do anything from a gastronomic tour of Tuscany to a strenuous trek on Mont Blanc, staying in comfortable hotels and eating plenty of good food. There are lazy strolls, energetic rambles or challenging hikes. You can go by yourself or join a group, carry a pack or have your luggage sent on ahead. You can even find fairly funky walking gear.

Walking, of course, is about the most environmentally friendly activity of all. You might leave footprints, but they won't be carbon filled – especially if you've reached your starting point by boat or train. And it's one of the few holidays where you'll also come back with firmer thighs – even if you've indulged in large quantities of the local food and wine.

My trip to Samos – the Greek island that was once home to Aesop and Pythagorus – was a self-guided holiday with Headwater, one of a number of specialist walking operators. The packages it offers make walking breaks easy: the company books the flights, hotels and transfers for you, and provides detailed notes to help you follow each day's walk. In my experience these are generally pretty good, keeping 'which way now?' squabbles with your partner to a minimum. A typical break involves several days of linear walks, in which you go to your next base following the route provided, while your luggage is sent ahead separately – cutting out the need to lug a hefty backpack around. But there will also generally be one or two places where you'll stay for a couple

of nights and do a circular walk, so you can explore an area in more detail.

The advantage of these self-guided trips is that you take the walks at your own pace. You can always miss one out if you just don't feel up to it – simply travel to your next base with your luggage and spend a lazy day with a book instead. We did this on Samos one day, when unseasonably high temperatures of nearly (38°C) 100°F made the five-hour walk a less than enticing prospect. The next day we set off very early, so we could walk in the cool of the morning – a great time, as it turned out, to spot some of the local birdlife.

Samos, just 1.6km (1 mile) from the coast of Turkey, is – incorrectly – dismissed in many guidebooks as a tourist hub. But the walks show you that this island has some stunning landscapes, pine forests, Byzantine churches and

This page: A fishing boat moored in the golden sun-lit waters around Samos; Mt Kerketefs, rising above a quiet bay on the Greek island of Samos

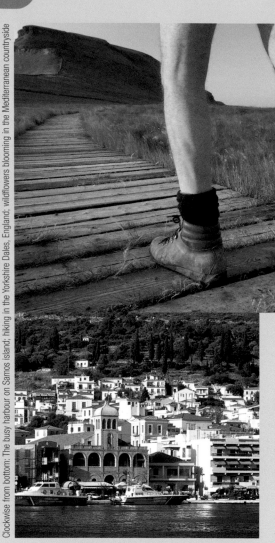

Clockwise from bottom: The busy harbour on Samos island; hiking in the Yorkshire Dales, England; wildflowers blooming in the Mediterranean countryside

suggests, accommodation with Inntravel is often in good country inns and small hotels. I travelled with the company to Basilicata, tucked away on the instep of Italy's boot and traditionally one of the country's poorest regions. The walks took me to places I'd never have discovered by myself, like poppy-filled meadows in the Pollino National Park, and along herb-lined pathways near the village of Viggianello.

While self-guided trips give you freedom and control, group tours mean that you don't have to worry about getting lost, as you'll have a guide with you all the time. This allows you to relax and enjoy the scenery – and chat to your companions. Group sizes vary quite a bit and it's worth checking the details before you book, so you know whether you'll be with a small group – perhaps limited to eight people – or a large one with up to 20.

rural vineyards. It's the same with other destinations – they only reveal their hidden faces if you explore them on foot.

Inntravel, another walking specialist, also offers self-guided walking breaks throughout Europe – again with luggage transfers, detailed route notes and maps. Most of its trips last around a week, but it also has some four-night short breaks that are ideal if you're short of time. As its name

These trips, like self-guided holidays, are generally carefully graded, so you can pick one appropriate to your level of fitness and agility. Choose carefully and ask for advice from the operator. I once joined a group trip to France in which everyone had to sit down for a lengthy break every couple of kilometres, even though the terrain was as flat as a crêpe – fine if that's what you want, but frustrating if you were hoping for a bit more exertion.

Trips range from trails in Sardinia to the mountains of Montenegro, and you soon become aware of the extraordinary diversity of landscapes in Europe. They often have a special theme, too. Ramblers, for instance, offers tours that focus on everything from birdwatching to wine-tasting, while Explore often organizes tougher expeditions to places like Iceland. Then there's ethically conscious ATG. This walking specialist has a wide range of upmarket group and self-guided trips, and was established on sound ethical principles. It runs holidays only to areas that are socially and environmentally robust enough to withstand the visitor impact, and it carries out conservation projects in many of these localities. Now that's a very eco-friendly footprint.

ECO**FILE**

Location: Samos is a Greek island in the eastern Aegean.

Getting there: Many operators offer the choice of rail travel from London if it's practical. For Samos, there are direct flights from London.

CO_2 emissions: Rtn flight to Samos via London from New York 2.12 tonnes; London 0.58; Sydney 6.20.

Offset cost: $31.50; £4.30; A$116.05.

Staying there: Accommodation is included in packages, and ranges from rural inns, former convents and small guesthouses to 4-star hotels.

Rates: Walking breaks range from £229 (US$460) per person for 4 nights in Derbyshire, to £3,800 (US$7,600) for 18 days in Italy. Headwater's Samos trip costs £699–799 (US$1,400–1,600) per person for 7 days.

Best time to go: Go when the weather is neither too hot nor too wet. For Samos, early May is best.

Further information:
www.headwater.com
www.inntravel.co.uk
www.ramblersholidays.co.uk
www.explore.co.uk
www.atg-oxford.co.uk

Responsibility: Going on a walking holiday means that you explore your destination in the most eco-friendly way possible. Staying in small, locally owned inns and hotels, and eating in small, local restaurants supports trade in more isolated rural communities.

mitArt

Linienstrasse 139–140, 10115 Berlin, Germany
+49 (0)30 283 90430 / www.mitart.de / mitart@t-online.de

IT once housed the GDR's National Military Printing Press, producing a ready supply of military propaganda. Now it's Berlin's first green hotel, offering a showcase for all sorts of up-and-coming contemporary artists who might not otherwise be exhibited. How times change. mitArt, the name a play on its location in the lively and cosmopolitan Mitte district of the city, is essentially a sleek urban *pension* – ideal for art and culture lovers wanting a base in the funky heart of Berlin.

The owner, Christiane Waszkowiak, started out running a modern art gallery that offered accommodation for the new artists she exhibited. Gradually it grew into a small hotel. In 2005, she expanded the operation by moving to this unassuming turn-of-the-20th-century building, decorating the interior in cool contemporary style with eco-friendly paints and plaster, and gentle varnishes on the polished wooden floors. The courtyard at the entrance is filled with all sorts of plants – from herbs that might be used in the kitchen, to lemon bushes, fig trees and even a banana palm. The rooms, which vary in size and range over three

floors, are all individually decorated. However, they're stylish and uncluttered, with dark wooden furnishings, crisp white bedding and contemporary artworks. The cleaning products and guest soaps used are organic, biodegradable and not tested on animals, while the en suite bathrooms have dual-flush toilets to limit water wastage.

The building is listed, which limits installation of many eco-features. However, Christiane does all she can. Electricity comes from renewable sources and low-energy light bulbs are fitted. Recycling of everything from plastics to cans is standard practice (as you'd probably expect in Germany), and any waste organic matter from the kitchen is collected in separate containers for communal composting.

The café on the ground floor, which offers lunch as well as breakfast, serves only organic food – sourced as much as possible from local suppliers. For breakfast you can choose from sausages, cheeses, eggs, vegetarian pâtés, wholegrain breads and home-made marmalade. Teas and coffees are organic and from fair-trade sources.

The hotel can give you plenty of information on things to do and see in the area, and Christiane is particularly knowledgeable on the local art scene. In five minutes you can walk to the city's most compelling cultural hub – Museum Island, a striking collection of classical buildings that house paintings, sculptures and antiquities. Then there are iconic sights like the imposing Brandenburg Gate, Norman Foster's shiny new Reichstag and the poignant Mauermuseum at Checkpoint Charlie. The Mitte district, with its great selection of lively bars, restaurants, shops and galleries, sits conveniently between the smart west of Berlin and the up-and-coming east. mitArt, with its historic legacy, trendy artworks and eco-friendly attitude, seems to sum up this fascinating city perfectly.

ECO**FILE**

Rooms: Five singles, 25 doubles.
Rates: €110–180 (US$150–245) per double per night, including breakfast.
Location: In the heart of Berlin.
Best time to go: In the autumn, when Berlin's many trees turn gold and bronze. Closed at Christmas.
Getting there: Fly into any of Berlin's airports. All have public transport links to Orienburger Tor, the nearest metro station to the hotel.
CO2 emissions: Rtn flight to Berlin from New York 1.79 tonnes; London 0.22; Sydney 5.25.
Offset cost: $26.55; £1.70; A$98.20.

Responsibility: mitArt makes a concerted effort to operate in an environmentally sound fashion, not just offering organic food and fitting a few low-energy light bulbs, but also recycling its waste, trying to reduce water wastage and using biodegradable products. It is looking for more ways to reduce its carbon footprint, and it supports new local artists.
Environmental: ⌀⌀⌀⌀⌀
Social: ⌀⌀⌀⌀⌀

Albergo Amici

Via Garibaldi 80, Varese Ligure, 19208 (SP), Liguria, Italy
+39 (0)187 842139 / www.albergoamici.com / info@albergoamici.com

ECOFILE

Rooms: 23 doubles and 3 singles.
Rates: €55 (US$75) per double per night, excluding breakfast (€5/US$7); €104 (US$142) per double per night, including all meals.
Location: In Varese Ligure, in the Val di Vara in Liguria. 117km (73 miles) from Pisa
Best time to go: Early summer.
Getting there: From Pisa, drive 1.5 hours to Varese Ligure, or travel by train for 110 mins to Sestri Levante and then 45 mins by bus to Varese Ligure. Alternatively, travel by Eurostar from London to Paris, then 13.5 hours by rail to Sestri Levante via Florence and Pisa, and finally 45 mins by bus to Varese Ligure.
CO_2 emissions: Rtn flight to Pisa from New York 1.86 tonnes; Sydney 5.46. Rtn Eurostar to Paris from London 0.01. Rtn transfer from Pisa by car 0.70; from Sestri Levante by bus 0.005. Train figures for Italy n/a.
Offset cost: $27.80; £2.10; A$101.35.

Responsibility: The hotel is at the heart of a whole community's efforts to be environmentally friendly. With water heated by solar panels, stringent recycling of rubbish and a reliance on locally produced organic food, it's made a good start.
Environmental: ⦸⦸⦸⦸⦸
Social: ⦸⦸⦸⦸⦸

OWNED by the same family since 1760, the unfussy Albergo Amici is a hotel that knows what it does best, and sticks to it. The large reception area, which also functions as the residents' lounge, has a comfy jumble of chairs, a ticking grandfather clock, and walls hung with old photographs of the family and their historic hotel. Guests sit here and chat, watch TV and sip drinks from the little bar. Pride of place goes to a large wood-burning stove, the fuel for which is collected locally.

The rooms themselves are simple and uncluttered, with few frills but everything you could require. But this isn't a place where you'd want to spend much time stuck in your room, for there's so much to explore outside. The Albergo Amici is in the heart of the historic market town of Varese Ligure, in the largely undiscovered mountains that stretch inland from Liguria's well-trodden coast. For centuries the town provided a retreat for wealthy residents of Genoa and other coastal areas, who came here to escape the oppressive summer heat. Now the municipality has got such a reputation for being environmentally friendly that it's become the first community in Europe to receive official EU accreditation for its eco-management measures. And the area in which it sits, the Val di Vara, is popularly known as Italy's 'Organic Valley'.

You don't have to go far to see these policies in action. The hotel has solar panels that heat the water, separates and monitors its waste for recycling, and uses as many eco-friendly cleaning products as possible. The staff are all involved in the process of trying to make the hotel a carbon-neutral establishment. Wander round the picturesque town –

of which the hotel's owner is mayor – and you might also spot photovoltaic cells on rooftops, although you won't notice the fact that the town's drinking water is now sterilized through an ultra-violet process rather than with chlorine. The community also has wind turbines up in the mountains, which produce a large proportion of the power it needs.

The hotel has an excellent reputation for its food, attracting large numbers of Italians from the coast for Sunday lunch. It makes great efforts to serve traditional dishes using produce that is locally sourced, seasonal and, ideally, organic, including meat, wine, cheese and olive oil. Pasta and bread are home-made. If you thought the only Ligurian dish was pasta pesto, think again. You'll find regional specialities like thick meaty stews, vegetable pies and sauces made from pine nuts.

The valley, with its organic farms and picturesque hill towns, is well worth exploring. Or you can get a bus down to the bustling coastal resort of Sestri Levante, sit by the Bay of Fairytales and indulge in an ice cream – you can always work it all off with a walk in Varese Ligure's clean mountain air.

Casa del Grivo

Borgo Canal dei Ferro 19, 33040 Faedis, Udine, Friuli-Venezia Giulia, Italy
+39 (0)432 728638 / www.grivo.has.it / casadelgrivo@libero.it

THERE'S no pretension about Casa del Grivo. It's a relaxed family home in a little hamlet in the far north of Italy, with a smallholding that's run on natural organic principles. This simple and welcoming country inn – home to Toni and Paola Costalunga, who live here with their three children and several animals – has plenty of rustic charm. It's also set in a part of Italy that's not on the tourist trail.

The house itself, with its wooden shutters and little balcony, was built around 1920 and has been renovated using traditional materials such as hand-made bricks, local stones and chestnut beams, as well as natural varnishes. There's a wooden staircase, and the very thick walls and layers of granulated cork provide excellent insulation. The couple have also ensured that the interior reflects the vernacular style, with wooden furniture from Friuli, a stone sink, and a fireplace in every room.

This style is continued in the guest rooms, which have traditional mattresses that are filled with wool and vegetable fibres. Only one has a private bathroom; the other three rooms – decorated in green, pink and white, respectively – share two bathrooms. Water is warmed by

solar power, and the house is partly heated by burning wood collected from the nearby forests. The Costalungas help to keep their environmental impact low by cleaning the house with biodegradable products, recycling their waste and composting as much as possible.

Toni grows all sorts of fruit and vegetables in the organic kitchen garden, and also has a vineyard in which he grows grapes that the couple use to make their own wines: Refusco, a dry red; Tocai, a dry white; and Verduzzo, a white dessert wine. Paola cooks for guests using lots of the family's produce, as well as other local and organic foods. You might have warming plates of polenta with wild mushrooms in the evening, or fresh bread (made in the wood oven) with home-made jams and the farm's fresh apple juice for breakfast.

Casa del Grivo is in Friuli-Venezia Giulia in the far north of Italy, a region that's squeezed between Austria and Slovenia and whose people have a distinctive dialect – Friuliano. There are plenty of walks, cycle paths and clean rivers by which to picnic. The nearby medieval town of Cividale del Friuli is well worth exploring, with its 15th-century cathedral, medieval buildings and Celtic hypogeum – a sort of cellar that some think was a tomb, others a jail. Afterwards, you'll be ready for a relaxed evening back at the farm, with a home-cooked dinner and a glass of that wine.

ECO**FILE**

Rooms: Four doubles.

Rates: €28 (US$38) per person per night, including breakfast; €45 (US$61) per person per night, including breakfast and dinner. Minimum stay of 2 nights.

Location: 20km (12 miles) from Udine in the Friuli-Venezia Giulia region of northern Italy.

Best time to go: Summer. Closed Christmas and New Year.

Getting there: Fly to Trieste, then drive 70 mins to Faedis; or take a bus or taxi from the airport to Trieste Centrale station, then travel by train for 1 hour to Udine, where someone can come and pick you up.

CO_2 emissions: Rtn flight to Trieste from New York 1.89 tonnes; London 0.27; Sydney 5.30. Rtn transfer by car 0.05. Train figures for Italy n/a. **Offset cost:** $28.90; £2.45; A$100.20.

Responsibilty: Casa del Grivo has a responsible approach to the environment, and makes a positive effort to minimize its carbon footprint. Measures such as using solar power and burning wood to heat the house reduce its impact – as, of course, does the organic garden.

Environmental: ⌀⌀⌀⌀⌀
Social: ⌀⌀⌀⌀⌀

Locanda della Valle Nuova

La Cappella 14, 61033 Sagrata di Fermignano, Pesaro e Urbino, Le Marche, Italy
+39 (0)722 330303 / www.vallenuova.it / info@vallenuova.it

THOSE who have discovered the glorious landscape of Le Marche tend to keep quiet about it. They don't want hordes of tourists descending on these deliciously green hills and exquisite towns and cities. Guests of the Locanda della Valle Nuova have done much the same, hoping to keep this 75ha (185-acre) organic farm to themselves. Owned and run by the Savini family, who have been producing organic free-range beef since 1981, the farm offers sleek contemporary guest rooms in a tranquil rural setting.

The Savinis' commitment to green living is comprehensive. The house, built in the 1920s, was restored in 1998 using traditional materials like stone and wood, with thick walls, double glazing and cork insulation to ensure good energy conservation. It is heated by a wood stove using fuel from the family's own woodlands, as well as some solar power, and by 2008 they plan to have solar panels to supply their electricity. More energy is saved with low-consumption light bulbs, and there are recycling bins for plastics, cans and paper.

The rooms are city-chic, rather than rustic, in style and are themed by colour

– one is bright and yellow, one is a soft pink, and another is cool and green. Soap dispensers help to cut wastage, and the laundry is washed with small amounts of concentrated soap that's not tested on animals.

In addition to raising beef, the Savinis also have a vineyard, produce some organic cereals (they have a small mill), keep free-range hens, and grow a wide variety of fruit and vegetables. Wander around the farm and you'll find apricot and plum trees, juicy watermelons and plump tomatoes. The food served is predominantly organic, seasonal and locally grown, and the family also collect wild herbs, sloes and nuts to use in cooking. You breakfast on home-made bread and jams, local honey and organic cheese, and in the evening enjoy freshly made pasta or the farm's own Marchigiana beef, accompanied by local wines and perhaps a home-made walnut liqueur. In the autumn, there's the possibility of delicious white truffles from the family's woodland.

Truffle-hunting is the only kind of hunting done on the farm, making it a real haven for wildlife. Porcupines, badgers, wild boar and deer all live here, and you might also see fireflies, which thrive in the garden. If you're feeling active you can go horseback riding at the farm's own riding school, or take a dip in the outdoor swimming pool. The family will also give you plenty of information on walks and cycling trails nearby. The beautiful city of Urbino is just a short drive away, while wildlife lovers will want to visit the Furlo Gorge Nature Reserve, home to rare orchids, raptors, reptiles, and even wolves.

ECO**FILE**

Rooms: Six (5 doubles, 1 twin), plus a self-catering apartment (sleeps 2).
Rates: €52 (US$71) per person per night, including breakfast; €78 (US$106) per person per night including breakfast and dinner (minimum stay of 3 nights). Self-catering apartment €680 (US$930) per week.
Location: Near Urbino, in the Marche, Italy. 60km (37 miles), from Rimini, 90km (56 miles) from Ancona.
Best time to go: Oct, for truffle-hunting. Closed Dec–May.
Getting there: Fly to Rimini or Ancona, then hire a car. The drive from Rimini takes 50 mins, and from Ancona takes 70 mins.
CO2 emissions: Rtn flight from New York 1.92 tonnes; London 0.30; Sydney 5.34. Rtn transfer from Rimini 0.04; from Ancona 0.05.
Offset cost: $29.40; £2.70; A$100.

Responsibility: The Locanda della Valle Nuova makes a consistent effort to work in harmony with the land and its wildlife. Energy consumption is low, and the farm continually tries to reduce its carbon footprint, as well as recycling waste and growing organic food.
Environmental: ✿✿✿✿✿
Social: ✿✿✿✿✿

Anna's House

Tullynagee, 35 Lisbarnett Road, Comber, Co. Down, BT23 6AW, Northern Ireland, UK
+44 (0)28 9754 1566 / www.annashouse.com / anna@annashouse.com

THE reed-fringed lake is home to moorhens, swans and the occasional heron. The garden, with its secret nooks and thick hedges, is lush and green. You feel as if you're miles from anywhere. Tranquil. Calm.

But Anna's House is just a 20-minute drive from busy Belfast, and is a wonderfully accessible green haven. The house itself was originally a two-room cottage, but has been sympathetically extended over the years into a large, comfortable guesthouse — run by Anna Johnson and her husband, Ken. The latest addition is a lovely light living area, with huge windows and stunning views. It's cleverly and efficiently heated by

a geothermal system that pumps the earth's natural heat up and under the floor. Energy is further conserved by solar panels, which Ken installed and which heat all the water; low-energy light bulbs; and the family car — a hybrid Prius. Eventually, the couple hope to have their own wind turbine, which will reduce their carbon footprint even more.

Anna and Ken have created a relaxed retreat, making you feel at home by offering welcome cups of tea and home-made cakes when you arrive. Guests often ask Anna for her recipes, which she happily passes on – in return for a donation to the local children's hospice. The couple also make a point of serving guests as much local and organic produce as possible. Breakfast – full Irish or something lighter if you prefer – is likely to include Anna's home-made bread and yogurt, as well as free-range eggs from a nearby farm and organic tea and coffee. She will happily cater for vegetarians and vegans, as well as people with special medical requirements such as coeliacs.

The four guest rooms are fresh and clean, with Irish linen sheets on the beds, en suite bathrooms and Wi-Fi access. Two of the rooms have a balcony, and one on the ground floor provides wheelchair access and has a wet room (shower room) in addition to a private terrace.

The Johnsons' flower-filled 0.8ha (2-acre) garden is completely organic, including the vegetable plot, which is nourished with their own compost. They also have another 7.3ha (18 acres) of land that Anna eventually plans to plant with indigenous trees and other species that will attract wildlife.

Stay here and you might find yourself spending ages just strolling round the garden, lying on the hammock among the pine trees, or spotting different species of birds and butterflies. However, there's plenty more to see, and birdwatchers will certainly want to pack their binoculars and head for Strangford Lough – a watery paradise for migrating wildfowl. Then there's Belfast itself to the north, with its historic buildings, shops and restaurants; or the Mountains of Mourne to the south, which offer plenty of opportunities for exhilarating walks. In the evening you can dine at one of the many local pubs, before heading back to the guesthouse and snuggling down for a good night's sleep.

ECO**FILE**

Rooms: Four rooms (2 doubles and 2 twins).

Rates: £70–85 (US$140–170) per room, including breakfast.

Location: 5km (3 miles) outside Comber, south of Belfast.

Best time to go: Early summer for the flowers, autumn for the trees.

Getting there: From Belfast, hire a car or taxi for the 15-min journey to Anna's House. Alternatively, from England, take the ferry from Liverpool, Stranraer or Douglas to Belfast, and drive from there.

CO_2 emissions: Rtn flight to Belfast from New York 1.41 tonnes; London 0.14; Sydney 5.68. Rtn ferry from Liverpool 0.005. Transfer by car 0.01.
Offset cost: $21.15; £1.15; A$106.35.

Responsibility: Anna's House has significantly reduced its carbon footprint with its use of geothermal heating as well as solar panels. The owners are committed to minimizing their impact on the environment still further and continually look for ways to become even greener. They also source local and organic food.

Environmental: ∅∅∅∅∅
Social: ∅∅∅∅∅

On your bike

Don't let Scotland's mountains put you off the idea of a cycling holiday here. As **Robin Barton** found, there's a route to suit everyone, with plenty of magnificent scenery along the way.

Quiet lanes, filling food, majestic scenery and plenty of hills: it's as if Scotland was designed by a committee of cyclists. The country has some of the finest cycle routes in the world, including purpose-built mountain-bike trails and long-distance coast-to-coast routes. But novice cyclists can rest assured, as there are easy circular loops that will leave you wanting more. Whatever your tastes, cycling is a great way to experience Scotland, and one of the most eco-friendly ways to travel.

Great for mountain-bikers: Glentress
The 7Stanes is a series of seven mountain-biking centres strung across the Scottish Borders, and Glentress, in the Tweed Valley, is the project's figurehead. It is one of the most popular visitor attractions in Scotland thanks to a wide range of trails, from easy-going blue routes for begin-

This page: Spectacular scenery along the V-trail at Glentress in Scotland's Tweed Valley

ners to the 19km (12-mile) red route and the testing 32km (20-mile) black route. Every mountain-biker should make at least one visit to Glentress; you're bound to leave a better rider. Not sure whether you're up to it? Mountain-biking courses are available from ex-pro racers Emma Guy and Tracy Brunger, who manage the Hub in the Forest shop and café. The clearly marked trails offer superb views over the Pentlands, the hills south of Edinburgh. There is plenty for non-cylists to do. Glentress is just 2km (1 mile) away from the thriving town of Peebles, where it's worth stopping to refuel at one of the town's excellent restaurants, such as the Sunflower.

Great for natural scenery: Great Glen Way

Expand your horizons with a trip into the Highlands on the Great Glen Way, a 130km (80-mile) route through the majestic Great Glen, the setting for many battles over the centuries. The route starts in the adventure town of Fort William, host to sporting events such as the Mountain Bike and Trials World Championships, and finishes on the east coast at Inverness. But it's not all about serious cycling here. Using canal towpaths, lanes and cycle tracks, this is a rugged but straightforward low-level route, as popular with long-distance walkers as with cyclists; a hybrid or mountain-bike is recommended. The easiest sections are those closest to Fort William: the 23km (14-mile) ride from there to Loch Lochy is a good introduction.

Maps can be obtained from VisitScotland offices at either end of the Great Glen, and the signposted path is patrolled by rangers. Fort William makes a convenient base, although the remote Loch Ossian Hostel on Rannoch Moor is in a great spot.

Great for families: Glen Trool

Gentle gradients and wide, easy trails are the hallmark of the Glen Trool mountain-biking routes, one of the 7Stanes centres. Using forest tracks and quiet lanes, the two waymarked routes – one short, one long – explore the beautiful woodland and lochs of Galloway Forest Park. Novice cyclists can pick up confidence on the unchallenging tracks that radiate from the forest visitor centre. And there's plenty more to do in the area, with water sports on

This page: The best and most eco-friendly way to see Scotland. Page 148: Cyclist on a 7Stanes trail

the forest park's lakes and two interesting towns nearby: Castle Douglas, beloved of foodies; and Kirkudbright on Solway Firth, a favourite haunt of artists.

Great for history: Orkney

The Orkneys are rich in history, from the neolithic burial chambers that pepper the islands to the wartime stories of Scapa Flow. And what better way to immerse yourself in it than by getting around on a bicycle?

The historic highlight of Orkney is undoubtedly Skara Brae, northwest of Kirkwall, the site of an ancient settlement dating back to 3100BC. Maes Howe, on the road from Stromness to Finstown, is a neolithic chambered cairn with UNESCO World Heritage status. The 30km (19-mile) ride from Kirkwall to Stromness via Orphir can include detours to both of these sites, as well as to stone circles and other burial chambers. On a clear day,

the views of the mountains fading gently into the sea are stunning; on a rough day, you'll want to be safely tucked up indoors.

Great for wimps:
Speyside Way

Cycle paths alongside rivers tend to be flat and traffic-free, and this route alongside the River Spey is no exception, making it ideal for novice or young bicycle riders. You join the Spey – one of Scotland's finest salmon rivers – at Craigellachie, then follow it southwest through Aberlour and past the Knockando and Tamdhu whisky distilleries. There are picnic tables at Blacksboat if you want a break, otherwise continue across the old railway bridge into Ballindalloch, the halfway point of this 19km (12-mile) ride. Next, either retrace your tracks along the riverside path or follow the B9102 to the north and east – it returns you to Craigellachie by way of a few hills.

Further information:
www.green-business.co.uk
www.sustrans.org.uk
http://cycling.visitscotland.com
www.7stanes.gov.uk
www.firstgroup.com/scotrail

Responsibility:
Few modes of transport are as eco-friendly as cycling. Your legs provide the power and calories provide the energy, and there are no waste products or emissions. Even mountain-bikers leave little evidence of their passing, although riding off established trails is discouraged.

ECO**FILE**

For Mountain-bikers: Glentress
Getting there: From Edinburgh, drive or catch a bus to Peebles, 29km (18 miles) to the south.
CO_2 emissions: Rtn flight to Edinburgh from New York 1.45 tonnes; Sydney 5.59. Rtn train to Edinburgh from London 0.08. Rtn transfer by car 0.17; by bus 0.005.
Offset cost: $24.15; £1.90; A$109.15.
Staying there: Castlehill Knowe (+44 (0)1721 720805; www.castle-hill-knowe.co.uk; from £25/US$50 per person per night).

For scenery: Great Glen Way
Getting there: From Glasgow, take a train to Fort William or drive there (169km/105 miles). Alternatively, catch an overnight train direct from London's Euston Station.
CO_2 emissions: Rtn flight to Glasgow from New York 1.43 tonnes; Sydney 5.05. Rtn train to Fort William from London 0.10. Rtn transfer by train 0.02; by car 0.10.
Offset cost: $22.85; £0.70; A$94.85.
Staying there: Huntingtower Lodge (+44 (0)1397 700079; www.hunting-tower.co.uk), 3km (2 miles) south of Fort William (£85/US$170 per double room per night); Loch Ossian Hostel (+44 (0)8701 553255; www.syha.org.uk), 30km (20 miles) east of Fort William (from £13.50/US$27 per person per night).

For families: Glen Trool
Getting there: From Glasgow, drive 130km (80 miles) to Glen Trool.
CO_2 emissions: Rtn flight to Glasgow as above. Rtn train to Glasgow from London 0.08. Rtn transfer 0.08

Offset cost: $22.50; £1.20; A$95.90.
Staying there: Number 3 (+44 (0)1557 330881; www.number3-bandb.co.uk) in Kirkcudbright (from £30/US$60 per person per night); Rusko Holiday Cottages (+44 (0)1557 814215; www.ruskoholi-days.co.uk; from £216/US$432 per week self-catering).

For history: Orkney
Getting there: From Aberdeen, fly to Kirkwall, Orkney, or take a ferry or drive (427km/265 miles).
CO_2 emissions: Rtn flight to Aberdeen from New York 1.46 tonnes; London 0.17; Sydney 5.00. Rtn transfer by plane 0.06; by ferry 0.001; by car 0.26.
Offset cost: $25.50; £3.15; $98.20.
Staying there: Westrow Lodge Bed and Breakfast (+44 (0)1856 811360; www.rovingeye.co.uk) in Orphir (from £28/US$56 per person per night).

For wimps: Speyside Way
Getting there: From Inverness, drive the 82km (51 miles) east to Craigellachie.
CO_2 emissions: Rtn flight to Inverness from New York 1.43 tonnes; Sydney 5.03. Rtn train to Inverness from London 0.09. Rtn transfer 0.05.
Offset cost: $21.95; £1.05; A$94.95.
Staying there: Craigellachie on Victoria Street (+44 (0)1340 881204; www.craigellachie.com; from £135/US$270 per double room per night, including breakfast); Minmore House Hotel (+44 (0)1807 590378; www.minmorehousehotel. com; from £64/US$128 per person per night).

Aqua City Resort

Sportova 1397/1, 05801 Poprad, Slovakia
+44 (0)1582 748840 / www.aquacityresort.com / reservations@aquacityresort.com

ECO**FILE**

Rooms: 58 in the 3-star Seasons;
46 in the 4-star Mountain View.
Rates: SKK4,090–5,620
(US$170–235) per double room per
night in the Seasons, including break-
fast and dinner; SKK4,590–6,190
(US$190–255) in the Mountain View.
Location: Poprad, Slovakia.
Best time to go: Winter.
Getting there: Fly to Poprad, from
where it's a 10-min taxi ride.
CO2 emissions: Rtn flight to Poprad
from New York 1.96 tonnes; London
0.33; Sydney 5.08.
Offset cost: $29.30; £2.55; A$95.10.

Responsibility: Aqua City keeps its
carbon footprint small by harnessing
natural energy in imaginative ways, as
well as recycling waste. It has its own
organic farm, run by local people, is
committed to using locally sourced,
fresh food wherever possible, and it
intends to get greener.
Environmental: ⊘⊘⊘⊘⊘
Social: ⊘⊘⊘⊘⊘

A RESORT and water park with saunas,
steams rooms, Jacuzzis, and both indoor and
outdoor heated pools might sound like an
environmental glutton, continually guzzling
vast amounts of precious energy. But Aqua
City is a resort with a difference. This family-
friendly water park – which also has two
hotels, a gym and a cryotherapy centre – gets
most of its power by harnessing the natural
properties of subterranean springs. The resort
has been built around two boreholes, which
channel the water from geothermal mineral
springs to feed the nine swimming pools and
heat the saunas. This geothermal water is
also converted to electricity, which powers
much of the resort. In addition, the owner,
entrepreneur Jan Telensky, has installed solar
panels and has plans for wind turbines, which
should eventually make the resort both self-
sufficient in energy (by, as he says, 'earth, wind
and fire') and emission-free.

You'll find Aqua City in Poprad, in eastern Slovakia, an area that's becoming increasingly popular for its winter sports. It's an angular, modern building with light, understated interiors and a dramatic backdrop provided by the High Tatras Mountains. Rooms in the four-star Mountain View hotel are crisp and contemporary, with balconies, LCD screens and spacious bathrooms, the latter supplied with an endless flow of hot geothermal water. The three-star Seasons hotel has smaller, more functional-looking rooms but is still very comfortable.

Both hotels give you easy access to the Aquapark, which aside from the pools (one Olympic sized) also has flumes and a toboggan ride. The water is purified with ultraviolet light and the pools are lined with stainless steel, so very little chlorine is needed, saving you from itchy red eyes as well as saving the planet. In the spa you can relax in the inhalation rooms, filled with fragrant vapours, or sit in a Jacuzzi or hot tub and then cool off in an ice cave, surrounded by real snow.

The resort's restaurant serves as much local and organic produce as possible; it even has its own farm, on which cattle and pigs are raised, and its own bakery, where bread is made in the traditional way. Waste, such as plastic, is recycled and the cleaning products used are organic. Jan is also committed to ensuring that tourism benefits the community through a variety of measures, such as employing local people and sponsoring nearby sports clubs.

Of course, you can't wallow in water all day – you'd go all wrinkly. Luckily, there are lots of appealing towns and villages just a short journey from your eco-friendly bubble. Electric trains run from Poprad to Tatranska lomnica, where you can take a cable car up into the Tatras Mountains. Or you can head to the former spa town of Stary Smokovec, then take the funicular train to Hrebienok – a popular skiing area that also offers good walks in summer. And if your muscles get stiff, there's always plenty of hot water back at the hotel.

The Hoopoe Yurt Hotel

Apartado de Correos 23, Cortes de la Frontera, 29380 Málaga, Andalucía, Spain
+34 (0)952 117 055 / www.yurthotel.com / yurthotel@mac.com

IF you thought staying in a yurt meant sacrificing comfort for eco-cred, then think again. The yurts at the Hoopoe just ooze stylish indulgence. Dotted among shady groves of cork and olive trees, these circular canvas caves are filled with more than a hint of eastern promise. Each one has its own acre of private meadow, filled with herbs and wildflowers, where you can sit and snooze in the Spanish sun.

Step inside and you find yourself transported to deepest Mongolia, with hand-painted decorations on the beams, exotic Mongolian artefacts and richly coloured textiles. Beds are large and comfortable, with crisp white sheets and jazzy cushions. Each yurt stands on a raised platform, so you don't have to worry about it being squishy underfoot or sharing your sleeping quarters with most of Andalucía's insects. Instead, you walk on polished wooden floorboards scattered with rugs.

For those who hate the communal ablutions aspect of camping, there's a pleasant surprise in the form of private bathrooms – each equipped with its own eco-friendly composting toilet and hot shower. You've got electricity too – solar-powered – and each yurt has both overhead and bedside lighting, as well as electric sockets for mobile phones and laptops.

There are four yurts to choose from, each slightly different inside. The Mongolian yurt is decorated in deep orange shades, the Afghani yurt has a rich red ceiling, and the Jaipur yurt is lighter and brighter. There's also the Safari yurt, which offers striking views of Gaucín – a traditional Andalucían white village. Outside, there's a natural spring-fed swimming pool, which is kept free from chlorine.

This romantic retreat is an ideal place for birdwatchers, as the mature trees and wildflower meadows attract a rich variety of species – including the hotel's exotic namesake, the hoopoe. Lay quietly in a hammock and you might spot anything from warblers and woodpeckers to vultures and eagles. At night you may also hear an owl – or at least the bells of a passing goat.

Yurts are the traditional dwellings of the nomadic peoples of the Mongolian steppes, but the Hoopoe Yurt Hotel is the brainchild of British couple Ed and Henrietta Hunt. Several nights a week they offer guests evening meals, which are eaten outside under the flickering lights of Chinese lanterns. The produce is either bought locally or grown in the Hunts' kitchen garden. They also provide guests with a continental breakfast that includes local honey and fresh fruits.

You might not want to stir far from your meadow, for the site offers stunning views of the Grazalema Mountains, but there's plenty to see in the surrounding area. In 20 minutes you can walk to the traditional white village of Cortes de la Frontera, with its bars, restaurants and shops; drive to the Moorish town of Ronda; or head out into the mountains for some birdwatching with a local guide. You never know, you might even be lucky enough to see a hoopoe.

ECOFILE

Rooms: Four yurts, all doubles.
Rates: €140 (US$190) per yurt per night, including breakfast.
Location: Near Cortes de la Frontera in Andalucía.
Best time to go: Spring, for the wildflowers. Closed Nov–Mar.
Getting there: Fly to Gibraltar or Jerez then hire a car. It's 1.5 hours' drive from Jerez and 2 hours from Gibraltar. Alternatively, walk across the border into Spain from Gibraltar, then take a 15-min taxi ride to San Roque and a 50-min train trip to Cortes de la Frontera. The owners will pick you up from there.
CO2 emissions: Return flight to Gibraltar from New York 1.62 tonnes; London 0.39; Sydney 6.01. Rtn transfer by car 0.03.
Offset cost: $24.65; £3.15; A$112.90.

Responsibility: This chic retreat keeps its environmental impact low by using solar power, reducing water wastage with eco-toilets, and leaving most of the land uncultivated to act as a haven for plants, butterflies and birds. The owners also ensure that the food they eat and serve to their guests is locally sourced.

Environmental:	✿✿✿✿✿
Social:	✿✿✿✿✿

To offset or not?

THE carbon-offsetting industry has taken off, fuelled by the idea that you can 'offset' a tonne of CO_2-equivalent (or CO_2e) emissions by either absorbing a tonne of existing CO_2, or preventing a tonne of future CO_2 being released from elsewhere in the atmosphere. The idea has attracted support from many people looking for a way to minimize their carbon footprint – and also much debate.

A rapidly growing number of carbon-offset companies can calculate the amount of CO_2 you emit through activities such as driving a car, heating your house or catching a plane, and will then quote the cost of offsetting this emission. The money you pay them will then go towards projects to reduce or prevent CO_2 emissions. If you choose to pay one of these companies, say £40 (US$80) to offset the emissions of your flight from London to Sydney, you can claim the flight was 'carbon neutral', which might help to ease your eco-guilt. But is offsetting really a practical solution?

Critics argue that carbon offsetting does nothing to reduce the amount of overall CO_2 emissions. As Leo Hickman, author of *The Final Call*, puts it, 'At best it falls into the "better than nothing" approach to

tackling climate change, but at worst it lulls us into a false sense of security. It fails to address the heart of the issue: that we need to reduce emissions, not just neutralize them.'

Offsetting schemes fall into two broad categories. The first aims to prevent future carbon emissions through renewable energy schemes, such as wind farms, or through energy-efficiency projects, such as installing energy-saving technologies in housing developments. The second aims to absorb existing emissions through carbon-sequestration projects such as reafforestation.

However, there is uneasiness about some of the projects being used to generate offsets. In a joint statement, Greenpeace, Friends of the Earth (FoE) and the World Wide Fund for Nature (WWF) expressed 'strong concerns over the environmental credibility of the credits and the contribution of the projects to sustainable development'. Although popular, forestation schemes are particularly problematic, as it is almost impossible to guarantee that a new forest will not be cut down or succumb to disease within the 100 years it needs to live in order to soak up the already-released CO_2. Some misguided tree-planting schemes are accused of replacing old-growth forests with monoculture spruce and eucalyptus plantations, disrupting local hydrology and replacing traditional farming lands in the process. Tree-planting schemes also do nothing to address our reliance on fossil fuels.

Schemes that invest in renewable-energy technologies in the developing world bring electricity to communities not served by the fossil-fuel grid and prevent the release of future carbon emissions. By encouraging this growth towards an alternative energy system, Michael Buick from Climate Care argues that offsetting can be 'a way to fund the transition to a low carbon economy'. Despite their criticism of off-setting schemes, Greenpeace, FoE and WWF still offset their emissions, but only through projects that have been certified by the rigorous Gold Standard. This is the strictest available standard for CO_2e credits – an 'independent, transparent, internationally recognised benchmark for high quality carbon offset projects', according to the organizations. The Gold Standard certifies only renewable-energy and energy-efficiency projects with sustainable development benefits for local people (for a list of companies that sell Gold Standard credits, see page 315).

Perhaps the most important outcome of the carbon-offsetting debate is the growth in our carbon literacy. We are starting to think about the size of our personal carbon footprint and how not only travel, but all aspects of our lives, have an impact on it – from the food and clothing we buy, to the amount of energy we use at home. Where flying is the only realistic option, it's worth considering how we can reduce our carbon footprint in other areas of our lives. Supporting a good carbon-offsetting scheme is better than ignoring the problem; but, ultimately, the first thing we must do is change our behaviour.

The Lodge

Semilla Besada, Apartado de Correos 19, 18420 Lanjarón, Granada, Andalucía, Spain
+34 (0)958 347 053 / www.holisticdecisions.com/thelodge / aspen@holisticdecisions.com

PERCHED high up in the Sierra Nevada Natural Park, 25 minutes' drive from the nearest village and with no public services, the Lodge feels incredibly remote. It's a two-bedroom self-catering apartment on the first floor of a farmhouse owned by British couple Aspen and David Edge. The house is around 500 years old, and is made mainly of stone and mud walls with chestnut beams.

Aspen and David run their 0.8ha (2-acre) farm as a research project, investigating small-scale and traditional farming practices, the idea being to work in harmony with the local environment. It's a serious exercise in self-sufficiency, too, and they'll show you round if you wish. They grow all their own vegetables and fruit, and also keep sheep, chickens, geese and goats. If they've got any surplus produce they'll happily sell

you some to cook in your apartment. But there may be little need, as a complimentary basket of items like homemade bread, fresh goat's milk and organic eggs is provided on arrival.

The apartment, like the farmhouse, has a decidedly low impact on the environment. In winter when it's chilly, it's heated with a wood-burning stove – dead wood found on the mountain

and prunings from the farm's own olive, almond and chestnut trees provide the fuel. Electricity comes from solar panels, as does hot water for your shower. The bathroom has a regulated flushing toilet, but if you're keen to do the full 'back to nature' bit you can always use the outdoor composting toilet. There's no TV but you're provided with plenty of books and board games, as well as a wind-up radio. The farm has a natural spring that provides drinking water, and there's also a small plunge pool – a cloudy blue colour as it isn't treated with chemicals.

With temperatures rising above 40°C (104°F) in summer, and only around six months of rainfall a year, water at Semilla Besada is a precious commodity. Aspen and David irrigate their land by collecting greywater from the house. They also use an open channel laid down by Moorish settlers almost a thousand years ago that harnesses snowmelt and river water.

The Lodge is the ideal base for walking in the mountains or horseback riding – there's a trekking centre just ten minutes away. The fragile landscape – dry *maquis* (scrub), with low-growing plants and aromatics like lavender and thyme – supports a wide range of insects, reptiles and birds. You might see whitethroats, bee-eaters, rare ibex or golden eagles.

If you want to explore farther afield, you can drive or walk into Lanjarón, the nearest village. This has a market and shops where you can stock up on supplies, as well as a mineral spa offering various treatments. Then head back to your apartment for dinner on the balcony, looking across to the distant Atlas Mountains of Morocco.

ECO**FILE**

Rooms: Self-contained apartment with 2 twin rooms.
Rates: €370 (US$500) per week; preferred minimum of 7 nights.
Location: Above Lanjarón village, 96km (60 miles) south of Granada in Andalucía.
Best time to go: Late spring or early autumn.
Getting there: From Málaga, hire a car for the 3-hour drive to the Lodge, or take a 1.5-hour bus trip to Granada and then change for another 1.5-hour trip to Lanjarón. It's 25 mins from Lanjarón to The Lodge. Alternatively, fly into Granada.
CO2 emissions: Rtn flight to Málaga from New York 1.64 tonnes; London 0.38; Sydney 5.98. Rtn transfer from Málaga by car 0.08. Bus to Lanjarón via Granada 0.02.
Offset cost: $25.60; £3.45; A$113.25.

Responsibility: The Lodge shows how it's possible to live a comfortable, sustainable lifestyle that has minimal impact on the surroundings. It is self-sufficient in power, which is solar, no water is wasted, and only biodegradable cleaning products and toiletries are used.

Environmental:	∅∅∅∅∅
Social:	∅∅∅∅∅

Whitepod

Les Cerniers, Batt. Postale 681, 1871 Les Giettes, Switzerland
+41 (0)79 744 6219 / www.whitepod.com / reservations@whitepod.com

THE pods look like a George Lucas interpretation of an igloo, a constellation of 21st-century domes clustered around a 19th-century farmhouse-cum-chalet high in the Swiss Alps. With smoke curling from their little chimneys, they perch on a mountainside cloaked in snow and fir trees, peering across the Rhône Valley to the massive peaks opposite.

Welcome to Whitepod, a high-tech eco-camp that appears each winter near the village of Les Cerniers like a snow bunny's Brigadoon. The brainchild of returned local Sofia de Meyer, Whitepod is just what the skiing world was crying out for: a stylishly simple, low-impact approach to the fragile alpine environment that leaves the smallest possible footprint in the pristine Swiss snow. To get here, you'll need to strap on your skis or your snowshoes for the final leg of the journey, as there are no coach-clogged roads around here to spoil the view.

Whitepod caters for a maximum of just 24 guests in nine space-age geodetic dome tents, lessening the load on the local environment while providing a sense of intimacy. These tents offer much more than a sleeping bag, with sheepskins, wood stoves and warm duvets to keep you snug as you reflect upon the day's activities. The pods are veiled in white canvas to help them blend into the landscape, and are set on wooden platforms that reduce the impact on the ground beneath. Modern insulation technology keeps them warm through the wintery

nights, and the big, round windows mean there's not only plenty of natural light during the day, but the sort of head-spinningly epic view that makes you want to burst into song as you wake up each morning.

Not all pods were created equal and guests have three kinds to choose from: the Expedition Pod, with a double bed and a small terrace; the Pavilion Pod, with a mezzanine level and a bathtub with a view; and the Group Pod, with room for eight people. The 19th-century chalet is the only part of the resort that uses electricity, and is the hub of the Whitepod 'village', housing the dining room, lounge and bar, bathroom facilities, and that alpine essential, the outdoor hot tub.

In keeping with Whitepod's philosophy, everything on the menu and wine list is locally produced and organic. Whitepod employs local staff, relies almost entirely on local produce and suppliers, runs a small grocery store that's open to locals, and pumps money into local charities and organizations.

Whitepod is perfect for winter pursuits. Snowshoe tours, dogsledding and ice-skating are all available, along with the option of paragliding from your pod's front door. A spa at the chalet adds that touch of sybaritic bliss.

During the evening, Whitepod's staff quietly attend to your stove. By the time you've walked back along the freshly carved path to your pod to retire for the night, it will be as warm as toast, letting you lie beneath your duvet contentedly listening to the silence of the alpine night. Peace in a pod.

ECO**FILE**

Rooms: Nine geodetic dome tents (6 Expedition, 2 Pavilion, 1 Group).
Rates: CHF325–1150 (US$270 –950) per pod per night, including transfers from Aigle.
Location: Above Les Cerniers at the foot of the Dents du Midi. The nearest train station is at Aigle and the nearest airport is Geneva.
Best time to go: Winter. Let it snow, let it snow, let it snow!
Getting there: From Geneva, take an 1.5-hour train trip to Aigle, where guests are collected twice daily. Alternatively, travel 2.5 hours from London to Paris by Eurostar, then take a TGV train for the 3-hour journey to Aigle.
CO2 emissions: Rtn flight to Geneva from New York 1.73 tonnes; London 0.19; Sydney 5.54. Rtn transfers to Les Cerniers by train and car 0.02. Rtn by rail from London to Aigle 0.02.
Offset cost: $26; £1.50; A$103.85.

Responsibility: Whitepod takes the whole 'think global, act local' philosophy seriously. With its strong support of local produce and suppliers, its sparing use of electricity, its waste recycling, its small number of guests and its platform-based pods, this is the ski world's ultimate in low impact.
Environmental: ∅∅∅∅∅
Social: ∅∅∅∅∅

Yediburunlar Lighthouse

Yediburunlar Mah, Bogazici Koyu, Fethiye, Turkey
+44 (0)208 605 3500 / www.exclusiveescapes.co.uk / admin@exclusiveescapes.co.uk

CRIMSON cushions make your hammock look deliciously inviting. You stretch out and sway gently in the breeze, while far below you pine-clad crags drop to a turquoise and indigo sea. Goat bells jangle gently as you pick up your book and read while trying to decide whether to go for a walk, take a dip in the pool – or just have a little snooze.

This is Yediburunlar; not, in fact, a lighthouse, but a rustic retreat perched on a clifftop on Turkey's dramatic Lycian coast. Reached only via a rocky dirt road, and around 20 minutes' walk from the nearest hamlet, this is surely about as remote as you can get in Europe. The owners, Leon Hitge and Semra Akdeniz, built and furnished the house themselves using natural materials like stone and wood. The main house – where they and their rescued cats live – has four guest rooms, while a separate building across the courtyard has two larger rooms that are quieter and more private. All have private bathrooms.

With virtually no mobile phone reception, no television and the nearest big town, Fethiye, an hour's drive away, Yediburunlar really does offer you the chance to get away from it all. It's so remote that most guests stay here for a full week and holidays are bookable only through operator Exclusive Escapes, which lays on all the transfers.

Leon and Semra appreciate the need to minimize their impact on this stunning landscape. They have solar panels that heat the water, and

ECO**FILE**

Rooms: Four doubles in the main house, 2 larger rooms in the annexe.
Rates: YTL1,175–2,000 (US$900–1,500) per double per week, including breakfast and dinner, flights from London and transfers.
Location: On the Lycian coast of Turkey, between Fethiye and Kalkan. 115km (71 miles) from Dalaman.
Best time to go: In summer – it stays cool up here. Closed Nov–Apr.
Getting there: From Dalaman, transfer for the 2-hour bus trip to Yediburunlar, where you will be collected. Jeep hire is recommended.
CO2 emissions: Rtn flight to Dalaman from New York 2.40; London 0.62; Sydney 4.75. Transfer 0.02.
Offset cost: $35.95; £4.80; A$89.15.

Responsibility: Yediburunlar is a remote eco-retreat whose owners respect and work with both the environment and local community. Visitors are served imaginative, fresh vegetarian food that impresses even hardened meat-eaters, and solar panels keep energy usage low.
Environmental: ØØØ*ØØ*
Social: ØØ*ØØØ*

they recycle as much waste as possible. Meals here are a highlight, incorporating ingredients that are fresh and, ideally, both local and organic. Everything is vegetarian, except for a weekly meal of fish. Milk, yogurt, olive oil and honey are all produced locally, and Semra uses local flour for the bread she makes every day. Breakfasts, often taken on the terrace, are a feast of fresh bread, yogurt, Semra's own jams and fresh fruit. You can buy light lunches here, but be sure to leave room for dinner – five or six courses, all freshly prepared.

You're given plenty of opportunities to get to know the local area, as Leon offers guided walks. You might explore a section of the long-distance Lycian Way, stopping to rest under carob trees and examining the stone tombs of the early Lycian peoples. Or you might go for a trek down to a secluded bay, or visit the ancient ruined city of Tlos. Once during the week you are taken into Fethiye for the day, where you can take a cruise on a *gulet* (wooden boat) or explore the busy harbour town while Leon and Semra stock up on fresh vegetables and organic eggs. As the minibus bumps its way back along the rocky road to Yediburunlar, you feel the silence wrap itself around you once again.

Africa & the Middle East

Main picture: Antelopes, Kalahari Gemsbrook National Park, South Africa. Left, from top: Buffalo Ridge Safari Lodge; view from Kasbah du Toubkai; Guludo Beach Lodge; education project, Anjajavy l'Hôtel

Locator map & budget guide

- Budget (up to US$100)
- Moderate (US$100–250)
- Expensive (US$250–500)
- Blow out (more than US$500)

Prices are for a double room, or two people, per night

Sp
Portugal Mad
Lisbon

Rabat
Casablanca
Morocco
A
5 4

ATLAS MTN

*Canary
Islands*

**Western
Sahara**

Mauritania

Senegal
Gambia   **Burk**
Guinea-Bissau **Guinea** **F**
                    *Guinea
                    Plateau*
Sierra Leone   **Ivory
                        Coas**
Liberia

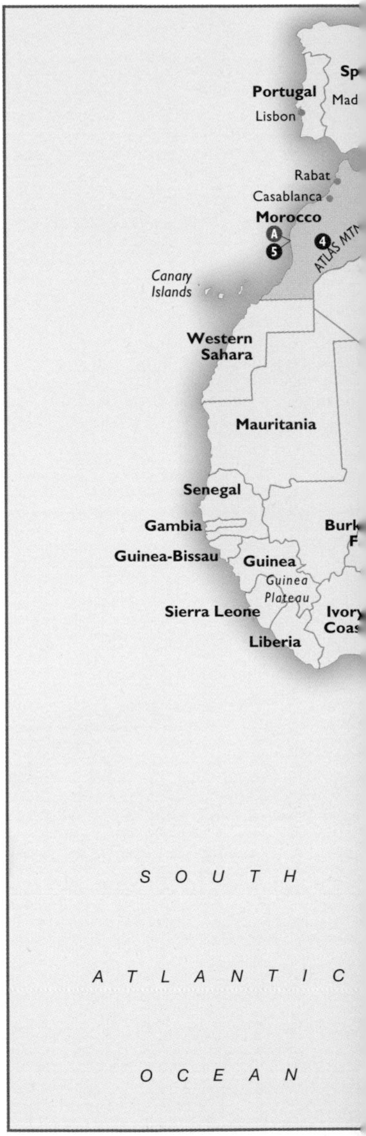

S O U T H

A T L A N T I C

O C E A N

Barcelona

Italy
Rome

Mediterranean Sea

Greece
Istanbul

Turkey
Anatolian Plateau

Turkmenistan

Algiers Tunis

Tunisia

Cyprus

Syria

Tehran

Lebanon

Baghdad

Iraq

Iran

Tripoli

Israel **Jordan**

Kuwait

ZAGROS MTNS

Algeria

Alexandria

Qattara Depression ⑰ Cairo

Egypt

Saudi Arabia

Qatar

Libya

⑱

U A E

Sahara

Jiddah

Oman *Arabian Sea*

Mali

Niger

Chad

Red Sea

Khartoum

Eritrea

Yemen

Chad

Sudan

Gulf of Aden

Benin

Nigeria

Addis Ababa

Togo

Lagos

Ghana

Central African Republic

Ethiopia
Ethiopian Highlands

Cameroon

Somalia

Equatorial Guinea

Gulf of Guinea

Gabon

Congo

Zaire

Uganda

Kenya

INDIAN

Victoria Nairobi

Congo Basin

Rwanda

① ②

Burundi

⑮

Kilimanjaro ⑭

Kinshasa

Tanzania

⑬

OCEAN

Luanda

Tanganyika

Dar es Salaam

Angola

Nyasa ⑦

Zambia

⑥

Malawi

③

Madagascar

⑨ ⑯

Harare

Mozambique

Mozambique Channel

Mauritius

⑧

Namibia Ⓑ Ⓒ

Zimbabwe

Réunion

Botswana

Kalahari Desert

⑫

⑩

Swaziland

Johannesburg

Lesotho

DRAKENSBERG Durban

South Africa

Cape Town
Cape of Good Hope

⑪

Basecamp Masai Mara

Basecamp Nairobi Head Office, Ole Odume Road, PO Box 43369 Nairobi, Kenya
+254 20 577 490 / www.basecampexplorer.com / info@basecampexplorer.co.ke

TUCKED up in bed in your cosy tented hut, you listen as a cast of mysterious creatures fills the darkness with a chorus of chirrups, squeaks and peeps. This is night-time at Basecamp, a wonderful ecolodge on the Talek River on the edge of the Masai Mara National Park. At sunrise you'll wake, sip some strong coffee, then set off for a dawn game drive – on which you're sure to spot some of the extraordinarily rich local wildlife: lions, elephants, wildebeest, maybe a black-backed jackal, an elegant giraffe, a jewel-coloured bird or a bustling mongoose. Then you'll head back to camp for a hearty breakfast with freshly baked bread and welcome cups of tea.

Basecamp is situated on land that is leased from the local Maasai people, and the Swedish operators work extremely closely with them – not simply employing Maasai to act as guides and drivers, but also initiating and supporting a range of projects that benefit the community and the environment. They've established a workshop, for example,

so that local women can make traditional beaded and leatherwork goods and then sell them at the camp. They've also planted trees, with the aim of making the camp self-sustaining in wood; they participate in a cheetah conservation project; and they support educational pro- grammes for local children.

The camp blends easily into the environment, with 15 thatched tents ranged around a grassy lawn. Each one has raised wooden floors, verandas and private – open to the sky – showers, the water heated by solar panels. There are simple comfy beds, bedside lamps and tradi- tional fabrics. Each tent also has a private composting toilet. The camp has a central restaurant hut where everybody gathers – and where staff have to keep an eye out for the occasional thieving baboon. Waste from the camp is carefully collected and recycled. The food is excellent and plentiful, with meals of hearty bean stews, fresh vegetables and fruit.

During your stay you're given plenty of opportunity to meet local people, with a trip to the nearby village and school. You can also have lazy siestas after lunch, before your late-afternoon game drives – in which you'll gain loads of information from your knowledge-able guide. The highlight of any trip though is an overnight stay at the bushcamp, a short distance from Basecamp. This is a real back-to-the-savannah site where you eat outdoors, sit around a campfire, swap stories with your Maasai guides, and sleep in Boy Scout tents. And early in the morning your guides, armed with their spears, will take you for a walking safari, telling you about native plants and trees, and showing you how to identify the tracks of different animals. Unforgettable.

ECO**FILE**

Rooms: 15 double tented huts.
Rates: From KSh61,500 (US$925) per person for 3 nights, including all meals, safaris and road transfers.
Location: On the edge of the Masai Mara National Park, 275km (170 miles) from Nairobi.
Best time to go: Jul–Oct for the animal migration.
Getting there: From Nairobi, fly 45 mins to the Masai Mara National Park. The company also offers a 5-hour overland transfer.
CO2 emissions: Rtn flight to Nairobi from New York 3.60 tonnes; London 1.92; Sydney 3.70. Rtn transfer by plane 0.06; by car 0.16.
Offset cost: $55.95; £15.65; A$72.25.

Responsibility: Basecamp Masai Mara is a shining example of green tourism. The camp has extremely close relationships with the local community, is run so as to make as little environmental impact as possi- ble, and offers its guests the chance to see Kenya's wildlife at close hand without harassing the animals.
Environmental: ⌀⌀⌀⌀⌀
Social: ⌀⌀⌀⌀⌀

Campi ya Kanzi

PO Box 236-90128, Mtito Andei, Kenya
+254 45 622 516 / www.maasai.com / lucasaf@africaonline.co.ke

IT has probably been noted from time to time that there are worse ways to start your day than to sit on a veranda, sipping fresh Kenyan coffee and watching the pink light of dawn painting the slopes of Mt Kilimanjaro while the first giraffes of the day quietly navigate their way through the mist-veiled acacias. It did the trick for Ernest Hemingway.

It also did the trick for Luca and Antonella Belpietro, the driving forces behind Kenyan ecolodge Campi ya Kanzi, or 'Camp of the Hidden Treasure'. Situated on a 1,000sq km (390sq mile) Maasai-owned ranch near Kilimanjaro in the Chyulu Hills (the 'Green Hills of Africa' that so possessed Hemingway), Campi ya Kanzi is a joint project between the Belpietros and the local Maasai to bring tourism to the area, sharing the profits and helping to preserve the community's way of life, its land and the stunning diversity of wildlife that roams across it.

The lodge was built entirely by the Belpietros and the Maasai – no outside contractors were used – and most of the staff are also locals. Guests stay in six tented cottages – or the suitably grander Hemingway and Simba tented suites. The cottages are spaced far enough apart

from each other to ensure privacy, and each one is pointed at a stunning view ranging from the Chyulu to Kilimanjaro itself.

The centre of the camp is the Belpietros' home, Tembo (Elephant) House, which offers more than a nod to colonial elegance with its library and backgammon boards, its menu of Italian cuisine and its lashings of Mozart.

The lodge is set in mountainous country that ranges sharply in altitude from 1,000m (3,000ft) to nearly 2,100m (7,000ft) above sea level, which means there is biodiversity in spades. All of the 'big five' species – elephant, lion, leopard, rhinoceros and buffalo – regularly set Hemingwayesque hearts aflutter around here. Zebra, giraffe, impala, wildebeest, hartebeest, oryx and gazelle make regular appearances, and rarer residents include cheetah, kudu, gerenuk and wild dog.

Exploration can be done with a combination of walks and open-top Land Rover – all in the company of a professional guide and a Maasai tracker. There's also the option of an air safari by light plane over the hills and volcanic slopes, and your Maasai tracker can take you to one of the local villages to give a much more complete picture of this world.

ECO**FILE**

Rooms: Six tented cottages and 2 suites.
Rates: From KSh28,600 (US$430) per night per person twin share, including all meals but excluding conservation fee (US$40 per day).
Location: In the Chyulu Hills of southern Kenya, 56km (35 miles) from Mt Kilimanjaro. The camp is 320km (200 miles) from Nairobi.
Best time to go: Year-round.
Getting there: From Nairobi, take a 1-hour flight or a 6-hour 4WD transfer.
CO2 emissions: Rtn flight to Nairobi from New York 3.60 tonnes; London 1.92; Sydney 3.70. Rtn transfer by plane 0.25; by car 0.19.
Offset cost: $57.20; £16.25; A$73.85.

Responsibility: Local Maasai benefit from revenue and employment from the joint venture, as well as a trust that employs Maasai game scouts, puts teachers into local schools and nurses into local dispensaries, builds schools and medical facilities, and awards scholarships. Maasai farmers are compensated when livestock is killed by lions, thereby preventing revenge killings. Local materials are used for the buildings, and lighting and water heating are solar-powered. Food is cooked on eco-friendly charcoal, organic waste is recycled and water is collected from the roofs. Wastewater is filtered naturally and used on the gardens or pumped into ponds where gazelles and lions drink.
Environmental: ⌀⌀⌀⌀⌀
Social: ⌀⌀⌀⌀⌀

Anjajavy l'Hôtel

Anjavavy, Boina Sakalava, Madagascar
+33 (0)1 44 69 15 00 (Paris head office) / www.anjajavy.com / contact@anjajavy.com

TSINGY – the dry, serrated remains of ancient coral reefs – cut through the arid landscape. Surpirsingly, an extraordinary variety of plants and animals have made this harsh environment their home, including bulbous baobab trees, taking root directly in the *tsingy* rocks. Gold-coloured lemurs nonchalantly swing through their branches and purplish lizards scutter through undergrowth, while hairy crabs, squadrons of butterflies and luridly coloured parrots busily fuss through the jagged stones.

The remote Boina Sakalava region in northwestern Madagascar is famous for this unique topography and wildlife, but getting there isn't straightforward. Making the journey overland is virtually impossible, so most people fly in from the capital, Antanarivo, instead. It's a rapid introduction to the island's diverse scenery, from the lush, verdant interior to the dry forest environment of secluded Boina Sakalava. The dry forest, so named for its lack of rainfall and the plants that have adapted to live here, has been designated one of the world's most crucial regions for conservation by the WWF. Working towards its conservation is Anjajavy l'Hôtel.

Anjajavy looks like a boutique hotel that has been deconstructed, its 25 sea-facing villas scattered through a mix of formal gardens and untrammelled nature. The heady pinks, trumpets of yellow and pools of lime green splashed across the vegetation might have been created on an artist's palette. Quiet breezes off the Mozambique Channel cool the air and nudge huge white parasols around the pool. Geckos, enamelled and jewel-like, provide idle entertainment as you sip an evening drink on the terrace.

As well as being a stylish eye-opener to the visitor, the project has been a revelation

ECOFILE

Rooms: 25 luxury villas.
Rates: MGA400,000–670,000 (US$225–370) per person per night, including all meals.
Location: Anjajavy is located in the northwest of Madagascar in the Boina Sakalava region. The nearest international airport is Antananarivo.
Best time to go: Apr–Dec. Note that Feb is cyclone season.
Getting there: From Antananarivo, fly 1.5 hours to Anjajavy.
CO2 emissions: Rtn flight to Antananarivo from New York 4.40 tonnes; London 2.63; Sydney 2.96. Rtn transfer 0.12.
Offset cost: $67.30; £20.70; A$57.60.

Responsibility: Anjajavy l'Hôtel has had a profound and beneficial effect on a poor and remote community. Educational and health programmes sponsored by the hotel in conjunction with NGOs have been a success, as have their various conservation initiatives in the surrounding dry forest.
Environmental: ØØØØØ
Social: ØØØØØ

to the local communities. Until eight years ago, Anjajavy and Amber Ampasy were impoverished fishing villages with soaring unemployment and all the associated problems of poverty. To help combat this, the hotel, in conjunction with an NGO, has instigated health and education programmes, as well as bringing new levels of employment. Produce can be sourced locally now that vegetable farming has been introduced, and the fishermen inevitably sell a large proportion of their catch to the kitchens.

Fish is something of a speciality on the hotel's outstanding seasonal menu. Although the cuisine is essentially French-inspired, Malagasy dishes are offered too. At lunchtime, flocks of brilliant parrots keep you company as you eat, while languorous suppers can be taken alfresco against the constant chitter and ticking of insects.

Anjajavy has made a positive contribution to more than just the local community; the surrounding environment has done well too. The hotel sponsors an initiative to encourage the use of easily replaceable, quick-growing timber as an alternative to hardwood trees, and supports a 450ha (1,100-acre) dry forest, where the principal endemic species of Malagasy flora and fauna thrive.

Guided walks through the forest should not be missed; warm thermals of scent spiral out of nowhere, bright red ants climb coral-rag spurs, baobabs and frangipanis fence in the paths, and tiny hummingbirds show off in the flowering bougainvillea bushes.

World harmony

In a celebration of his global citizenship, **Nick Maes** danced and swayed to the rhythms of local and international sounds at Morocco's five-day Gnaoua World Music Festival.

A bus station seething with hopeful-looking 20-somethings brandishing bongos, backpacks and bedrolls can only mean one thing: a music festival is afoot.

At Marrakesh coach terminus, the throng, like me, are headed to Essaouira, a coastal town that has never quite got over a visit paid by Jimi Hendrix back in the 1960s. Since that memorable stopover, his spirit has been adopted as an unofficial totem for the sleepy fishing port and haunts the Gnaoua Music Festival held in the town each June – the sole reason for this exodus. Gnaoua is something of a latter-day Woodstock-on-sea for revellers looking for a different kind of festival.

It's not just Moroccan youth who pile into the festival. Marrakshi

sophisticates, tanned and Raybanned, saunter past a few surfer types with sun-bleached locks and didgeridoos. Families from Fez pushing buggies, with grandma and toddlers in tow, merge with local fishermen and women draped in pink or turquoise-blue veils. It's perhaps the most egalitarian and inclusive music festival: a huge free celebration that attracts enormous and diverse crowds from

Left to right: Musicians playing traditional Moroccan instruments at the festival; crowds enjoying the line-up

all over Morocco – as well as tourists from all over the world.

Half a million people show up at the festival over five days, swelling Essaouira's population nearly tenfold, a statistic that might be a little alarming for some. Yet somehow the town copes, happily absorbing the masses. The attendance figures are more than double those at Glastonbury – Britain's premier music festival, which is held at the same time. But rather than suffering the rain and miserable seas of mud traditionally associated with its UK counterpart, Essaouira guarantees sunshine all the way. And rather than being cooped up behind security fences, the crowds here are free to roam the beaches and throughout the town.

Hidden deep in the *medina* (old quarter) is the Marché aux Grains, a small piazza that temporarily abandons its usual function as a market in favour of the Maalems. These are the traditional Gnaoua musicians who inspire the festival. A little after 11pm on a balmy night, Maalem Kbiber

from Marrakesh begins to entrance his audience as he strums and beats his *gembri*, a guitar-cum-drum with both strings and a skin covering. Rhythmic drumming and the discordant clanging of small cymbals pulsates from the stage, electrifying the crowd. This is the original trance-dance music, repetitive, hypnotic and sacred.

Gnaoua music was created in the 16th century by slaves in the Guinea Empire and is rooted in the concepts of mysticism, regaining freedom, and the pain of suppression. The practitioners today are regarded as intermediaries or spiritual healers, people who are still highly revered throughout North Africa. During private ceremonies, the Maalems induce trances in the possessed, bringing about an exorcism and freeing their spirits. At the festival, everyone's spirits are liberated.

The crowds go crazy, singing along with, and dancing to, the drumbeats. Dervish whirls and Levantine congas swirl around the stage. Boys nod their heads, impressively swinging tassels a

beach is now festooned in nylon tents; they spring up like fluorescent mushrooms. Past the two main stages is another camp, this one a wonderful village of Bedouin tents that looks like a gathering of brown cloth elephants hunched around a red-carpeted square.

Stoned Moroccan hippies drift along the shore in fragrant clouds of smoke, stopping to chat with friends dressed like psychedelic folk dancers. The crowds sport an impressive array of afros and mini-Mohawks; Hendrix, Guevara and Marley T-shirts are ubiquitous; and music seems to pump evocatively and mysteriously out of nowhere, conjuring up a palpable sense of expectation for the coming night's festivities.

After dark, the town is illuminated by lights from every tourist shop and every grocer, butcher and kiosk. The streets are even more energetic than in the day,

metre long in perfect circles from decorated caps. Some of the Lilas, the Maalems' musicians, are elaborately dressed in cowrie-embroidered clothes that look like the garb of exotic pearly kings. Their charisma and seemingly endless energy is infectious and sweeps the audience along for hours of good-natured carousing.

I find that no matter how hard I dance, exhaustion never seems to bite in; or not, at least, until the next morning. Recovery over a late breakfast sets me up for a day spent leisurely strolling along the prom. What had been a

with a purposeful rush to do business. It feels like the place has turned itself inside-out: carpets hang from walls, yellow goat-skin slippers tumble onto pavements and strings of beads glisten in alleyways. Even with these sensual distractions, there's still time to grab a *tagine* from one of the many restaurants before heading off to the next venue.

Place el Khayma is a small square located near Essaouira's museum. The sense of uninhibited excitement from the dancing and clapping crowd is reason enough to draw you in, but then Maalem Said el Bourqui takes to the stage. As he strikes up, the audience surges in unison and soon falls under his enigmatic spell. The music is intoxicating.

It's not just traditional performers who play; the festival is equally famous for attracting headlining world musicians too. In 2007's line-up, Baaba Maal from Senegal was joined by artists from Burkina Faso, Iran, Argentina, France, Cuba, Brazil and Britain, whose Asian Dub Foundation played a mesmerizing set. Intriguingly, many of these great musos are drawn by the chance to collaborate with the Maalems and Lilas – an opportunity that's also been grabbed by mainstream performers like Led Zeppelin, Sting and Carlos Santana.

The music never quite finishes though, even after the final encores on stage. Small sound-systems set up around town and on the beach lure those keen to keep going. As day breaks, there are still a few die-hards strumming guitars, playing pipes and singing – quiet, somnolent entertainment that catches the subtle spirit of the event.

Festival addicts the world over can do no better than join in. Just make sure you've shaken out your loon pants, re-dipped the tie-dye and dusted off the love-beads – Jimi Hendrix lives.

ECOFILE

Location: Essaouira, on Morocco's Atlantic coast, around 200km (125 miles) southwest of Marrakesh.

Getting there: From Marrakesh, the best way to reach Essaouira is to travel approximately 2.5 hours by Supratours bus, taxi, or one of the local buses. It is also possible to fly 40 mins to Essaouira's local airport.

CO_2 emissions: Rtn flight to Marrakesh from New York 1.63 tonnes; London 0.51; Sydney 6.09. Rtn transfer by bus 0.04; by taxi 0.12; by plane 0.07.

Offset cost: $26.06; £4.71; A$116.

Staying there: Essaouira has many good hotels and *riads* (see Lalla Mira on pages 178–9), but the intrepid should pitch a tent on the shore to soak up the atmosphere.

Rates: The main festival is free.

Best time to go: The festival is held in the third week of Jun. Check the Gnaoua website for exact dates.

Further information: www.festival-gnaoua.net Other African music festivals that are worth investigating include Mali's Festival in the Desert (www.festival-au-desert.org) in Jan, and Zanzibar's Busara Music Festival (www.busara-music.com) during Feb.

Responsibility: The festival has had an enormous effect on the local economy, accelerating development in the area and bringing in the equivalent of a year's income for some traders. As well as promoting musical traditions from all over the world, the Gnaoua festival helps to maintain the music, traditions, and culture of the Gnaoua brotherhood.

Kasbah du Toubkal

Imlil Valley, High Atlas, Morocco
+33 (0)5 49 05 01 35 (France head office) / www.kasbahdutoubkal.com /
kerrie@discover.ltd.uk

CUSHIONS of spring flowers and sulphur-yellow lichens lie around a gnarled and ancient juniper tree festooned with bright butterflies. The tree provides gentle shade for possibly the most memorable picnic you're ever likely to eat: a small, simply laid table, Moroccan rugs, mint tea, delicious salads and subtly spiced meat dishes are arranged in a stupendous setting atop the 2,400m (7,872ft) Tizi M'zzir.

Getting to the top of the mountain is no mean feat, especially the last 200m (650ft), which involves a scramble up scree and vertiginous paths to the summit. But once there, relax and enjoy the views; they are simply overwhelming. A good 700m (2,300ft) below lies the Imlil Valley, a verdant

patchwork of steep terraced fields and tiny mud homes that could well have been transplanted from the Himalayas. And above, in the distance, stands the awesome Mt Toubkal, snow-covered even in North Africa's summer sun. But it's the luxury of the waiting picnic that somehow sears itself into your memory.

Of course, not all lunches here will be so impressive; this is trekking country and most days spent out in the High Atlas will be broken by your guide with somewhat more humble cuisine. The views, however, will match or even better your introduction.

The Kasbah du Toubkal is part of one of the area's hilltop villages, perched at the far end of the Imlil Valley on a promontory that has far-reaching views. The ancient structure used to be the fortified summer home of Caid Souktani, a local ruler, but was abandoned in 1959. Scroll forward a few decades, and the atmospheric ruin has been sympathetically renovated into a comfortable base for the superlative hiking in the region.

Tiled roof terraces and a tearoom catch warm summer breezes and provide space for other tasty meals. Indoors is a cool, candlelit room for *tagine* suppers. It's worth noting that local custom frowns upon alcohol, although guests may bring their own wine for dinner, provided they're discreet and don't expect a member of staff to serve it.

All those who work at the Kasbah du Toubkal are local. Their salaries provide much-needed income in an area that had hitherto been reliant on peasant farming. But this is done with the utmost respect for the egalitarian Berber tradition, providing a superb example of sustainable tourism that runs harmoniously within the indigenous culture.

Berber culture has provided some of the design cues in the hotel, too. Earthenware crockery and mugs, and the ubiquitous carpets and rugs, make for stylish surroundings, but the baths need a special mention. More like sarcophagi than mere tubs, they're surrounded in black marble spattered with ghostly grey fossil shells, and are the perfect foil to a hard day's trekking – even if you did stop for a spot of luxurious picnicking.

ECO**FILE**

Rooms: 14 rooms.
Rates: From Dh1,460 (US$180) per room per night, including breakfast.
Location: The Imlil Valley is an hour's drive south of Marrakesh. The nearest airport is Marrakesh.
Best time to go: The summer months are perhaps best, although spring and autumn are also very good. It is possible to trek in the surrounding mountains during winter, but only expert climbers with snow experience should embark on more adventurous climbs. Cross-country skiing is also popular during winter.
Getting there: From Marrakesh, either take a taxi, or ask the hotel to arrange your transfer.
CO_2 emissions: Rtn flight to Marrakesh from New York 1.63 tonnes; London 0.51; Sydney 6.09. Rtn transfer 0.06.
Offset cost: $25.15; £4.25; A$115.

Responsibility: Kasbah du Toubkal is an excellent example of tourism in a remote and culturally sensitive environment. It buys all goods and services locally, which has a profoundly beneficial impact on the local community. Some 50 local people are directly employed in the venture, and freelance guides earn a significant proportion of their income from the hotel. Awareness of the environment and good mountain-climbing practice are standard.
Environmental: ∅∅∅∅∅
Social: ∅∅∅∅∅

Lalla Mira

14 rue d'Algerie, Essaouira, Morocco
+212 24 475046 / www.lallamira.ma / info@lallamira.net

ALONG Essaouira's labyrinthine streets, daytime business is carried out in the cool of night. Extended families trawl the colonnaded avenues and souks, picking over barrows of fresh mint and brightly coloured spices, plastic buckets and innumerable cuts of meat. This is definitely the time to mix with the locals and bombard your senses with the thrill of being in a bustling North African market.

And therein lies Essaouira's charm, for even though this idyllic fortified port has a healthy tourist business, it's still very much a working town. Fishing is the main industry, and a morning trip to the harbourside is the perfect start to the day. The offloading of boats is something of a spectator sport, as human chains deftly transfer the catch of sardines in plastic laundry baskets to refrigerated trucks. Yet for all their modern navigation systems and radar beacons, the boats are exactly as they were centuries ago: big wooden tubs that resemble a child's toy.

Founded in the seventh century BC by the Phoenicians, the town might also never have changed had it not been for a late 18th-century French designer. His perfect fortifications pleased the local sultan so much that he gave Essaouira its name: it means 'Well Designed'.

Design is still important today as wrecked buildings are renovated or renewed, as was the case with the Lalla Mira hotel. Tucked neatly on a sidestreet off rue Mohammed el-Qorry, this modern building blends

seamlessly with its older neighbours. Traditional chalk-plastering methods have been combined with state-of-the-art solar panels to create Morocco's first eco-hotel. Here, underfloor heating and hot water are both powered by the sun.

The hotel's *hammam* is the only original part of the structure and is the oldest bath-house in town. Originally used by West African slaves some 200 years ago, it gives the hotel its name: Lalla Mira is a spirit of Gnaoua, a mystical musical tradition that has its roots in sub-Saharan Africa. Gnaoua music is still alive today, drawing huge crowds to the town's annual festival, held in June (see pages 172–5).

Even without the festival the streets are never quiet. Respite can be found on the hotel's roof terrace, where the superb views are accompanied by the tapping of traditional metalsmiths below, whose works have been used to furnish the hotel. Its 13 rooms are simply equipped, and their organic, allergy-free bedding and kapok-stuffed mattresses (somewhat like futons) make for a good night's sleep. It's not just the bedding that's organic; the hotel's restaurant uses produce from its own pesticide-free farm in the nearby hills.

You don't have to eat in all the time, as Essaouira has many restaurants. The best of these are the outdoor grills in Place Moulay Hassan and Souk Jedid – strolling back along twisting lanes as you feast on sardines makes for a memorable meal indeed.

ECO**FILE**

Rooms: 13 rooms.
Rates: From Dh436 (US$53) per person per night, including breakfast.
Location: Essaouira is 200km (125 miles) southwest of Marrakesh.
Best time to go: Year-round. Essaouira's microclimate keeps temperatures mild during Morocco's searing summer heat, although it can get cold in winter.
Getting there: From Marrakesh, the best way to reach Essaouira is to travel 2.5 hours by the Supratours bus, a local bus, or taxi. It is also possible to fly 40 mins to Essaouria.
CO_2 emissions: Rtn flight to Marrakesh from New York 1.63 tonnes; London 0.51; Sydney 6.09. Rtn transfer by bus 0.04; by taxi 0.12; by plane 0.07.
Offset cost: $26.80; £4.70; A$116.

Responsibility: Lalla Mira has a firm environmental and ethical commitment. Plans are afoot for introducing a solar-powered desalination plant and the hotel is also closely involved with various local cooperatives – notably a women's co-op that produces argan oil, herbs and medical spices – and with the Trans-Mediterranean Energy Cooperation (TREC), an organization endeavouring to establish clean energy in North African countries.
Environmental: ∅∅∅∅∅
Social: ∅∅∅∅∅

Guludo Beach Lodge

Cabo Delgado, Mozambique
+44 (0)1483 288769 (UK head office) / www.guludo.com /
contact@bespokeexperience.com

THE bright orange skiff skips across waters so ridiculously blue you have to pinch yourself to make sure you're not hallucinating. The last stand of mangroves is home to an imperious azure bird. He stands nonchalantly on one leg and would look more at home sipping cocktails and smoking cigarettes in a Manhattan drawing room than he does standing querulously in the Indian Ocean.

Soon, other distant islands come into view, looking like white lines etched onto the farthest edges of the sea – a taster of the beaches to come. But the boat trip doesn't last long enough, and after about half an hour Guludo Beach Lodge hoves into view. It lies on a seemingly

endless stretch of white coral sand amid tangles of bush and coconut palms. The tropical-charisma quotient doesn't get any better, and nor do the eco- and ethical credentials.

The creation of Brits Amy Carter and Neil Allcock, Guludo Beach Lodge has been carefully designed to have minimal impact on the environment. The pair boast that, should the place ever close down, it would simply disintegrate, leaving no trace of its presence whatsoever. Let's hope that never happens, for there's way too much to lose.

Award-winning thatched *bandas* – large tents covered with *makute*-thatch roofs – merge into the bush along the seafront. The accommodation is simply equipped with furniture made by local craftsmen, and includes alfresco bathrooms with solar-heated showers tucked behind bamboo screens. The state-of-the-art dehydrating Enviro Loos fit the lodge's ethos perfectly.

But the greatest luxury at Guludo is space. The pristine 12km-long (7-mile) beach is utterly deserted except for a few fishermen and curious kids. Long walks along the sand engender a heady sense of tranquillity, and it's easy to lose track of time and daydream. While lazing on the beach you might also spot one of the dugongs that bumble through the waters in these parts.

There's plenty of other wildlife here, too. Leopards, rare African wild dogs, elephants, warthogs and buffaloes all creep through the undergrowth, while dolphins, turtles and any number of exotic fish splash through the wet stuff. Needless to say, the snorkelling and diving are excellent.

Those who can drag themselves away from beach activities should visit nearby Ibo Island. The former Portuguese capital of Cabo Delgado province has now fallen into ruinous beauty, and a trip there is essential. Bush walks and picnics in the Quirimbas National Park – established as a protected area at the request of its inhabitants and high in biodiversity – are also winning diversions.

Guludo village is about 2km (1 mile) away from the lodge. After a morning spent here chatting to the residents you feel as though you've found friends for life. You'll meet up with them again on Friday night if you head to the local disco and dance to the music under the stars.

Life at Guludo Beach Lodge is ineffably chilled. As you loll over a drink watching the last vestiges of the sunset, it seems hard to believe that the orange boat is already set to take you home in the morning.

ECO**FILE**

Rooms: Nine thatched *bandas* (tents).

Rates: From MT10,500 (US$205) per person per night, including all meals, but excluding transfers.

Location: Guludo is in the north of the Quirimbas National Park close to the Tanzanian border. The nearest airport is Pemba, 120km (74 miles).

Best time to go: May–Dec (Aug and Dec are peak months). Jan–Apr are the hottest months but also constitute the rainy season.

Getting there: From Dar es Salaam (Tanzania), take a local flight to Pemba. Alternatively, fly from Maputo (Mozambique) to Pemba. The 2-hour transfer from Pemba to Guludo is by road.

CO_2 emissions: Rtn flight to Pemba via Dar es Salaam from London 2.3 tonnes. Rtn flight to Pemba via Maputo from New York 4.47; Sydney 3.57. Rtn transfer 0.07.

Offset cost: $67.55; £17.80; A$68.05.

Responsibility: Guludo Beach Lodge is a true ecolodge, adhering to strict fair trade in tourism principles. It invests heavily in training and education programmes, and contributes 5 per cent of its income to the Social and Environmental Regeneration Fund (SERF), a charity that aims to relieve poverty and protect the fragile environment. It is an excellent example of ecotourism and a vital source of local employment.

Environmental: ⊘⊘⊘⊘⊘
Social: ⊘⊘⊘⊘⊘

Vamizi Island

Cabo Delgado, Mozambique
+258 272 21299 / www.maluane.com / reservations@maluane.com

THE old lady breathed heavily as she concentrated on digging a large pit in the sand. Most 70-somethings would normally spend their night-time hours on less exerting activities, but this senior citizen was different. Well over a metre (3ft) in length, the olive-coloured green turtle had travelled thousands of kilometres back to the sandy beach on which she had been hatched all those years before to lay her own eggs. About a hundred rheumy eggs the size of ping-pong balls were laid in the hole, before she laboriously covered them up with sand and slipped back into the warm waters of the Indian Ocean.

Several hundred hawksbill and green turtle nesting sites have been counted on Vamizi Island alone. Eggs are laid between July and April, so

there's a good chance of witnessing this special event. It represents a gratifying measure of both the ecological health and biodiversity of this pristine habitat.

Vamizi is one of three coral-ringed islands included along with 33,000ha (81,500 acres) of mainland that make up the Maluane Project, an unspoilt wilderness set along Mozambique's northern coast. It's perhaps unique as a low-impact tourism destination and scientific conservation project, as the Mozambican government, the Zoological Society of London and the local community have formed a partnership to manage the location. On the north side of Vamizi, gazing through coconut palms towards Rongui Island in the distance, is its exclusive hotel.

Lazy lunches of fresh calamari, crab, lobster or prawns often take place outside the dining room and bar. It's then a short walk along the white talcum-powder beach to your airy villa for a siesta. Created to cause minimal environmental impact, the villas incorporate traditional design elements of *makute* thatch and Arab-inspired furniture, which in turn are complemented by contemporary details.

The seas surrounding crescent-shaped Vamizi are home to exceptional diversity: 350 species of fish inhabit the unbleached corals that provide superb snorkelling and diving. Twitchy crabs wielding blue-tinted claws vie with sea urchins, while octopuses show off their dazzling ability to change colour to uninterested clams. In deeper waters, gamefish like tuna, sailfish and marlin are plentiful, as is the legendary bonefish.

But the attractions are not just ocean-based. Walks along the immense beach take time because there are so many tiny coves to explore. If the sun gets too hot, scramble up a path into the forest to seek out a quiet pool of shade – although your solitude will be broken by birdsong and the acrobatics of the endemic samango monkeys.

In the evening, after watching a turtle lay her eggs, it's time for you to sink into your huge, comfortable bed. The strange lullaby of hiccups and hums from a night-time choir of insects guarantees a deep sleep.

ECO**FILE**

Rooms: Ten luxury thatched villas.
Rates: From MT14,300 (US$560) per person per night, including all meals, but excluding transfers.
Location: 290km (180 miles) north of Pemba in Cabo Delgado province, and 60km (40 miles) south of the Tanzanian border.
Best time to go: May–Dec (Aug and Dec are peak times). Jan–Apr are the hottest months, when the rainy season (short, intermittent showers) also occurs.
Getting there: From Dar es Salaam (Tanzania), take a local flight to Pemba. Alternatively, fly from Maputo (Mozambique) to Pemba; Vamizi Island has its own plane for the 75-min transfer from there.
CO_2 emissions: Rtn flight to Pemba via Dar es Salaam from London 2.30 tonnes. Rtn flight to Pemba via Maputo from New York 4.47; Sydney 3.57. Rtn transfer to Vamizi 0.31.
Offset cost: $71.10; £19.58; A$72.50.

Responsibility: Environmental concerns are taken very seriously on Vamizi Island. Built almost entirely from sustainable local materials, the hotel comes under the watchful eye of the Maluane Project in partnership with the Zoological Society of London. This project has had a huge effect in helping to preserve the exceptional fauna and flora here.
Environmental: ☒☒☒☒☒
Social: ☒☒☒☒☒

Goodwill hunting

On a Kalahari hunting trip, **Rupert Isaacson** was privileged to spend time with the Ju/'hoansi, and in return contributed much-needed money to the tribe's Nyae Nyae Conservancy.

It's winter in the Kalahari, the grasses yellowed by the sun, the trees black and bare, and the sky an unremitting, dazzling blue. The three Ju/'hoansi Bushman hunters – lean, whip-thin men, – climbed down from the thorn tree in whose spiky branches they had just secured the quarters of the wildebeest they had killed. The rest of the meat, cut into thin strips, was stuffed into sacks cut from the wildebeest's own hide and strung together with the dry, tough reeds that grew thereabouts, ready for the long walk home.

The two older hunters, Bo and Fanzi, took the knapsacks while Xau, a lad of perhaps 18, used one of the sharp-ended digging sticks to spear the two heavy racks of ribs in the tree and swing these over his right shoulder. On the ground, where the carcass had lain, all that

This page: The Jo/'hoansi Bushmen hunters, preparing poisoned arrows and digging for roots

remained was the dung cleared out of the intestines. We set off, heading 10km (6 miles) through the dry bush to the village where we were to feast that night.

It had been a day like none I had ever known: up at dawn and into the wide, singing bush behind the three hunters. They had begun tracking almost immediately, walking fast, casting what seemed merely cursory glances at the ground. Yet, unerringly, they had brought us to within metres of their antelope prey. Just two days before, I'd been sitting on the Tube in London.

To go hunting with the Bushmen was, for me, the fulfilment of a childhood dream. These people have traditionally avoided contact with the outside world where possible. That they are now willing to accommodate tourists

reflects a common crisis faced by all the Bushmen clans of the five countries of the Kalahari.

For the great grassland's last remaining pockets of wilderness are being encroached upon by aggressive groups of cattle herders, and by the more insidious attentions of the diamond-mining industry. In the Nyae Nyae region of Namibia, where the Ju/'hoansi live, the invaders are the Herero tribe, whose herds have overgrazed their own lands to the south. Benjamin Xishe, an English-speaking Ju/'hoansi, outlined the problem.

'The Herero come, they say to one of the village headmen, "Look after my cattle for me and I will pay you and give you meat and milk." And the headman is afraid and agrees. Then the Herero do not pay, and they kill off the game

This page: An arrow poisoned in preparation for the hunt; the Eushimen on the Nyae Nyae conservancy

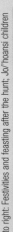

and the cattle trample out the wild foods and then the Ju/'hoansi have nothing.'

Benjamin and the other Ju/'hoansi hope that tourism will help to stem the Herero encroachment. If the San can earn money simply by practising their traditional culture, the Hereros' initial bargaining power would be taken away. The Ju/'hoansi also realize that the mere presence of foreigners shames the local authorities into taking action, and demonstrates to the government (whose view of Bushmen has traditionally been, at best, dismissive) that the hunter-gatherer way of life can attract much-needed tourist dollars.

The government has taken notice. In 1998, it acceded to the Ju/'hoansis' request for the area to be declared a game conservancy, with severe restrictions on livestock-keeping. The Herero have been moved back to their own lands to the south and the Bushmen given control of the tourism and the game.

It's a great relief – because elsewhere in the Kalahari the governments have been actively disposing the Bushmen to make way for new diamond mines. In neighbouring Botswana, for example, San people have been routinely tortured, dispossessed and starved to force them off their ancestral lands, and human rights workers and journalists have been banned from even entering the country. Namibia, by taking a much more enlightened approach, has secured a future for this oldest, most ecologically integrated of human cultures.

This is no throw-away claim: both geneticists and anthropologists reckon that no older human culture exists.

It is impossible to overstate the magic of spending time with the Bushmen, a gentle people who practise pacifism, gender equality and natural healing. At Nyae Nyae, during the long walk home from the hunt, the three hunters, Bo, Fanzi and Xau, stopped to rest every few kilometres. Tom,

my companion, and I had shared our tobacco and water with them until our supplies of both ran dry. Seeing this, Fanzi, the second-oldest hunter, pointed to a small twig poking up from the dry, cracked earth. Taking a digging stick, he began to hack at the ground and in less than a minute unearthed a large round tuber, whose flesh, when he cut into it, dripped with moisture. He handed the pieces round, allowing everyone to quench their thirst. Just then, a piercing cry made us look up. About 20m (60ft) above the thorn trees, two eagles were chasing a smaller hawk out of their territory, spiralling into the unrelenting blue.

Much later, bellies full of the meat we had brought back, the whole clan came to our camp to dance, the women clapping and singing, the men weaving slow, stomping patterns in the firelight until the moon had passed its apex, and hyenas began to whoop in the distance. Then, like moths, the Ju/'hoansi rose in a fluttering rush and drifted off into the darkness, leaving us alone. Long after they had gone, Tom and I sat up, listening to the night sounds and wondering how we would ever describe it when we got home.

ECO**FILE**

Location: North-eastern Namibia, 450km (280 miles) from Windhoek. The camps move each year, but are usually on within 10km (6 miles) of the Tsumkwe-Botswana Border Rd.

Getting there: From Windhoek, drive 8 hours to Tsumkwe, then transfer to the camp (20km/12 miles). Arrange through a responsible operator such as Safari Drive or Okavango Tours (see below).

CO_2 emissions: Rtn flight to Windhoek from New York 3.55 tonnes; London 2.41; Sydney 3.68. Rtn transfer 0.27. Alternatively, offset your trip by donating to the Nyae Nyae Conservancy, to develop non-desertification land-use projects.

Offset cost: $56.20; £20.15; A$73.85.

Staying there: Accommodation is in tented camps organized through Safari Drive or Okavango Tours and Safaris (see below).

Rates: Self-drive safaris from N$21,500 (US$3,000) per person per week; guided safaris from N$18,000 (US$2,500) per person per week, including all meals.

Best time to go: Mar–Sep, when the elephants migrate in and there's less foliage – best for game-viewing.

Further information:
www.kalaharipeoples.org
www.safaridrive.com
www.okavango.com

Responsibility: The Bushmen manage this fragile ecosystem without encroachment of livestock and subsequent desertification, allowing animal migration routes to stay open. Money from tours goes direct into the hands of the locals.

Damaraland Camp

Haub River Valley, Namibia
+27 (0)11 807 1800 (South Africa office) / www.wilderness-safaris.com

THE rocky wilderness is scarred with dry riverbeds, their empty channels looking like stony paths leading blindly into a sea of sand. Abstract granite domes loom in a silent landscape that might easily be construed to be bereft of life, the scattered remains of a petrified forest only exaggerating the effect. But you'd be wrong to assume this apparently waterless hinterland was long dead – life still holds a fragile grip. For here, an extraordinary ecosystem has evolved around the morning mists that form when cold air off the Atlantic meets the warm mainland.

The name Damara is derived from a Nama word meaning 'Who Walked Here', and refers to the footprints left by the Damara people around waterholes. Likewise, desert plants, rare desert elephant and black rhino, oryx, kudu and springbok have all adapted to this inhospitable environment. Even lion and cheetah occasionally risk a visit.

This unique arid setting is also home to the award-winning solar-powered Damaraland Camp. Its nine tented rooms each have their own verandas and share a natural rock-pool that provides cool respite from the sun. The main restaurant and bar are built from local rock and canvas, a sympathetic design that cleverly wraps the desert under the sails of a landlocked clipper. The international and African desert-style suppers here are made from fresh produce regularly brought in from Windhoek.

This exceptional region remained unprotected until 1981, when an NGO initiative supported by the community developed a game-guard

system that halted illegal poaching. In 1996, a partnership forged between the Damaraland people and a commercial enterprise, Wilderness Safaris, brought the camp into existence, and 10 per cent of its revenue and ground rent goes directly into the community. Since then, the 180,000ha (445,000-acre) Torra Conservancy has been established and the numbers of desert elephant and rhino have increased. It's one of the most successful community tourism set-ups in Africa, meeting all management costs and reinvesting profits into community projects without donor funding.

In the Torra Conservancy you'll find terrific nature walks and drives in spectacular scenery. Geological features like the basalt organ pipes and volcanic Burnt Mountain are an intriguing backdrop for mountain-biking, birding, rhino-tracking and visits to the Twyfelfontein rock engravings, which date from 10,000–20,000 years ago. Game-spotting is also an option, although this isn't the type of safari you might expect in South Africa or elsewhere, as the animals travel vast distances for food and water and are harder to find. Instead, its appeal comes in the detail. Nothing is too small to overlook: the battles waged by the insect population against the desert extremes are every bit as monumental and dramatic as those fought by larger animals.

The sense of space and sheer elemental beauty here is unbeatable. In the quiet of night, when the camp is lit with lanterns and the sky glitters with countless stars, the world seems like the smallest place in the cosmos.

ECO**FILE**

Rooms: Ten large tented rooms.
Rates: From N$2,310 (US$300) per person per night, including meals and safaris, but excluding transfers.
Location: On the north face of the Haub River Valley, 90km (55 miles) from Torra Bay on Namibia's Skeleton Coast. The nearest airport is Windhoek.
Best time to go: Year-round. The high season is from Jul to mid-Nov.
Getting there: From Windhoek, fly 100 mins to Damaraland by light plane. Alternatively, drive to the camp (route directions can be provided on booking).
CO_2 emissions: Rtn flight to Windhoek from New York 3.55 tonnes; London 2.41; Sydney 3.68. Rtn transfer by plane 0.63; by car 0.15.
Offset cost: $62.05; £22.85; A$80.55.

Responsibility: This ecolodge is a great example of a community-based safari operation. The tangible financial benefits for the local people are exemplary, notably in terms of local enterprise, employment and training. Conservation and environmental concerns are also strong points, the success of the camp being instrumental in the creation of the Torra Conservancy.
Environmental: ∅∅∅∅∅
Social: ∅∅∅∅∅

Skeleton Coast Camp

North of Möwe Bay, 20km (12 miles) from the Skeleton Coast, Namibia
+27 (0)11 807 1800 (South Africa office) / www.wilderness-safaris.com

WINDBLOWN sand whips at the bleached whale bones and eroded husks of long-forgotten ships stranded on the lonely Skeleton Coast. Sand dunes moan as the harmattan whirls over them and through endless dusty plains, canyons and saltpans.

This immense primeval territory is physical testimony to the forces of nature, carrying geological scars from the tectonic upheavals that split ancient Gondwanaland and divorced continents in the process. In its northern sector, some 300,000ha (741,000 acres) have been leased exclusively to the Skeleton Coast Camp for low-volume safaris. The camp's footprint is hardly discernible: it sleeps a maximum of 12 people in six tented rooms, which works out at a generous 22,000ha (55,000 acres) per guest.

Built on stilts on an island in the dry Khumib River, 20km (12 miles) from the coast, the solar-powered Skeleton Coast Camp is an example of award-winning ecotourism. None of its tented structures are permanent, so the site will revert back to nature should it ever be dismantled. Water resources are scarce (they are trucked in from the Hoarusib River), so are rigorously metered and carefully conserved. Environmental and community issues are paramount here. The camp employs more than 80 per cent of its employees from the local Himba people and provides ongoing support for conservation work, notably the Kunene Predator Research Project, preservation of lichens, and monitoring of the behaviour of desert elephants and giraffes.

It takes a while to acclimatize here, especially when on safari – for example, it's not always apparent when an animal has come into view in the enormous landscape. The small pride of

ECOFILE

Rooms: Six tented rooms.
Rates: From N$29,600 (US$4,135) per person per night for a 3-night stay, including all meals and safaris but excluding transfers.
Location: North of Möwe Bay, about 20km (12 miles) from the Skeleton Coast. The nearest airport is Windhoek.
Best time to go: Year-round. The high season is Jul–Oct.
Getting there: From Windhoek, transfers to the lodge are only by a 2.5-hour light plane flight.
CO2 emissions: Rtn flight to Windhoek from New York 3.55 tonnes; London 2.41; Sydney 3.68. Rtn transfer 0.10.
Offset cost: $54.20; £18.85; A$70.65.

Responsibility: The Skeleton Coast Camp takes its environmental and social responsibilities seriously, and has had a beneficial impact on a very poor region, especially economically and with the building of a school. Its low impact, coupled with its support for the Himba, stylish accommodation and unique situation, make for a very special vacation.
Environmental: ⊘⊘⊘⊘⊘
Social: ⊘⊘⊘⊘⊘

lions that recently set up their territory in the Hoarusub Canyon is a significant development — lions haven't been in the area for a decade. The felines were feeding chiefly on cattle belonging to the local Himba people, but the camp reimburses them for their losses, balancing conservation with social responsibility. There's speculation that the pride will soon reach the sea and another source of food: the seal colonies, a thought that might be a little too real for the squeamish.

Access to the region for tourists is strictly limited, minimizing environmental impact and creating a sense of overwhelming isolation. This may not appeal to everyone, but the desolate seclusion is also the camp's magic. Days here are unlike a regular safari — when you leave camp in the morning, you're gone until evening to cover as much ground as possible in 4WDs. Trips to the coast and treks here are sensational. *Welwitschia* (the world's oldest living plant) and *Lithops* ('flowering stones') look otherworldly amid the lichen fields and dunes.

After a long day out in the wilderness, welcome suppers are eaten under an ancient leadwood tree. Nightfall quickly blinds the world, and only the crackling of the campfire breaks the darkness.

Buffalo Ridge Safari Lodge

PO Box 4617, Halfway House, 1685, South Africa
+27 (0)18 365 9908 / www.buffaloridgesafari.com / reservations@buffaloridgesafari.com

AS the engine stopped, what was merely oppressively hot air suddenly got heavier in the abrupt silence. Gradually, the rhino and calf came into view, and the heat and humidity were forgotten. At a year old the toddler was already the size of an upright piano, its mother a concert grand. Caked in mud and sporting hefty horns, the magnificent creatures stopped for an impromptu photo op and then sauntered on their way, leaving in their wake a safari vehicle full of ecstatic tourists.

Rhino-tracking in the fascinating Madikwe Game Reserve is thrilling stuff. This 75,000ha (185,000-acre) region was nothing more than poor grazing ground for cattle until 20 years ago, when the Lowveld bushveld and Kalahari thornveld ecosystems were restored. Today, its wildlife is superbly diverse after the largest translocation of animals ever – all 10,000 of them. The reserve is renowned for its rare African wild dog and cheetah (the 'big five' almost come as standard), and you'd never guess the land had been anything other than wild.

The utter transformation of Madikwe is noteworthy, but the story behind Buffalo Ridge Safari Lodge itself is remarkable, for it's the first camp of its kind in South Africa to be wholly owned by a rural community – the Balete. During apartheid these people were forcibly resettled in Lekgophung (west of Madikwe) and lost everything, but then in conjunction with Nature Workshop they won a 45-year lease of land at Tweedepoort and opened the lodge. Individual employment is an obvious benefit, but the lodge has brought prosperity to the whole community.

Buffalo Ridge Safari Lodge is perched atop Tweedepoort Ridge and commands far-reaching views across the Madikwe. The split-level main lodge is approached over a bridge that crosses a stone-strewn ravine filled with rock figs; here you'll find the restaurant, swimming pool, bar and viewing decks. The sleeping accommodation is luxurious, yet informal. Built from local materials, the eight thatched suites fit snugly into the surroundings. Their sliding doors open directly onto the bush, conjuring up an indoor/outdoor vibe.

And it's outside where most guests want to be. Walking and open-vehicle safaris are led by Balete guides, who have the intimate knowledge of the land that comes with growing up here. Flattened grass, the movement of birds and telltale droppings are some of the tiny clues that lead the experts towards animals. Dung is central to a tracking/walking safari, and holds all sorts of information, although actually locating an incontinent pachyderm is sometimes easier said than done. The birdwatching is also excellent, as is the botany for those who want a more sedentary holiday. But there's one creature most folk are thrilled not to see on safari; surprisingly, in the Madikwe Game Reserve you'll not find a single mosquito.

A superb day of game-spotting is eventually rounded off with a delicious meal and drinks back at Buffalo Ridge. But take time after supper to look into the massive African night sky. Surely there are more stars here than anywhere else on the globe.

ECO**FILE**

Rooms: Eight luxury chalets.
Rates: From R2,100 (US$320) per person per night, based on double occupancy and including all meals, safaris and return transfers to Madikwe airstrip.
Location: Madwike Game Reserve, North-West Province. Near the border with Botswana, 200km (125 miles) west of Johannesburg.
Best time to go: Year-round. The rainy season (Oct–Mar) has hot days and warm nights, while the dry season (Apr–Sep) has warm days and cold nights – good for viewing game.
Getting there: From Johannesburg, fly 45 mins to Madikwe airstrip with Federal Air or Madikwe Air Charters. Alternatively, drive 4 hours to the camp. Request a map on reservation.
CO_2 emissions: Rtn flight to Johannesburg from New York 3.97 tonnes; London 2.63; Sydney 3.30. Rtn transfer by plane 0.06; by car 0.12.
Offset cost: $60.75; £20.65; A$63.90.

Responsibility: Buffalo Ridge Safari Lodge is the ultimate in feel-good stories, as the Balete community owns the camp and is its main beneficiary. The social and training initiatives are genuine, and the ongoing environmental concern has had a striking effect on what was once pasture. The success of Buffalo Ridge has prompted Nature Workshop to undertake a similar partnership with another community in the southeast corner of Madikwe.

Environmental: ØØØ ØØ
Social: ØØØØØ

Hog Hollow Country Lodge

Askop Road, The Crags, Plettenberg Bay, 6600, South Africa
+27 (0)44 534 8879 / www.hog-hollow.com / info@hog-hollow.com

DENSE forest spills down from the hills and out of the canyons but stops abruptly when it reaches the softly contoured dunes of Plettenberg Bay. The broad beaches below are misty with wind-blown sand and pounded by huge waves. A whipping, salty wind invigorates the senses. An idle walk along these stretches will bring you to huge rock-pools riddled with tiny fish and crawling with crabs.

The seashore around here is wonderful, but the landscape inland is even more dramatic. Bloukrans Pass meanders off the highway through spectacular canyons carpeted thickly with trees and punctuated with boulders. A drive in this neighbourhood should be compulsory. Although those of a nervous disposition will resist a dive, Bloukrans Bridge is the site of the highest bungee-jump in the world.

Nearby is the Matjies River Gorge, and perched high on a ridge above it is the four-star Hog Hollow Country Lodge. Despite the impressive landscape, the area (known as the Crags) was for many years a little-visited district given over to wattle, an invasive Australian plant that destroyed the rare indigenous forests and *fynbos* (scrubland). In 1993, the lodge changed all that. It was built on the site of an old wattle plantation, and the owners paid special attention to clearing the

foreign invader and restoring the original habitat. Today, 15 luxurious suites are scattered around the main house in extensive grounds that also house a pool and *boma* – an area where fires are lit at night.

Hog Hollow's ecological credentials are commendable, but its ethical policies are nothing less than impeccable. This member of the Fair Trade in Tourism South Africa (FTTSA) organization is party to exacting demands concerning the empowerment and welfare of poor local communities. The lodge also plays an important role in the local economy, as it buys in only local services and produce.

The local produce is pretty good too, borne out by the excellent reputation garnered by the kitchens here. Sociable candlelit gourmet meals accompanied by wines are served at a huge communal table in the main house.

Hog Hollow does, however, have a lot more going for it than its food. Xolani, a local guide and font of knowledge, can take you on an individual township tour. Stopping off for a beer and a chat with locals in one of the taverns should not be missed. The area also offers great walking, horseback riding and cycling trails, boat tours, whale-spotting trips and scuba-diving excursions. But it is memories of the deep green landscape and wide sea vistas that will remain with you long after leaving, and the sight of the Tsitsikama Mountains looming above the long beaches that will all but guarantee your return.

ECOFILE

Rooms: 15 cottage suites.
Rates: From R1,160 (US$160) per person per night, including breakfast.
Location: 18km (11 miles) east of Plettenberg Bay in Western Cape Province. Hog Hollow is 566km (351 miles) from Cape Town. The nearest airport is George (130km/80 miles).
Best time to go: Year-round, although the lodge closes in Jun.
Getting there: From Cape Town, drive 6 hours to the lodge via the N2 road. Alternatively, fly to George and then then hire a car.
CO2 emissions: Rtn flight to Cape Town from New York 3.87 tonnes; London 2.83; Sydney 3.29. Rtn transfer by plane 0.12; by car 0.34.
Offset cost: $62.55; £23.80; A$67.80.

Responsibility: Hog Hollow Country Lodge is a member of the Fair Trade in Tourism in South Africa organization, and as such adheres to strict ethical principals. It is particularly socially responsible, exclusively employing local people from the Plettenberg district, investing heavily in training programmes, and buying in local services and produce to provide a top-quality product. Unlike many such resorts, it is also child-friendly.
Environmental: ∅∅∅∅∅
Social: ∅∅∅∅∅

Vuyatela

PO Box 338, Hluvukani, 1363, Mpumalanga, South Africa
+27 (0)13 735 5118 / www.djuma.com / djuma@djuma.co.za

AN elegant giraffe nervously dips her head down to the water's edge, but something disturbs her. She pulls away and haughtily catwalks into the bush, apparently above whatever inconvenience it was that bothered her. How does a creature so tall vanish so completely into the straw-coloured bush? It's a disappearing act that is hard to credit. The disturbance reveals itself – a solitary hippo raises his knucklehead out of the water and snorts.

The watering-hole at Vuyatela is a magnet for all sorts of wildlife: elephant, waterbuck, kudu and zebra all make an appearance during the day. They need refreshment as the sun beats down relentlessly here, but you can watch these everyday African wildlife stories unfurl before you from the comfortable shade of a parasol on the terrace of the bush lodge.

Vuyatela is tucked deep in the classic African savannah of the Sabi Sand Game Reserve. Eight chalets with sun-decks and plunge pools looking across the bush create a sense of informal exclusivity. They're built of mud and thatch, inspired by indigenous building techniques,

and sensitively constructed from local materials. But Vuyatela also has a strong contemporary feel, fusing elements of quirky, modern South African culture with the traditional. And when it comes to social awareness and eco-credentials, this bush lodge is cutting edge.

Vuyatela is a member of the Fair Trade in Tourism in South Africa scheme, a strictly regulated body that audits all aspects of tourism businesses. These include the working environment, employment equity, workplace skills and wider community involvement, as well as ecological concerns. It is a notoriously difficult organization to join, and membership is a cast-iron guarantee of tourism best practice. Vuyatela needs to be saluted for its endeavours, as the vibe in this place is unequalled and the staff are excellent.

Expert local guides accompany guests on early morning and late-afternoon game drives, where you're pretty much guaranteed to see the 'big five': lion, leopard, buffalo, rhino and elephant. You might also catch sight of cheetah and some of the 200 species of birds, 85 reptile species and dozens of different mammals in the area.

The bush walk – a gentle ramble around the lodge – is totally winning. A bizarre-looking plant, elegant with post-modern pom-poms, turns out to be a kind of catnip for baboons. Dung beetles put on extraordinary performances, burying gobbits of manure twice their size in a matter of minutes. This may all be a lot less flashy than a leopard, but somehow it's just as interesting.

Plans for the next day's safari are discussed before supper at a communal table, which sits beneath an enormous chandelier made from recycled Coke bottles. It's an informal affair of hearty well-cooked fusion cuisine, with Malay, Zulu, Afrikaans, Shona and British influences. A final nightcap beside the campfire is accompanied by the constant electronic thrum of insect noise.

An early morning coffee before the game drive is mandatory. But it's briefly disturbed by the strangest of noises. A bass didgeridoo honking echoes across from the watering-hole: it's the hippo waking up to a new day.

ECO**FILE**

Rooms: Eight luxury chalets.
Rates: From R3,570 (US$500) per person per night, based on double occupancy, and including all meals, safaris, a guided walk and taxes.
Location: Djuma Game Reserve in Mpumalanga Province, northeastern South Africa, adjacent to the Kruger National Park.
Best time to go: Year-round. Summer (Dec–Feb) is the birthing season, inevitably bringing predators. Aug and Sep are the driest months when the vegetation dies down and the game-viewing is excellent.
Getting there: From Johannesburg, fly to Kruger-Nelspruit, where a light plane will transfer you to the lodge.
CO_2 emissions: Rtn flight to Johannesburg from New York 3.97 tonnes; London 2.63; Sydney 3.30. Rtn transfers 0.10.
Offset cost: $60.50; £20.50; A$63.55.

Responsibility: Vuyatela is a member of Fair Trade in Tourism in South Africa. Its social/community programmes are excellent, and it actively helps with schools and the N'wa Tumberi Day Care Centre in Utha. Its ecological and environmental care is also strong, with long-term goals for preserving the local habitat. In addition, Vuyatela has positioned a network of live cameras around the park, making it the world's first virtual game reserve.
Environmental: ⌀⌀⌀⌀⌀
Social: ⌀⌀⌀⌀⌀

A walk on the wild side

Do voluntourists provide support for wildlife conservation, or take jobs away from locals? **Richard Newton** tracked lions and wrestled with his conscience in Botswana's Okavango Delta.

What am I doing here? It's an ethical question that has suddenly assumed compelling urgency. I am sitting on the roof of a Land Rover within metres of a lion pride. It is early evening and they are rousing, stretching, preparing to hunt. I feel acutely vulnerable up here. And also guilty. Eye to eye with seven lions, I am wondering if someone else should be in my place. Am I depriving a deserving local of a job?

In truth, the question has been nagging me since my arrival in Botswana. No special skills or qualifications are required for my adopted role as an assistant to a pair of lion researchers, and my briefing lasted just five minutes. Equipped with a pair of headphones and an antenna, I took up my perch and, as we drove away from camp, listened to an audio trail of strengthening beeps, twitching my dangling feet left or right according to the direction of the signals. Following my cues through the windscreen, Chistiaan Winterbach, at the wheel, took us across rough bush, dodging termite mounds and rutted hippo trails.

Many volunteer projects exist to help conserve native and endangered African wildlife

Finally the source of the transmission is located: a radio collar worn by one of the lionesses.

When we find them, the big cats are asleep in tree shade. We wait, something I will get used to over the coming days. Wildlife research requires infinite patience, and is a stark adjustment from the usual tourist safari, in which the goal is to pack in as many sightings as possible in a three-hour game drive. Here the schedule is not built around photo opportunities and gourmet meals. For the duration of my stay with husband-and-wife team Christiaan and Hanlie Winterbach, I am not a tourist. I am a voluntourist.

At its best, voluntourism – the combination of a paying holiday with voluntary work – provides a much more satisfying experience than an average vacation. It is often uncomfortable and can involve plenty of strenuous or tedious work. Yet by contributing directly to conservation or development projects, you are rewarded with a genuine sense of personal achievement, and also a deep and lasting connection with the place and its people.

But at its worst, voluntourism is colonialism in a new guise. Unskilled, privileged westerners arrive in Africa to 'help'. Their motives are well intentioned, but they can inadvertently undermine the local labour market. When a bunch of foreign voluntourists spend a couple of weeks building a classroom or an orphanage, they are effectively depriving local builders of work. In the longer term, Africans become increasingly dependent on outside assistance, and the economy stagnates.

In Botswana, I arrived in the tourist gateway town of Maun, where the unemployment rate is around 20 per cent. Many of the inhabitants were lured here by the prospects of the thriving tourism industry in the nearby Okavango Delta. However, there

ECO**FILE**

Location: In the Okavango Delta, 80km (50 miles) northwest of Maun, Botswana.

Getting there: From Johannesburg (South Africa), fly 100 mins to Maun in Botswana. Access to the camp is by a short 15-min charter flight or 5-hour drive.

CO2 emissions: Rtn flight to Maun via Johannesburg from New York 4.17 tonnes; London 2.84; Sydney 3.51. Rtn transfer by plane 0.03; by car 0.10. **Offset cost:** $63.50; £22; A$67.35.

Staying there: Lion Camp is a working wildlife research base. You stay in a walk-in safari tent with an adjoining outdoor bathroom.

Rates: From £2095 (US$4,200) per person for 11 days in the low season, including accommodation, all meals, flights from London and transfers (booked exclusively through Discovery Initiatives; see below). The same company also offers a 9-day elephant, leopard and wild dog study trip in Botswana's Tuli Block, costing from £2,595 (US$5,200) per person, excluding flights.

Best time to go: The low season is Feb–Mar and Nov; the high season is Apr–Oct and Dec–Jan.

Further information:
www.botswana-tourism.gov.bw
www.discoveryinitiatives.co.uk
www.earthwatch.org

Responsibility: The Okavango Delta is one of the great wilderness areas of Africa; a vast wetland surrounded by the Kalahari Desert. Christiaan and Hanlie Winterbach have been studying the region's lions since 1997.

are only so many jobs to go around, and though Maun benefits from the ancillary businesses that have sprung up to supply the lodges and research camps, there are still many people left idling on dusty street corners.

And now, along with the tourists, here come voluntourists like me. From here I will fly by light aircraft to the Winterbachs' camp. The money they earn from paying volunteers is vital; without it, they would be unable to continue their study of the delta's lions. Their findings are essential for maintaining a healthy lion population, the lions draw the tourists, and tourism creates new jobs.

But how am I viewed by the unemployed of Maun? Admittedly, not every jobless person here would leap at a position that entailed spending hours sitting unguarded atop a Land Rover close to wild lions; though for the right person it could be a stepping stone towards a career in wildlife research or the safari industry.

Voluntourism is fraught with ethical quandaries. With an increasing number of such tours available, prospective voluntourists must look carefully at the merits of each project, and at their role within it. Does the project meet a genuine local need? Are local people directly involved in it? Are there any adverse impacts on the community? Is your role – and the money you contribute – important to the project's success?

One long-established volun-tourism organization, the non-

and composition of the local lion population, and extrapolating behavioural differences between Okavango lions and those in other parts of Africa.

To achieve these aims, they process huge amounts of raw data using complex mathematical formulae, pie charts, graphs, maps and tables. It turns out that a

profit Earthwatch Institute, has a distinguished record in this field. Each year, more than 4,000 paying volunteers participate in its projects around the world, usually working alongside local people. The institute has 27 projects in Africa, including a study of inverte-brates in South Africa, the development of a conservation strategy for crocodiles in Zambia, and the establishment of clean water supplies for villages in Kenya.

These are life-changing experiences for all involved. My time with the Winterbachs is no exception. I had always tended towards an idealized view of field research. The first mistake was to assume that researchers lead carefree lives, roaming the bush at will. In reality, they are tied down by their research aims. For Christiaan and Hanlie, these include monitoring the numbers

wildlife researcher is essentially a mathematician in khaki.

Nor is daily life in the wilder-ness idyllic. The Winterbachs' base, Lion Camp, is a five-hour drive from Maun, or 20 minutes by aircraft. Out here, they must be self-contained, prepared to deal with any vehicular, computer or health emergency themselves. Despite their remoteness, they cannot escape the financial headaches of the modern world. Their work is perilously funded by a combination of neighbouring safari camps, international donors and, latterly, voluntourism.

As I sit on the roof of the Land Rover watching the lions head out across the floodplain at the start of a hunt, I can take comfort from the fact that without volun-tourists like me, the Winterbachs would not be here at all. This is voluntourism at its best.

Chumbe Island Coral Park

PO Box 3203, Zanzibar, Tanzania
+255 (0)24 223 1040 / www.chumbeisland.com / info@chumbeisland.com

THE baobabs on Chumbe Island stood like ancient sentinels long before David Livingstone had even set eyes on Zanzibar. If he were around today, he'd recognize not only the trees but the whole place – excepting the late-Victorian lighthouse – because it has barely changed. And therein lies its charm; this tiny dot off the East African flank has managed against all odds to preserve not only its unique flora, but also the surrounding coral seas.

For many years Chumbe Island was a military base, and as a no-go area it unintentionally conserved the fragile land and marine ecosystems. The unique aquatic heritage is easily seen on a walk around the rock-pools at low tide. Baby conger eels glower in crevices at slinky starfish, plump sea anemones wave at sea urchins and tiny fluorescent fish dart past crabs. This is just a taster for the snorkelling that can be experienced farther out, for the luminous coral reefs

surrounding the island are regarded as some of the most beautiful to be found anywhere on earth.

This rarity and abundance of nature was enough of a prompt to lead to the opening of a small-scale ecolodge, although there's nothing diminutive about its aspirations. Seven comfortable solar-powered bungalows sit on the site, gazing across the royal-blue Indian Ocean. Their specially designed roofs collect rain, which is then filtered and stored in tanks below ground. Long-drop composting toilets require only a handful of leaves to be thrown in after use and soon decompose waste into fertilizer, ensuring that nothing escapes into the reef sanctuary. These excellent green credentials are topped off by specially filtered drinking water, doing away with the need for plastic bottles, and specialist disposal of rubbish. But don't let the haze of virtue cloud the simple fact that this is a lovely place to visit.

The island is covered in pristine coral-rag forest, some of the last in the Zanzibar archipelago. A guided walk through this diverse environment is enchanting. Land, rock and hermit crabs scuttle at your feet, fleshy plants ooze sticky white poison if broken, and fossilized corals and giant clams are evidence of ancient rich seas. But the most impressive creature you'll have the privilege of meeting here is the rare coconut crab, the largest land crab in the world.

An evening amble on the shoreline throws up any number of exquisite, jewel-like shells, although the collectors among us will have to resist the overpowering urge to take them away. Night falls swiftly near the Equator, and by the light of a solar-powered torch you find your way to the dining room, built in the old lighthouse keeper's cottage. Here, good Swahili-style and international cuisine made from locally sourced ingredients awaits, which with the staff's traditionally warm Zanzibari welcome will make you feel as if you've found a new home.

Lying in bed after supper, your mind wanders as you listen to the gentle waves, and it's easy to believe the island will remain pristine for another hundred years under its current guardianship. Livingstone would be proud.

ECO**FILE**

Rooms: Seven eco-bungalows.
Rates: From TZS200,000 (US$150) per person per night, including all meals, boat transfers and taxes.
Location: Chumbe Island sits off Zanzibar's west coast.
Best time to go: Open year-round. Dec–Apr is very hot; the rainy season runs mid-Apr to mid-Jun, when it is very humid.
Getting there: From Dar es Salaam (Tanzania), fly 20 mins or take a ferry approximately 1.5 hours to Zanzibar. Road transfers to Mbweni Ruins and the boat ride to Chumbe take a further 30 mins.
CO_2 emissions: Rtn flight to Dar es Salaam from New York 3.82 tonnes; London 2.13; Sydney 3.49. Rtn transfer by plane 0.05; by ferry 0.0002.
Offset cost: $57.55; £16.35; A$66.25.

Responsibility: The award-winning Chumbe Island Coral Park lies in a protected marine area. It has established numerous educational, research and outreach programmes designed around its unique habitat. The lodge's policy of training and employing local people, and its ecological education programmes for both schoolchildren and adults are exemplary, as is the extensive research into Chumbe Island's marine and forest environments.

Environmental:	🌿🌿🌿🌿🌿
Social:	🌿🌿🌿🌿🌿

Fundu Lagoon

Wambaa Peninsula, Pemba Island, Tanzania
+255 (0)77 443 8668 / www.fundulagoon.com / reservations@fundulagoon.com

IN the warm, shallow waters surrounding Misali Island, sea anemones undulate among the corals, accompanied by idle starfish, giant clams and schools of gaudy angelfish. The diversity of life is mesmerizing.

Misali is just one of several uninhabited atolls dotted along Pemba Island's remote west coast. The Indian Ocean here is absurdly blue and splashes refreshingly onto your face as you head by boat towards the Wambaa Peninsula. There's no other way of reaching Fundu Lagoon, the hotel on its northernmost tip – although you might feel you're speeding into pristine jungle as Fundu is all but invisible from the sea.

Palm trees burst out of sundecks and puncture the *makute*-thatch rooftops, becoming part of the architecture. Sandy pathways leading to the tented bungalows disappear into tropical thickets. Local wooden masks leer from walls and calico sails catch the breeze, providing welcome shade. This laid-back style, created by London fashion designer Ellis Flyte, cleverly combines the best of African tradition with sustainable local materials and sophisticated hippy-chic. It's made for idlers.

All sense of time vanishes here – perhaps the combination of equatorial heat and tranquil surroundings is responsible – and breaking the sleepy spell doesn't come easy. It's worth it though, as the scuba-diving in the Pemba Channel is widely held to be some of the best anywhere. Its dazzling undersea gardens are home to kaleidoscopic coral fans and aptly named brain corals, where thousands of reef fish, wrasses, turtles and barracudas graze. Serious divers from the world over are drawn to this area, but these tricky waters can only be dived by those with

ECOFILE

Rooms: 16 thatched tents.
Rates: From TZS350,000 (US$275) per person per night, including all food and drinks, but excluding transfers. Note: not suitable for children under 12.
Location: Wambaa Peninsula, Pemba Island, north of Zanzibar. The nearest airport is Chake Chake.
Best time to go: Jun–Apr. Closed mid-Apr to mid-Jun during the rainy season. Note that Christmas, Jan and Feb are very hot.
Getting there: From Dar es Salaam, fly to Chake Chake via Zanzibar. Transfers by road from the airport to Mkoani Port and then by speedboat to Fundu Lagoon take approximately 1 hour.
CO2 emissions: Rtn flight to Dar es Salaam from New York 3.82 tonnes; London 2.13; Sydney 3.49. Rtn transfers 0.06.
Offset cost: $57.65; £16.40; A$66.40.

Responsibility: Fundu Lagoon employs 85 per cent of its workforce from local villages; other staff come from Zanzibar and Dar es Salaam. The hotel has funded the building of a school, instigated local health and welfare programmes, and sunk freshwater wells for the community. It also has an ongoing commitment to the local marine environment, stopping dynamite fishing in the area and providing an alternative source of revenue for Misali Island residents.
Environmental: ⌀⌀⌀⌀⌀
Social: ⌀⌀⌀⌀⌀

experience. For guests keen to learn, the hotel has a fully equipped PADI dive centre; otherwise, time spent snorkelling at Misali will more than compensate.

Diving and snorkelling is tiring, thirsty work, so returning for a sundowner at the jetty bar is a welcome distraction. The three bars in the resort are at the heart of a convivial social scene of impromptu parties with other guests. And the local bar-staff, like everyone who works here, are a source of fascinating stories about the regional tradition and culture. Dinners of fresh fish and locally sourced produce are languorous affairs, inevitably washed down with good South African wines.

Waking early when everything is still and silent is a magical time of day. It's easy to imagine you're the only person on the island, but, of course, you're not. An accompanied trip to the local village will help you to learn about the local culture and people, and is an essential part of the experience of staying here. It's another absorbing aspect of this isolated, unaffected natural world.

Serengeti Under Canvas

Serengeti, Tanzania
+27 (0)11 809 4300 (South Africa office) / www.ccafrica.com / reservations@ccafrica.com

THE sun vanishes swiftly on the Equator, plunging the Serengeti plains into soupy darkness. At night-time, the potent sounds of the bush seem even more exaggerated. As you lie awake inside your tent, it's easy to imagine that every rustle is a stealthy hyena and it takes a while to acclimatize to these natural sounds – especially the big noises; falling asleep to the roars of a lion is an overpowering experience.

Sleeping in a tent in one of the world's most thrilling natural habitats can draw you closer to nature than you'd ever thought possible. But with Serengeti Under Canvas you'll find that familiarity with this new environment soon kicks in, bolstered in no small way by your substantial luxury safari tent. Camping is one of the most eco-friendly forms of accommodation and Serengeti Under Canvas is no exception to this, as no footprint is left after they've moved on. Only six en suite double tents and a mess make up the encampment, but with no electricity the site is atmospherically lit with paraffin lamps and the first-rate cooking is performed over open fires. Yet the set-up is far from rudimentary. Polished silver and crystal, crisp linen and a personal butler evoke the decadence of a 1920s-style African adventure.

Serengeti Under Canvas pitches on private sites throughout the region. The transient camps follow the herds on Africa's extraordinary

great migration, a unique wildlife exodus that sees the annual movement of more than 2 million animals. Zebra, wildebeest and Thomson's gazelle — along with all the associated predators — coalesce into one of the great spectacles of the natural world.

Expert local guides take guests out in semi-open vehicles, bumping through dry grass and scrub to get close to these vast herds. The drama, scale and numbers are difficult to comprehend as you enter a panorama so teeming with life that it's humbling.

With so many creatures about, security is paramount, both in the bush and in the camp. At night you're constantly escorted when moving between tents. It's easy to forget that the animals here are wild and dangerous, yet surprisingly, the camp guards aren't armed; instead they're practised in the art of scare tactics, deftly moving on unwanted visitors.

You'll also be accompanied on walking safaris in quieter areas. While it might not have the drama of the vehicle safaris, trekking through the bush allows you to forge a simple connection with nature that's just as memorable. But no scene is as compelling as when the vast wildebeest herds give birth to their young in February and March. Camping will never be the same again.

ECO**FILE**

Rooms: Six luxury safari tents.
Rates: From TZS690,000 (US$540) per person per night, including all meals, safaris, transfers and taxes.
Location: Following the animal migration, the camps gradually move through the Serengeti National Park. Jul: Western Corridor; Aug to mid-Oct: Mara/Wogakuria region; mid-Oct to Jan: central Serengeti plain; Feb–Mar: short grass plains; Apr–May: southern Serengeti; Jun: western Serengeti.
Best time to go: Wonderful year-round, but the birthing season in Feb–Mar is very special.
Getting there: From Dar es Salaam, fly to any one of five airstrips in the Serengeti National Park. The air and road transfers vary greatly in length depending on which campsite you visit; you'll be advised on details when booking.
CO_2 emissions: Rtn flight to Dar es Salaam from New York 3.82 tonnes; London 2.13; Sydney 3.49. Rtn transfer 0.13 (varies with location).
Offset cost: $58.70; £16.90; A$67.70.

Responsibility: The locally staffed Serengeti Under Canvas is unashamedly opulent, yet is a genuinely green experience. Its umbrella company, Conservation Corporation Africa, is responsible for many projects through its NGO, the Africa Foundation, which has raised more than US$4 million for community development projects, schools, education, environmental awareness and HIV/AIDS initiatives through tourism.
Environmental: 🌀🌀🌀🌀🌀
Social: 🌀🌀🌀🌀🌀

Should I give to beggars?

'GIVE ME!' 'Donnez-moi!' 'Pen, present, money, sweets.' 'Stylo, cadeau, l'argent, bonbon.' As you move around Africa, the language may change but the message remains persistent. In cities and in far-flung villages, foreign visitors often find themselves besieged by African poverty in the flesh.

The abstract numbers are shocking enough. More than 400 million people in sub-Saharan Africa – half the total population – subsist on less than US$1 a day. Confronted with a forest of outstretched palms, visitors are forced to deal with the problem face to face. It is uncomfortable, and it is also often heartbreaking.

In some cases, giving to beggars – especially to street children – can do more harm than good. These kids are often skipping school in order to reap what they can from tourists, and occasionally they are part of organized begging rings, with the proceeds going to ruthless gang leaders. It's possible that your gift to may not benefit the intended

recipient at all, and even if it does, it may do little to alleviate the beggar's situation.

An alternative is to give money to a local registered charity, especially one that works with the homeless and underprivileged. On their departure, visitors can also donate any unwanted currency left over from their trip to airport collection boxes or to schemes such as the British Airways Change for Good campaign, run in partnership with UNICEF, which has raised £18 million (US$36 million) since 1994.

A charitable donation can feel like a remote and unsatisfying response when we are faced with the vivid reality of African poverty. Undoubtedly, there are times when we will see people who are genuinely and urgently in need of help, and for whom the gift of money, or perhaps even some food, will make a significant difference – for that day at least.

While the horrors of poverty are all too apparent when we are in the midst of it, begging is a symptom of a problem that is beyond the means of individual tourists to tackle. Whether we choose to give to beggars or not while we travel, the greater challenge is to take our shock back home, and to act upon it. Out of sight, but not out of mind.

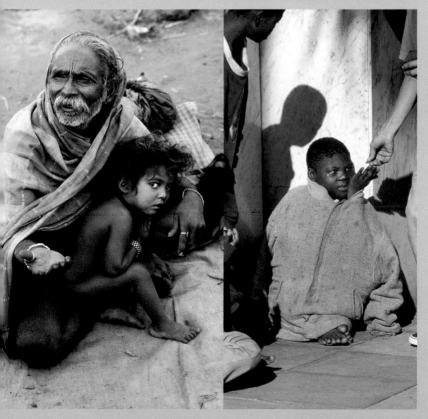

The Islands of Siankaba

PO Box 60845, Livingstone, Zambia
+260 3 327490 / www.siankaba.net / siankaba@zamnet.zm

THE majestic Zambezi River is so wide in places that it appears to merge into the horizon. Some stretches are rippled by stealthy currents that make the surface look like watered velvet, but a paddle breaks the illusion. Drifting slowly along in a gently rocking dugout canoe is mesmerizing. These ancient craft have been plying the swirling waters for all time and are a wonderful way to view the Zambezi. The river's name is enough to set most people dreaming of African adventure. It sounds like it is: big and meandering, an imposing waterway heading inexorably towards the famed Victoria Falls.

Kingfishers provide a delightful distraction; flashes of neon blue that contrast dramatically with the deep, dark waters. The area 45km (28 miles) upstream from the falls is famed for its birdlife. Here, trumpeter hornbills guffaw in the canopy overhead and rust-coloured paradise flycatchers show off elegant tail feathers that would put any hat at Royal Ascot to shame. Set in the middle of this idyllic scene are The Islands of Siankaba, a small, exclusive and perfectly positioned tented lodge.

Siankaba is built on two forested sand islands, which the owners, Simon and Bonnie Wilde, have been careful to respect. They boast that no trees were felled in its construction, just the odd branch lopped off where absolutely necessary. It's a job well done; with minimal environmental impact, Siankaba looks stylish. Victoriana is something of a theme. The roll-top baths in each of the seven luxury tents have come straight from the time David Livingstone was exploring the region, and the furnishings – a combination of colonial safari fittings and tropical drawing-room furniture – only add to the effect. The old explorer would have been impressed, as he was with this particular stretch of the river.

Building a place like this can be done only with the blessing and involvement of the local community, and just such a relationship has been integral to this development. In consultation with the local chief, HRH Sekuti, the Wildes have undertaken to employ only local people in the lodge. Yet it isn't just employment that's made a difference – the indigenous hardwood tree-planting initiative has been another successful community project.

The Islands of Siankaba are covered in mature waterberry, mahogany and ebony trees, creating a rich habitat that's a Mecca for the birds. Dangling between them and linking the two together are a series of elevated walkways and suspension bridges, reminiscent of a children's playground. On the larger of the two islands, you'll find a swimming pool, a lounge bar and a dining room.

Between meals, days here are spent on a variety of activities. Apart from the birding, anglers are drawn in the hope of bagging an elusive Zambezi tiger fish, although any catches have to be let go as Siankaba has a strict release policy. Those wanting an aerial perspective can opt for elephant-back safaris, and there are trips to Victoria Falls, Mosi-O-Tunya National Park, and Chobe National Park in neighbouring Botswana.

However, the best view of all is to be had at sunset, when you can sit back at Siankaba and watch as the Zambezi rusts the sky with tremendous deep reds and oranges that slowly leach into the heavens.

ECO**FILE**

Rooms: Seven luxury tents.
Rates: From ZK1.4 million (US$360) per person per night, fully inclusive. Note: not suitable for children under 12 or wheelchair-users.
Location: In the Zambezi River, 38km (24 miles) above the Victoria Falls and 48km (30 miles) downstream from Botswana's Chobe National Park. The nearest airport is Livingstone (Victoria Falls).
Best time to go: Year-round, although Apr–Sep is most pleasant.
Getting there: From Johannesburg (South Africa), fly to Livingstone in Zambia. Siankaba provides a 25-min transfer flight from there.
CO_2 emissions: Rtn flight to Livingstone via Johannesburg from New York 4.20 tonnes; London 2.86; Sydney 3.53. Rtn transfer 0.10.
Offset cost: $63.90; £22.25; A$67.85.

Responsibility: The Islands of Siankaba lodge has a very good social policy: apart from employing a significant number of local people and instigating a series of training and educational programmes, it has installed a maize-milling machine and cattle-dip for the local community, and helps the local school and clinic with supplies. Its ecological concerns are wide-ranging; in particular, its indigenous hardwood tree-planting initiative has been very successful.
Environmental: ⊘⊘⊘⊘⊘
Social: ⊘⊘⊘⊘⊘

Adrère Amellal Ecolodge

18 El Mansour, Mohamed Street, Zamalek, Cairo, Egypt
+20 2 2736 7879 / www.adrereamellal.net / info@eqi.com.eg

THE eight-hour bus journey from Cairo to the Siwa Oasis trawls through magnificent desert; a dusty ride clouded with ancient temples, mirages and unfathomable distances. Dead streams of dry earth appear along the way, a seemingly empty promise of water to come. But the muted ochres dissipate as Siwa's cool blue salt lake and verdant date palms come into view. The final 15km (10 miles) along a bumping track brings you to the ghostly face of Adrère Amellal (White Mountain) and the end of your journey. The sense of arrival is a welcome relief.

Beneath the soaring cliff, and almost camouflaged from the world around it, is Adrère Amellal Eco-lodge. Once a series of Siwan houses, the lodge has been sympathetically restored and remodelled using ancient building methods. Constructed entirely of mud, sand, straw and salt in a technique known as *kershef*, it looks as though it has been massaged out of the very earth on which it sits. But this isn't the only nod to antiquity; there's no electricity or phone either.

For all its apparent simplicity, Adrère Amellal Ecolodge shouldn't be mistaken for the kind of green accommodation that involves roughing it. Its reputation and consummate eco-credentials have captivated a discerning clientele that includes holidaying royalty. The attractions are easy to see: elegant building materials, locally manufactured Bedouin-style furniture and beautiful couches made from mud (the soft

contours are piled high with cushions) breathe a sophisticated desert-style luxury. Excellent locally produced organic food is served from traditional pots onto Limoges porcelain. But luxury aside, the social and environmental concerns are what makes this place exceptional.

From its inception, Adrère Amellal has brought about much-needed employment to the area. Other than employing local staff, a women's initiative has been set up in nearby Siwa, providing employment for more than 300 traditional embroiderers. All products and provisions used at the lodge are sourced from neighbourhood communities. In addition, the surrounding grounds are currently being developed into a desert park to preserve endangered flora and fauna.

Energy consumption is kept to a minimum, solar power being the mainstay; wastewater is treated aerobically and ultimately feeds the organic garden; and other waste is either recycled or composted. When it's needed on cold nights, heating comes from traditional braziers, while oil lamps and beeswax candles light the place at night, casting long, low, Levantine shadows.

Adrère Amellal offers other benefits for guests too, not least a sense of calm, which is soothingly hypnotic. When the heat is fierce, bathing in the restored Roman springs provides some respite. As you sit in the refreshing waters, you can almost reach out and touch the history of this charismatic oasis.

ECO**FILE**

Rooms: 39, including 10 suites.
Rates: From EGP2,500 (US$448) per person per night, based on double occupancy and including all meals, but excluding transfers and trips.
Location: Adrère Amellal is in the Siwa Oasis, 800km (496 miles) from Cairo. The nearest airport is Cairo.
Best time to go: Oct–Apr. Nights can get very cold, occasionally dropping to freezing point, and summer months can be extremely hot, reaching temperatures of 52°C (125°F). By travelling in the summer you avoid the tourist rush.
Getting there: From Cairo, take the West Delta bus service to Marsa Matroh, then a bus direct to Siwa Oasis (8 hours). Book tickets in advance. Private transfers can also be arranged from Cairo.
CO2 emissions: Rtn flight to Cairo from New York 2.62 tonnes; London 0.77; Sydney 4.57. Rtn transfers by bus 0.11 by car 0.36.
Offset cost: $44.25; £8.50; A$92.10.

Responsibility: Adrère Amellal is part of Environment Quality International, a company that has spent more than 20 years consulting on low-impact and social developments throughout Egypt, North Africa and the Middle East. The hotel has strong links with the local community and solid green credentials.
Environmental: ∅∅∅∅∅
Social: ∅∅∅∅∅

Feynan Eco-lodge

PO Box 1215, Amman 11941, Jordan
+962 6461 6523 / www.rscn.org.jo / tourism@rscn.org.jo

JAGGED dry-stone walls lying like broken teeth tumble down a steep gully, and exposed boulders are strewn across the harsh and unforgiving landscape like gravestones. But it's the scorching noon sun that is most memorable. It has done a perfect job of bleaching this land, as well as the half-dozen tourists scrambling towards a pine tree to seek shade. The five-hour walk down the Wadi Dana to the desert floor at Feynan passes through stark, elemental beauty and rocky desert-like hills – it's a novel way of reaching a bed for the night.

The trek through Dana Nature Reserve to the Feynan Eco-lodge is a wonderful introduction to its complex system of mountains and wadis, which cover some 320sq km (125sq miles). They plummet into the desert lowlands of the Wadi Araba and embrace a kaleidoscopic array of biodiversity. But don't worry if you're not up to the hike in, as you can do it the easy way instead, in a Bedouin truck or 4WD.

Arriving on foot, the sight of the lodge comes as welcome relief. It looks like everything you'd expect of a desert dwelling. Incorporating traditional adobe techniques, the building is a post-modern take on the arabesque architecture of the region. Lines of serrated rocks embedded into the walls break up the surface, lending it the feel of a citadel. Gloriously isolated, it's something of a triumph and blends comfortably into the surroundings.

Local Bedouin staff the lodge, an initiative created by the Royal Society for the Conservation of Nature (RSCN) as a response to protecting the environment and alleviating high unemployment and poverty. Candles light the place at night, creating dappled shadows and an atmosphere that verges on the monastic. Romantics beware.

The food is simple too. Delicious vegetarian dishes – think hummus, local vegetables and lentils – are liberally served up with traditional Bedouin hospitality. But it's the naturalness of the place, subtly reflecting the superb and austere desert views, that will live with you. Egyptian cotton bedsheets are perhaps the one concession to luxury.

Hiking in the surrounding countryside on trails ranging from easy to extremely tough is a must. A guide is definitely useful to help locate some of the archaeological remains that litter the place. Nabatean tombs, Iron Age sites and Byzantine churches vie with the Roman copper mines in Wadi Feynan, which are rated as being second only to nearby Petra in terms of importance. The wildlife is interesting, too, and you may be lucky enough to spot an endangered wolf or Nubian ibex. Birdwatching is another speciality, as 200 species have been recorded on the reserve, 33 of which have global importance.

Leaving the lodge is a lot easier said than done, but for those with time and energy there's no better way than to head out on another long-distance trail. Climbing out of a wadi up into the brilliant sunshine and watching a kestrel arc overhead is hard to beat.

ECO**FILE**

Rooms: 26 rooms.
Rates: From JD35 (US$50) per person per night, including breakfast.
Location: In the Jordan Valley 50km (30 miles) north of Petra. The nearest airport is Amman (approx 200km/125 miles).
Best time to go: Year-round, although it closes Jul–Aug.
Getting there: From Amman, drive 2.5 hours down the Araba (Dead Sea highway) to the lodge.
CO$_2$ emissions: Rtn flight to Amman from New York 2.67 tonnes; London 0.80; Sydney 4.44. Rtn transfer 0.12.
Offset cost: $41.55; £6.90; A$85.15.

Responsibility: The solar-powered Feynan Eco-lodge and the Dana Nature Reserve have had a big impact in the local area. Initiatives created by the RSCN have helped preserve not just flora and fauna, but also the traditional way of life of nomadic pastoralists with sustainable grazing lands. Other initiatives established by the RSCN include a women's candle-making cooperative and other micro-industries. In all, some 800 people directly benefit from tourism in this area.
Environmental: ØØØØØ
Social: ØØØØØ

Asia

Main picture: View of the Himalayas, Kalmatia Sangam Himalaya Resort. Left, from top: Kumaon village walk, Kalmatia Sangam Himalaya Resort; Thai ingredients, Gecko Villa; Boat Landing Guest House

Locator map & budget guide

● Budget (up to US$100)
● Moderate (US$100–250)
● Expensive (US$250–500)
● Blow out (more than US$500)
Prices are for a double room, or two people, per night

218

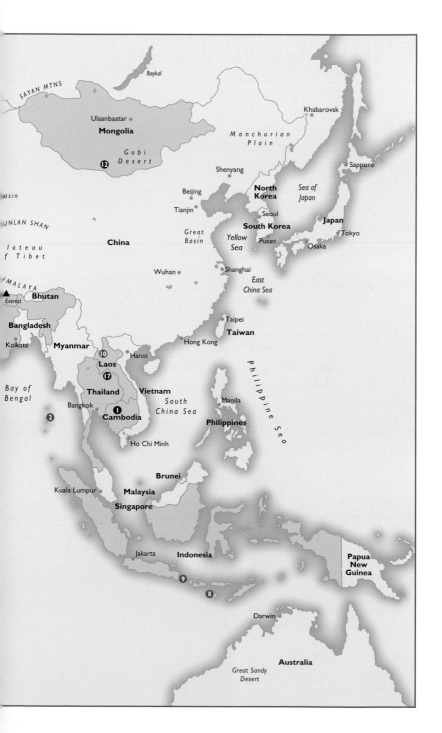

SAYAN MTNS

Baykal

Ulaanbaatar

Mongolia

⑫ *Gobi Desert*

Khabarovsk

Manchurian Plain

Shenyang

Beijing

Tianjin

North Korea

Sea of Japan

Sapporo

asin

UNLAN SHAN

China

Great Basin

Seoul

South Korea

Pusan

Japan

Tokyo

Osaka

lateau f Tibet

Wuhan

Shanghai

Yellow Sea

East China Sea

MALAYA

Everest

Bhutan

Bangladesh

Kolkata

Myanmar

⑩

Laos

⑰

Thailand

Hanoi

Taipei

Taiwan

Hong Kong

Philippine Sea

Bangkok

❶

Cambodia

Vietnam

South China Sea

Manila

Bay of Bengal

❷

Ho Chi Minh

Philippines

Brunei

Kuala Lumpur

Malaysia

Singapore

Jakarta

Indonesia

❾

❽

Papua New Guinea

Darwin

Australia

Great Sandy Desert

Hôtel de la Paix

Sivutha Boulevard, Siem Reap, Cambodia
+855 63 966 000 / www.hoteldelapaixangkor.com / info@hoteldelapaixangkor.com

THE rash of new development that has engulfed Siem Reap has been compared to an Asian version of Las Vegas. The mass migration of tourists coming to see the spectacular ruins of nearby Angkor Wat has spawned towers of brash angular concrete, seemingly in defiance of the refined ancient architecture of the temple complex. The Hôtel de la Paix, however, is one sparkling exception: a five-star monument to minimalist modern taste with a retro-chic nod to colonial splendour.

Guided by the hip hand of architect and landscape designer Bill Bensley, famous for Bangkok's innovative Bed Supperclub, this is a hotel that indulges, pampers and delights. The rooms, which range from the Deluxe standards to the Courtyard Garden and Pool suites, are all lavish in size, immaculate in concept, flawless in design and fastidious in attention to detail, from the vast terrazzo bathtubs to the fully loaded iPods. The Deluxe Spa Suite includes a private rooftop garden and plunge pool, accessed by a wrought-iron spiral staircase.

ECO**FILE**

Rooms: 107 luxury rooms.
Rates: From KHR765,000 (US$190) per room per night.
Location: Central Siem Reap, 7km (4 miles) from Angkor Wat.
Best time to go: Nov–Feb has the best weather.
Getting there: From Siem Reap international airport, transfer to the hotel by private car, *tuk-tuk* three-wheeler or motorbike.
CO2 emissions: Rtn flight to Siem Reap from New York 4.40 tonnes; London 2.87, Sydney 2.05.
Offset cost: $65.45; £21.50; A$38.40.

Responsibility: While it is short on eco-conscience, Hôtel de la Paix is long on social responsibility, setting new standards for the luxury hotel industry and proving that such developments can have a positive impact on the local community.
Environmental: ⌀⌀⌀⌀⌀
Social: ⌀⌀⌀⌀⌀

And when it comes to eating, the hotel's Meric restaurant – named after a unique variety of Cambodian pepper – showcases a similar vision for funky style, offering innovative Khmer dishes with a French twist.

While the Hôtel de la Paix may have made few obvious concessions to environmental sustainability, when it comes to initiatives within the local community its efforts are exemplary. The emphasis is on a proactive interaction between guests and the local Khmer families, thereby fostering a level of cross-cultural understanding that is hard to find in this bracket of the industry anywhere, and fuelling the opportunity for visitors to see direct, tangible benefits to their hosts through sponsoring a variety of programmes already supported by the hotel.

Working with a number of local NGOs, the hotel opens channels for guests to contribute wherever they choose, from providing a child with all the school supplies he or she needs for as little as US$10, to digging wells and installing pumps, or even building a family home for US$1,000. Some 90 wells have been completed so far, and the lives of hundreds of families have been transformed through better education, housing and healthcare facilities. These outreach endeavours are all described on a 'connecting menu' – a list of community-based projects guests are encouraged to support. This list educates visitors and opens up viable, trusted routes for them to make a positive impact.

There is no denying that, by anyone's standards, the Hôtel de la Paix is accommodation for the privileged – but its strong social conscience should be saluted. So, while you are summoning the courage to try some of the restaurant's more unusual dishes, you can ponder the impact of your stay here on the local community, and feel a little warm glow that will outshine the lights of the nearby Asian Vegas.

Barefoot at Havelock

MB - 5, 1st Floor, Atlanta Point, Port Blair 744101, Andaman and Nicobar Islands, India
+91 (0)3192 236008 / www.barefootindia.com / reservations@barefootindia.com

WITH his trunk raised in front like a ready-made snorkel, Rajan propels his buoyant bulk through the water with ease. Elephants are surprisingly graceful swimmers and have been at it on the Andamans for millennia, leading some to conclude that they evolved from the water. After a lifetime of lifting logs, this retired male tusker seems to enjoy the feeling of weightlessness. An elephant with a penchant for ocean swimming sounds like a surreal circus act, but on these fantastic white-sand islands, anything seems possible.

Once described by oceanic explorer Jacques Cousteau as the 'invisible islands', the 572 Andaman and Nicobar islands remain one of the last frontiers on our rapidly globalizing planet. Only 36 of these are inhabited and more than 85 per cent of the land mass is still untouched, protected primary rainforest. A combination of strict government controls and the presence of an Indian naval force still makes the area largely inaccessible, while indigenous tribes who live on the more

remote Nicobar Islands remain hostile to intruders, fending them off with blowpipes, spears and poisoned arrows.

A visit to Havelock Island gives a tantalizing glimpse of these secretive islands, regarded as one of the world's anthropological and biological hotspots. There are some 700 plant species found here, more than 150 of which are endemic. Birdlife includes hornbills, sea eagles and fluorescent parrots. Along the shoreline are some of the most luxuriant mangrove ecosystems in the world, and in the waters are crocodiles, sea turtles and superlative gamefish. To soak up this rich abundance, you can trek through virgin rainforest, camp on deserted beaches, snorkel over the pristine coral reefs or even take part in ongoing research with local conservation groups. This experience is hands-on, enlightening and utterly original.

Accommodation at the island's Barefoot in Havelock resort is in its Nicobari Cottages and Andaman Villas, which provide the ideal synthesis of functionality, style and ecological sensitivity. The former are constructed from bamboo and local timbers, with conical palm-thatch roofs, and are fan-cooled and furnished with sustainably sourced teak. The air-conditioned Andaman Villas are built from plantation hardwoods, and boast views of the forest canopy through a glass panel in the roof of the en suite bathroom. Two further Duplex Cottages with mezzanine levels are spacious enough for a family.

In the restaurant, the chef will happily cook the spoils from your fishing trip while you listen to the strains of an extensive music library. Vegetables are organic, eggs and chicken are free-range, and the seafood is plucked straight from the mesmerizing big blue before you.

Water is drawn judiciously from a natural spring, rainwater is harvested and greywater is recycled for irrigation. Strict policies govern all forays into this delicate environment, and the extensive knowledge of indigenous trackers and experienced dive instructors is relied upon. With both guests and elephants taking to the water, it looks like the footprints at Barefoot may be minimized even further.

ECOFILE

Rooms: Ten fan-cooled Nicobari Cottages, 8 air-conditioned Andaman Villas and 2 Duplex Cottages.

Rates: From Rs3,000 (US$75) per night for the Nicobari Cottages, from Rs4,500 (US$110) for the Andaman Villas, and from Rs5000 (US$125) for the Duplex Cottages.

Location: Havelock Island, 3 hours by boat northeast of the Andaman Islands capital of Port Blair.

Best time to go: Year-round.

Getting there: From Kolkata (Calcutta) or Chennai (Madras), fly to Port Blair, capital of the Andaman Islands. Barefoot will arrange the 3-hour transfer by boat from there.

CO_2 emissions: Rtn flight to Port Blair via Kolkata from New York 4.22 tonnes; London 2.57; Sydney 2.95. Via Chennai from New York 4.52; London 2.67; Sydney 2.96. Rtn transfer 0.0003.

Offset cost: $62.80; £19.30; A$55.20; via Chennai $65.15; £22.20; A$55.40.

Responsibility: A sustainable and responsible approach to travel is deeply embedded in the policy of the resort, which carefully polices any interaction between visitors and the pristine ecosystems here. Strict government regulations prevent any intrusion on indigenous tribal areas. Barefoot makes a significant effort to tread lightly on the islands.

Environmental: ⊘⊘⊘⊘⊘

Social: ⊘⊘⊘⊘⊘

Cardamom House

Athoor Village, Dindigul District 624701, Tamil Nadu, India
+91 (0)4512 556765 / www.cardamomhouse.com / chrislucas@cardamomhouse.com

IN stark contrast to the bleak desolation of the Tamil Nadu plains, Cardamom House is nestled amid colour and abundance. After driving through a barren wasteland of hostile vegetation – all thorn acacias and spiky palmyra palms – the final approach is through fertile farmland dominated by a dragon's-back ridge of hills. A narrow tarmac strip turns into a bumpy, potholed track, before finally arriving at a silent lake.

For those accustomed to the parched browns of the frenetic highways, the dazzle of Cardamom House's electric-pink bougainvillea seems too bright to be real. This place is quiet. Very quiet. For a writer, an artist, or those seeking seclusion and good birdwatching, the ingredients are all there. The majestic views are broken only by birdsong, a few bleating goats and the resident quacking ducks. The diverse and colourful gardens are filled with flowering shrubs and trees, from a rare scarlet frangipani, to gardenias, flamboyants, laburnum and those bougainvillea.

At first sight, Cardamom House makes little impression on the eco-scale. Its brick, stone and concrete buildings appear to push the ecological footprint of the property up with their intrinsically inefficient construction materials. However, as pointed out by the proprietor, retired British physician Chris Lucas, the bricks were hand-made by a local family business and the stone dressed by local masons using only hand tools. Water is sprayed over the external rocks and on the brick floors of the living spaces, thus cooling them through evaporation.

In such an arid climate, one wonders about the wisdom of relying on water for lowering temperatures. However, rainwater is harvested wherever possible, solar hot-water collectors have been installed on all three buildings, and

ECO**FILE**

Rooms: Three houses, with 6 twin rooms and 1 double suite in total.
Rates: From Rs3,000 (US$75) per night. Minimum stay of 2 nights.
Location: Athoor Villlage, 65km (40 miles) northwest of Madurai.
Best time to go: Dec–Apr.
Getting there: From Chennai (Madras), Trivandrum, Kochi (Cochin), Madurai or Trichy, travel by train to Dindigul Junction, then take a 45-min taxi ride to Athoor. Alternatively, fly 1 hour from Chennai to Madurai, then take a 4-hour taxi ride to the lodge.
CO_2 emissions: Rtn flight to Madurai via Chennai from New York 4.33 tonnes; London 2.47; Sydney 2.77. Rtn transfer 0.04.
Offset cost: $64.95; £18.85; A$52.60.

Responsibility: Although the ecological footprint of the modern buildings could have been reduced, the owner's genuine commitment to responsible tourism is reflected in the interaction between Cardamom House and the local community.
Environmental: ⵁⵁⵁⵁⵁ
Social: ⵁⵁⵁⵁⵁ

a solar-powered pump provides water for an emerging organic farm, complete with an efficient drip irrigation system and vermiculture (worm-composting) to grow a variety of fruits and vegetables. All waste is composted or recycled efficiently, and traditional methods of pest control are used to protect the crops grown on the 1.4ha (3.5-acre) smallholding.

In addition to making Cardamom House more eco-friendly, Chris is diligent about the principles of what he calls 'non-invasive tourism'. The attentive staff are all local and will accompany small groups to the nearby village of Athoor (one guest described this as the 'absolute highlight' of his trip to India). All supplies are purchased from Athoor market and, to ensure that no local livelihoods are undermined, produce from Cardamom House itself is not sold to other foreign-owned houses.

Further non-invasive tourism around Cardamom House includes birdwatching: one group from the UK spotted more than 160 bird species around the lake in just four days. There are also walks around the lake, to a temple in a hillside cave, and to a fabulous waterfall and bathing pool. The serenity of the location provides a perfect antidote for those fatigued by life on the Indian road, while the roast potatoes and chicken served at dinner will be a welcome break for those tiring of the ubiquitous rice and curry.

Kalmatia Sangam Himalaya Resort

Kalimat Estate, Post Bag 002, Almora 263601, Uttaranchal, India
+91 (0)5962 231572 / www.kalmatia-sangam.com / manager@kalmatia-sangam.com

TAKE a break from foraging for wild chanterelle mushrooms to savour their apricot aroma as it mingles with the pine-scented breezes. Stand among quiet walnut groves, surrounded by pomegranates and flowering rhododendrons, while taking in the most majestic mountain views on the planet. After your mushroom-hunting, indulge in an aromatherapy massage or a well-deserved sundowner, looking out to the panoramic splendour of silver peaks stretching for 300km (200 miles) along the horizon. Is this heaven? Well, almost. You can just about see it from here, at Kalmatia Sangam in the Himalayan foothills.

Kalmatia Sangam is the ideal place to absorb the crisp high-altitude light and pervasive stillness of the Himalayas with quiet contemplation, or to indulge the senses in a kaleidoscope of colours, flavours, sounds and smells. When you're not trekking in the hills or admiring the lofty peaks, you can feast on the terrace, choosing from an international menu executed with innovative flair. Then retire to the wrought-iron fireplace of your toasty chalet and marvel at the array of stars splashed across the night sky above.

The Kalimat Estate dates from the late 1860s and its current incarnation is the vision of Dieter and Geeta Reeb, whose previous work with textiles is visible in the flawless taste of the furnishings used throughout the stone-built whitewashed chalets. Designer dhurries cover the beds, complementing the flagstone floors and elegant cane furniture, and works by local artists adorn the walls. The antique writing desks will inspire any literary muse to wax lyrical about a landscape that has drawn the likes of such novelists as DH Lawrence and JRR Tolkien.

ECOFILE

Rooms: Eight double cottages, 2 smaller cottages (sleep 1–2).
Rates: From Rs4,300 (US$108) per double per night.
Best time to go: Ideal hiking weather is mid-Sep–Apr.
Location: 380km (235 miles) northeast of Delhi and 7km (4 miles) from the hill station of Almora.
Getting there: From Delhi, drive for 8 hours to the resort, or take a 9-hour train journey to Kathgodam and drive 2.5 hours from there.
CO2 emissions: Rtn flight to Delhi from New York 3.56 tonnes; London 1.88; Sydney 3.09. Rtn transfer by car 0.22. Train figures for India n/a.
Offset cost: $56.30; £15.85; A$62.

Responsibility: Although the chalets are not overendowed with eco-technology features, the Reebs are very conscious about preserving the environment, its delicate ecology and the rich local culture. For example, local artists and handicrafts are supported, all treks are limited to four members (accompanied by a hotel porter) and local staff are employed throughout.
Environmental: ⌀⌀⌀⌀⌀
Social: ⌀⌀⌀⌀⌀

The inherently spiritual atmosphere of this region, which is close to some of the most sacred pilgrimage sites in India, may also engender even the most hardened cynic to a spot of contemplation – the hotel offers traditional Vipassana meditation, led by a professional teacher, in both indoor and outdoor spaces. The nearby Kasar Devi temple is a testament to the sanctity of the area, having drawn some of India's most illustrious spiritual heroes, from social reformer Swami Vivekananda to author of *The Way of the White Clouds*, Lama Anagarika Govinda.

To allow visitors an authentic experience of the area, Dieter and Geeta have partnered up with three homes in villages approximately six hours' walk apart within the Pahari community. While stays at these houses are not as luxurious as the resort itself – they have traditional charpoy beds, bucket showers and squatting toilets – the visual delights of the hike there far outweigh any discomforts, taking you past immaculate terraced paddy fields and brightly clad women winnowing rice. In spring and summer, the paths are lined with fruit blossoms and butterflies, while in winter cherry trees come into flower and red chillies dry on the roofs. During the monsoon, the skies may be overcast, but your eyes are more likely to be drawn to those bright yellow chanterelles, bursting through the green moss and pine needles beneath you.

Friends in high places

On a hiking tour through the Kumaon district in Himalayan foothills, **Rory Spowers** left behind little but bootprints along the trails and came away with a lifetime of memories.

After the dust, din and overwhelming heat of the Indian plains in late May, the ascent to Almora and the hills of the Kumaon district was more than just a breath of fresh air. The clarity of the light combined with the cooler temperatures and low population density to make me exhale deeply with audible sighs of relief.

There's something about walking. It could be that it makes you engage with the landscape at a natural pace, rather than the amplified speeds that come with motorized transport. Walking connects us to the earth, both physically and metaphorically. Our senses come alive to sights, sounds and smells that are elusive within the confines of a car, a train, or even on a bicycle. By walking, we become fully immersed in the presence of what surrounds us. It's meditation in action — and the most natural, most authentic, most enriching way to travel.

Nowhere in the world is this made more apparent than in the Himalayas. The terrain here clearly prohibits most other modes of travel, but thereby opens up possibilities that would be inconceivable

This page: Spotting wildlife between villages. Top right: The spices and colours of India

elsewhere. The Village Ways concept taps into this in the most simple, low-impact but rewarding manner, providing the perfect balance of physical exertion, visual stimulation and cultural exchange. This is not macho mountaineering exploration, encumbered with equipment, but gentle hiking from village to village, immersing every sense in some of the most dramatically beautiful scenery this side of heaven.

On my arrival at Khali Estate in the Binsar Wildlife Sanctuary, the start and finish point for all the treks, I was greeted by Raju and Hemu, two guides from the Village Ways team. I washed away the dust of the journey, took my first deep breaths of Himalayan air, then started discussing the programme for our two days of walking as the mountain sky filled with stars and the twinkling lights of Almora hill station stretched out below. I already felt like I had stepped into another world.

One of the many wonders of walking at altitude is the diversity and contrasts of vegetation and landscape, shifting through different permutations as passing cloud cover alters the play of light. One minute you are in the hills of Provence, then the Californian Rockies, the Australian outback or even the Scottish Highlands. This continual metamorphosis keeps the landscape alive and was fully at play as we struck off on a four-hour hike from Khali to Gonap, passing through a dense forest of gnarled old oaks and rambling rhododendrons that revealed glimpses of the valley below.

This page: Walks pass through villages without interrupting the daily lives of the locals

Although I knew the rains would not hit the north of India for at least a month, I could not help but scour the ground for yolk-yellow chanterelle mushrooms, which the monsoon would soon hatch to the surface. I made a mental note to return one day, during the prime foraging months of July and August.

A rocky ridge on the descent to Gonap provided the first panorama of the high Himalayas, a skyline of whipped cream peeking through the hazy light of late summer. Then down we went through dense forest and past the sinuous contours of terraced fields to the village of Gonap, a settlement of just ten families. Here, while we ate our 'tiffin' picnic of simple but delicious local curries, Mr Prem Singh told us how his father had purchased the village from a local landlord in 1944. That afternoon, we ambled on to the Village Ways house at Kaththdhara, along the way catching a glimpse of the Pancha Chulli range of five peaks, a rare sight at this time of year.

In keeping with the strict codes of the company's responsible tourism policy, the Village Ways houses have all been built and managed by local people, constructed in traditional style utilizing local stone rendered with mud mortar. Some interiors are distempered a stunning

This page: Money from Village Ways tours enables local people to stay with their families in their villages, rather than going to the cities in search of work

turquoise-blue, the timbers are local chir pine and the roofs are covered in thick slabs of slate. This vernacular style marries well with modern eco-technologies to create low-impact comfort: solar water heaters feed modern bathrooms and photo-voltaic panels provide all the lighting necessary. A traditional Bukhari wood-burning stove takes the chill off winter nights, and any aches and pains from the day are well absorbed by a good-quality mattress. Health and hygiene have also been well considered: each house comes equipped with a water filter; food and drinks are served using stainless-steel kitchenware; and the bathrooms are spotless.

You could easily stay in Kumaon for weeks, exploring the various Village Ways trails. Numerous set options are available, as are bespoke tours to suit your taste. Foodies will be drawn by the nine-day 'Temples and Tiffin' tour, which takes in Mahatma Gandhi's first ashram alongside a full repertoire of local delicacies. If you're looking for a good trek and some mind-spinning views, consider the 'Beyond Zero Point' walk, which incorporates all the ridges and high points of Binsar Wildlife Sanctuary (2,000m/6,500ft above sea level), stopping along the way at five villages. Those seeking minimal exertion may veer towards 'Ramsay's Ramble', which stops in just three villages over eight days but allows for maximum interaction with their residents.

In terms of company philosophy and impact, Village Ways is an exemplar in the field, providing the reciprocal benefits between host and guest that are key to sustainable and responsible tourism. Families previously fragmented by migration to cities have found new sources of local income, and each village has a committee responsible for implementing the Village Ways criteria. In addition, social and environmental awareness are on the rise locally, evident in the natural history knowledge of the guides and the pride they take in their rich cultural heritage. Walking through one of the most sacred parts of the Himalayas, it is easy to see why this should be so. By supporting Village Ways, you can be sure that your footprint will be light, your money will be well spent and your memories will be with you for life.

ECOFILE

Location: Khali Estate is close to Almora, 380km (235 miles) from Delhi. The nearest rail station is Kathgodam, to the south.

Getting there: From Delhi, take a long-distance taxi for 8 hours to Almora. Alternatively, travel by train for 9 hours to Kathgodam, then take bus or car 2.5 hours to Kahli Estate.

CO2 emissions: Rtn flight to Delhi from New York 3.56 tonnes; London 1.88; Sydney 3.09. Rtn transfer by taxi 0.22. Train figures for India n/a.

Offset cost: $56.30; £15.85; A$62.05.

Staying there: Accommodation is in traditional-style modern houses.

Rates: A typical 9-day tour starts at Rs48,000 (US$1,200) per person, all inclusive.

Best time to go: Oct–Nov, for views, warm days and cool nights.

Further information: www.villageways.com

Responsibility: Once you reach the villages, your only footprints will be those that you leave on the trails. Food is local, the guides are local, and the hot water and power are solar. A stringent system of responsible tourism guidelines applies to the whole operation, which is what the future of low-impact tourism should look like everywhere.

The Orchid Hotel

Nehru Road, Vile Parle East, Mumbai 400 099, India
+91 (0)2226 164040 / www.orchidhotel.com / samohmu@orchidhotel.com

THE mere thought of a five-star business hotel next to Mumbai's airport claiming to be eco-friendly seems to beggar belief. But if you're already worried about the impact your flight has had on the environment, you could certainly do worse than stay at the Orchid. As evidenced by the growing catalogue of awards this pioneering hotel continues to clock up, it is both innovative and impressive, providing a stopover that might lighten the impact of your carbon-loaded journey.

The design and construction features of the hotel are a fusion of common sense and cutting edge. The depressions and protrusions in the facade, for example, play an important role in passive energy conservation, since most of the dead space remains in shadow and thus minimizes surface radiation. There is a naturally lit central atrium, allowing the 72 rooms surrounding it to remain sheltered from external elements, and the rooftop pool adds insulation. Although the hotel appears to be built from conventional high-footprint materials, this again is a misconception. The two types of cement used contain high proportions of fly ash, which provides excellent thermal insulation and soundproofing from the incessant air traffic, and the interior wall panels are made from fertilizer waste.

This attention to low-footprint design and features extends to the triple-glazed windows, the recycled wood used in the restaurant, and the reconstituted rubber wood that makes up the window frames and

shutters. Water consumption is minimized through the use of aerators, restrictors, dual-flush cisterns, recycled greywater and drip irrigation, and the installation of energy-efficient lamps reduced the hotel's electricity bill by a staggering US$75,000 over the course of a year. An air-scrubber reduces airborne pollution from the hotel boiler and 'fuzzy logic' fridges optimize the efficiency of mini-bars and fridges.

Although the rooms outwardly conform to those of a standard five-star business hotel, closer inspection reveals the level of the Orchid's commitment to creating a benchmark in the industry. A switch on the air-conditioning master control automatically raises the temperature by 2°C (4°F) to save energy, the coat hangers are made from reconstituted sawdust, and fruit baskets and newspapers are delivered only on request to minimize waste. Natural ayurvedic products fill the bathrooms, and cloth bags for laundry and shopping are provided to reduce the use of plastic.

The level of innovation extends beyond the hotel into the local community. Here, various schemes supported by the Orchid have had positive impacts, including the Nirmalaya Composting Project, which takes all the waste from the annual ten-day Ganesh festival – from garlands to offerings and idols – and converts it into organic manure.

A stay at the Orchid is far more than just a regular stopover. Here, every detail seems to have been thoroughly considered, from the hotel's responsibility towards the local environment and community, right down to minutiae like the clove-wood toothpicks that are offered at the end of your meal.

ECO**FILE**

Rooms: 245 rooms, ranging from Deluxe rooms to Presidential suites.
Rates: Deluxe rooms from Rs14,000 (US$350) per night, including breakfast.
Location: Adjacent to the domestic airport at Mumbai (Bombay).
Best time to go: Year-round.
Getting there: From Mumbai's international or domestic airports, take a short 5–10 min taxi ride.
CO2 emissions: Rtn flight to Mumbai from New York 3.85 tonnes; London 2.03; Sydney 2.99.
Offset cost: $57.20; £15.25; A$56.

Responsibility: The Orchid has been well recognized as a benchmark for the urban five-star hotel, proving that a modern concrete development can still make significant advances in reducing its overall impact on the environment. While many such hotels rely on their PR machines to spin out 'greenwash' statements, the Orchid has shown that 'walking the talk' can improve more than just the bottom line.
Environmental: ⊘⊘⊘⊘⊘
Social: ⊘⊘⊘⊘⊘

Wildernest Nature Resort

Swapnagandha, off Sankhali, Chorla Ghats, Goa, India
+91 (0)8314 207954 / www.wildernest-goa.com / reservations@wildernest-goa.com

DESPITE what the backpackers may tell you, Goa is not just about beaches; it is also blessed with a hinterland that rivals any hill station in India. Wildernest is a naturalist's heaven that was born from an altruistic intention to preserve 180ha (450 acres) of pristine habitat from the invasive bauxite mining that has stripped much of inland Goa. At 800m (2,600ft) above sea level, the site has spectacular views down towards the coast, and sunsets over range upon range of hazy bluish hills.

The focus of the lodge is on the wildlife, which includes 140 species of birds, 30 different mammals and 150 medicinal plants. Local villagers trained as guides take guests on twice-daily treks to caves and cater-acts, including the Vazra Falls, which drop an impressive 142m (466ft). Resident ecologists are on hand to answer any queries, and zoological specialists are invited to the lodge to give illustrated talks in the evening, when visitors gather round the bonfire before dinner to share stories from their day's explorations.

Considerable thought has gone into creating the 16 low-impact cottages, some with views over the gorge, others suspended over the surrounding forest. Giant bamboo tubes conceal light fittings and create sturdy handrails, and old railway sleepers support the Cloud 9 bar and form rustic platform balconies. Australian acacia, first planted as a firewood crop, has been sourced from nearby social forestry projects

and provides most of the timber, including the louvred panel walls that do wonders for passive cooling. The rooms have a minimalist but tasteful feel, with white cotton blinds and terracotta tiles, while chunky no-nonsense taps and shower fittings dispense that rare Indian luxury – good water pressure. These design concepts extend to the restaurant, whose passive cooling features are enhanced by a two-tiered roof. Here, spread out on huge hardwood tree trunks, stunning buffets are served. Outside, the organic shape of the infinity pool blends with the landscape, allowing you to float above plunging vistas.

At present, six of the cottages are solar-powered, the others soon to be converted from the current generators. A wind data study has been conducted, and the proposed turbine will generate auxiliary power for the resort and the neighbouring village. Sewage is treated biologically and all plastic waste is recycled in the nearest town.

To help preserve the sanctity of the area further, a nature conservation facility has been established to monitor the Western Ghats environment over the long term. In addition, a biodiversity corridor has been created, allowing larger mammals the free-dom of movement they need. It has since been discovered that a few leopards and one roaming tiger have benefited from this initiative – this corner of Goa is shared with some of India's most impressive mammals.

ECO**FILE**

Rooms: 15 double-bedroom cottages and 1 family cottage.

Rates: Forest View Cottage from Rs6,000 (US$148) per night; Valley View from Rs7,000 (US$173) per night; Family Valley Cottage Rs10,000 (US$248) per night.

Location: Overlooking the Swap-nagnadha Valley, 27km (17 miles) off Sankhali and 65km (40 miles) from the Goan capital, Panjim.

Best time to go: Year-round, but the monsoon season (Jun–Aug) brings the jungle to life and draws the most serious nature-seekers.

Getting there: From Mumbai (Bombay), fly 1 hour to Goa and then take a taxi 2.5 hours to Wildernest. Alternatively, take the train 12 hours from Mumbai to Thivin, and a taxi from there.

CO2 emissions: Rtn flight to Goa via Mumbai from New York 3.97 tonnes; London 2.15; Sydney 3.12. Rtn trans-fer 0.03. Train figures for India n/a. **Offset cost:** $59.60; £16.45; A$59.

Responsibility: Wildernest was inspired by positive long-term inten-tions and is committed to providing a low-impact and educational experi-ence of the surrounding region. Specialists in a range of botanical and zoological fields ensure that guests receive maximum gains from their exposure to the habitat.

Environmental: ⌀⌀⌀⌀⌀
Social: ⌀⌀⌀⌀⌀

Yogamagic Canvas Ecotel

Bapougue, 1586/1 Grand Chinvar, Anjuna, Bardez 403509, Goa, India
+91 (0)832 562 3796 / www.yogamagic.net / info@yogamagic.net

YOGAMAGIC seems to have evolved as much from divine providence as from conscious intent. Owners Phil Dane and Juliet Leary met in Goa in 2003, when Phil possessed little more than a Rajasthani tent, had recently discovered a passion for yoga, and was developing embryonic plans for some sort of retreat centre on a piece of land he had been offered the use of in Anjuna. However, with a previous career as a song-writer and music producer, Phil had zero experience in running a tourist destination. Enter stage left: Juliet, ready to help bring the dream to fruition. The result was Yogamagic.

Four years on, it is hard to believe that the couple had no knowledge of building or design, since what they have created is innovative, aesthetically stunning and totally functional. During the centre's season, the main accommodation is in seven spacious canvas tents, each decorated in one colour from the rainbow spectrum, corresponding to the seven chakras, or energy centres,

ECO**FILE**

Rooms: Seven tents with double beds and the Maharani Suite.
Rates: From Rs2,750 (US$70) per tent per night, including breakfast.
Location: Just inland from the Goan beaches of Anjuna and Vagator.
Best time to go: Dec–Jan is peak season. Open 17 Nov–31 Mar.
Getting there: From Mumbai (Bombay), fly to Goa and then take a 1-hour taxi ride to Yogamagic.
CO2 emissions: Rtn flight to Goa via Mumbai from New York 3.97 tonnes; London 2.15; Sydney 3.12. Rtn transfer 0.04.
Offset cost: $59.55; £16.40; A$59.

Responsibility: Having laid the foundations for their low-impact yoga destination, Phil and Juliet are now turning their attention to a pro-gramme encouraging the cultivation of jatropha for use in the production of biodiesel. They intend this to be a large-scale cooperative enterprise, and will launch it in conjunction with a musical project to raise funds for bio-diesel production, which will take Phil back into the studio.
Environmental: ⬤⬤⬤⬤⬤
Social: ⬤⬤⬤⬤⬤

recognized by yogic systems. Each is equipped with an adjoining bathroom, integrated within the permanent tent sites, including a composting toilet, in which the waste is treated with effective micro-organisms and added to the rich compost heap every two days, leaving no odours whatsoever. Plans are now underway to expand the number of units, creating low-impact structures from ingeniously recycled materials.

The couple's design skills are perhaps best displayed in their house and in the Maharani Suite included within it. Built from locally sourced laterite blocks, chipped directly from the ground, the building has an earthy feel while retaining the sophistication of modern comforts. Attention to detail is seamless, from the reclaimed Rajasthani doors and embroidered cushions, to the beautiful home-made light shades.

The swimming pool is testament to the natural flair of this entrepreneurial pair, sculpted around an island with flowering plants and small palms planted amid the rocks. Submerged ledges provide seating in the sun and shade, or next to a poolside pavilion crowned with thatch from rice paddies. Smaller freshwater pools are integrated alongside the main pool and filled with flowering lotuses. The chlorinated system is soon to be replaced with either ozone filtration or salt water, thus removing the need for conventional chemical treatments.

The yoga pavilion is a long, low, open structure with a compacted mud floor and grass-thatch roof. A number of qualified instructors pass through over the season, but yoga is by no means mandatory – guests are free to dip in and out as they please. Other activities take in nearby beaches like the secluded coves of Vagator, or the weekly flea-market at Anjuna, the epicentre for the world-renowned full-moon parties.

Those seeking peace and seclusion will be pleased to note that the Yogamagic site is far enough removed from the action to prevent any interruption to their meditation. Here, there is nothing more to distract you from your tree pose than the rustle of palm leaves in the wind.

Nihiwatu

Kuta Poleng Complex Block C/2, Kuta 80361, Bali, Indonesia
+62 (0)361 757149 / www.nihiwatu.com / info@nihiwatu.com

FROM around the globe they come, suntanned, barefoot and bristling with anticipation, making the pilgrimage to Nihiwatu – a surfing Mecca in a remote corner of Indonesia. Faced with a 2km (1-mile) crescent of deserted beach, flanked by headlands and backed by 177ha (438 acres) of tropical forest, Nihiwatu is breathtakingly beautiful. But it's not until you're perched above the waves at the sandy-floored bar and restaurant that you'll really understand why the surfers come: stretching out across the bay is the powerful 'fat left break' for which Nihiwatu is renowned.

Disillusioned by the proliferation of what he calls 'surf slums', the low-budget dives that have ruined many Indonesian beaches and spawned waves of callous development, Claude Graves set out to make a difference. The result is Nihiwatu, a holy grail for those that make it to Sumba, a small island east of Bali. Claude's commitment to preserving the sanctity of this hallowed spot is such that only nine surfers are permitted to gather on the waves at one time.

Although the bar conversation may often revolve around 'gnarly tubes', Nihiwatu is by no means restricted to surfers. The fishing, diving and snorkelling are world-class, mountain-bike trails weave through the surrounding jungle, and you can trek to nearby waterfalls through Stone Age sites and traditional villages. To recover, slip into the infinity pool overlooking the bay, try some gentle Hatha yoga, or indulge in a massage in the spa. It's all here.

ECO**FILE**

Rooms: Seven double bungalows, 2 villas (up to 4 guests) and a large private villa (groups only).

Rates: From Rp3,652,100 (US$390) per bungalow per night, and from Rp7,866,200 ($840) per villa per night, including meals.

Location: Sumba is 400km (250 miles) east of Bali.

Best time to go: Year-round, although the rainy season is Jan–Mar.

Getting there: From Denpasar in Bali, fly to Tambolaka in West Sumba, from where Nihiwatu will arrange a road transfers (4–5 hours in total).

CO2 emissions: Rtn flight to Denpasar from New York 5.36 tonnes; London 5.84; Sydney 1.28. Rtn transfers 0.17.

Offset cost: $82.20; £30.10; A$27.10.

Responsibility: Nihiwatu is a world leader in setting new standards for responsible tourism. Its social work has transformed the lives of thousands of locals and has created a blueprint for replication in other parts of Sumba.

Environmental: ⬤⬤⬤⬤◐

Social: ⬤⬤⬤⬤⬤

The pursuit of this vision did not come easily. With his wife, Petra, Claude spent years seeking the tropical dream, literally hacking through jungle to discover Nihiwatu. The couple then lived on the site for seven years, in a simple shelter, battling with malaria while developing ties with the local community and conveying the essence of their low-impact plans. Seven luxury bungalows and two villas are now nestled among the trees, integrating bamboo and *alang-alang* grass thatch with sliding glass doors, and overlooking the spectacular Indian Ocean. Plans are afoot to convert the generators to run on biodiesel and there has been minimal interference with the native vegetation.

In addition to employing 98 per cent of the lodge's staff from the local community, Claude set up the Sumba Foundation in 2001 to pump money back into the local economy. To date, more than US$2 million has gone to fund projects ranging from building local schools and healthcare clinics, to reducing endemic malaria rates.

As tourism pushes into more remote areas, Nihiwatu is an example of a sensitive way forward. Whether you're riding the waves or just armchair-surfing with drink in hand, your visit will benefit the locals.

Panchoran Retreat

Nyuh Kuning Village, Ubud, Gianyar 80571 Bali, Indonesia
+62 (0)361 974028 / www.lindagarland.com / info@lindagarland.com

OVER the last 15 years, Linda Garland has established herself as a global authority on the wonders of bamboo, an ecological material par excellence. Fondly known as the Bamboo Queen, Linda has integrated her passion for this unexploited resource into housing, clothing, jewellery, food and even beer-making. At Panchoran Retreat in Bali, she has incorporated the material into every aspect of the spectacular built environment that has taken shape around her dreams.

Bamboo is evident everywhere, from the buildings to the candlesticks, beds, sofas and lampshades. This is the heart of Linda's bamboo kingdom, terraced with emerald rice paddies and bordering a plunging gorge, where waterfalls cascade into glassy bathing pools. Perched above this enchanted landscape is a series low-impact houses, including the River House, Waterfall House, and the New Waterfall House.

The lush, rambling property has been nurtured by Linda for the last 25 years, slowly allowing the garden and buildings to grow in symbiosis. The 10ha (25-acre) site is bordered by an equivalent area of protected forest, so the feeling of seclusion is preserved in perpetuity. One of the many attractions of staying here is that the trip to the restaurants and boutiques of nearby Ubud, the centre of Bali's rich cultural heritage, is just a short walk or bike ride through the Monkey Forest.

The sense of taste and style is immaculate throughout all three houses, creating a sumptuous yet simple elegance. The standards are high, from the crisp white linen to the superior bathroom fittings, but the

tone is earthy and understated. Showers are open to the starlit skies, built into boulders and lined with pebbles from the river. *Alang-alang* grass thatch for the roofs is grown on site, as were the bamboos and timbers used for construction. Blessed with some 42 natural springs, the property is able to feed Jacuzzis and natural pools with plentiful fresh water and thereby minimize the need for chemicals. One house comes complete with a huge swinging daybed poised above the river.

Panchoran ticks most of the boxes for sustainability, with a responsible recycling programme and plans to expand renewable energy projects with more solar and hydro power. Linda's passion for all things bamboo extends way beyond the retreat itself, and her Environmental Bamboo Foundation has been the catalyst for numerous projects within the surrounding community, other parts of Indonesia and the world at large. From her gene pool of 200 species, she can recommend which should be used for regenerating watersheds, for sequestering roadside pollutants, for building or for numerous crafts. No visit to Panchoran is complete without hearing her expound with infectious enthusiasm about the endless properties of this remarkable plant.

ECO**FILE**

Rooms: River House (3 doubles), Waterfall House and New Waterfall House (2 doubles each).
Rates: From Rp1,874,100 (US$200) per person per night.
Location: On the outskirts of Ubud, 30km (19 miles) north of Denpasar.
Best time to go: Year-round, although the rainy season is Jan–Mar.
Getting there: From Denpasar, travel 1.5 hours by taxi to the lodge.
CO2 emissions: Rtn flight to Denpasar from New York 3.36 tonnes; London 3.84; Sydney 1.28. Rtn transfer 0.02.
Offset cost: $79.90; £28.95; A$24.25.

Responsibility: Sustainability has long been deeply ingrained in the vision behind Panchoran, and is also key to outreach work done in promoting bamboo worldwide. The style of the operation is fluid, informal and organic, freely dispensing knowledge, plants and resources to those who are interested or who come to visit.
Environmental: ⊘⊘⊘⊘⊘
Social: ⊘⊘⊘⊘⊘

Should I visit Myanmar and the Maldives?

IN the same way that South Africa was off-limits for socially responsible travellers and businesses during the days of apartheid, so some countries today are considered best avoided owing to their repressive regimes and human rights abuses. Two current examples are Myanmar (Burma) and the Maldives. However, many will argue that taking such a stance towards ruling governments is merely depriving communities dependent on tourism of much-needed revenue. The question you must ask is, where is your money going?

With some of the most spectacular sights in Southeast Asia, such as the temples of Pagan, Myanmar is ruled by a junta that has repressed the people's democracy movement led by Aung San Suu Kyi for the last two decades. High-profile campaigns to boycott visits to the country have drawn the support of politicians, dignitaries and celebrities all over the world (www.burmacampaign.org.uk / www.uscampaignforburma.org). Aung San Suu Kyi herself has urged tourists not to visit Myanmar, and it is claimed that nowhere in the world is the link between tourism and human rights abuses more pronounced. Much of the recently developed tourist infrastructure, from new roads to hotels, has been built using child and slave labour. The regime claims that tourism earns the country US$100 million per year, but it effectively holds the

purse strings through state control of the industry. Since 50 per cent of the national budget is spent on the military and just US38¢ per person on health, it is hard to imagine that a visit to Myanmar will do much to improve the lives of the people.

Few cases for a potential boycott are as cut and dried as Myanmar. For example, although the Maldivian government is accused of being despotic, having imprisoned opponents of the regime, a total boycott may not be the answer there, and a responsible and ethical approach to tourism in the region could benefit local people. Groups like Friends of Maldives (www.friendsofmaldives.org) provide an updated list of resorts it considers worthy of a boycott owing to links with corrupt ministers in the ruling party. The UK organization Tourism Concern (www.tourismconcern.org.uk) also runs an ongoing campaign for fair living conditions and for shared benefits from tourism in the Maldives. It points out that while tourists enjoy luxury holidays, many of the locals are living in poverty. Fresh fruit and vegetables often go directly to tourist islands, bypassing the local people, and a UN report showed that as many as 30 per cent of Maldivian children under the age of five are suffering from malnutrition. At the same time, the Maldivian government imposes restrictions on expressions of freedom, so local people are unable to speak out about these injustices. Some hotels in the Maldives offer a more responsible approach to tourism (see Soneva Fushi, pages 246–7), proving that the industry can be a positive force in the Maldives. But, as ever, if there are doubts concerning the destination of your choice, it pays to do your homework.

The Boat Landing Guest House

PO Box 28, Ban Khone, Luang Namtha District, Luang Namtha Province, Laos
+856 86 313 398 / www.theboatlanding.com / theboatlanding@yahoo.com

ECO**FILE**

Rooms: Small and large twins, doubles, suites and a 4-person family room.

Rates: From LAK274,000 (US$28) per night, including breakfast.

Location: Ban Khone village in Luang Namtha,135km from Udomsai. The Guest House is adjacent to the Namtha River boat landing, 6km (4 miles) from town.

Best time to go: During the high season, Nov–Apr.

Getting there: From Laos' capital, Vientiane, fly 1 hour to Udomsai, then 3–5 hours by bus or car.

CO₂ emissions: Rtn flight to Udomsai via Vientiane from New York 4.31 tonnes; London 2.81; Sydney 2.30. Rtn transfer by car 0.08; by bus 0.04.

Offset cost: $65.25; £21.70; A$44.60.

Responsibility: The low-impact design and socially conscious approach of the Boat Landing has been integral since its inception, ensuring an organic evolution and a considered role within the greater community. The involvement of the local community in the project and the extended family atmosphere make for an authentic and responsible experience of the region.

Environmental: ∅∅∅∅∅

Social: ∅∅∅∅∅

ISOLATED from the outside world since the early 1960s, the Laotian province of Luang Namtha remains one of those rare destinations in the 21st century to be truly 'out there'. Bordered by China to the north and the Shan state of Mynamar (Burma) to the west, and home to a diverse collection of ethnic groups, from the Tai Yuan to the Akha and Hmong, this forgotten corner of Indo-China is also rich in biodiversity, stunning landscapes and possibilities for the adventurous traveller.

In recognition of this potential, the Boat Landing guesthouse operates in conjunction with its sister company, Green Discovery, to open up this fascinating region in a low-impact and responsible manner, creating a blueprint model for community-based eco-tourism. Through a collaboration between American aid worker Bill Tuffin and local

couple Sompawn and Joy Khantisouk, the ecolodge developed within an acacia grove beside the Namtha River. Initial plans for a French colonial-style mansion were soon abandoned in favour of vernacular architecture and natural, ecological materials. Wall panels are constructed from woven rattan, timber has been sourced sustainably and the use of cement has been kept to a minimum within the foundations.

From an environmental perspective, the Boat Landing development is a positive role model, from its use of solar hot water to waste separation and recycling. Used engine oil is applied to treat timbers, organic waste is composted, and various initiatives are in place to protect the biodiversity of the region from the use of chemical pesticides and herbicides. The activities on offer, from mountain-biking and kayaking to trekking and rafting, all involve local villagers and support the Nam Ha National Protected Area (NPA) through funds generated from access permits. Since 2001, both Green Discovery and the Boat Landing have worked in conjunction with the UNESCO Nam Ha Ecotourism Project, setting benchmark standards for tourism in the region and, in the process, bagging a whole swathe of awards for responsible practice.

The food in Laos is in itself almost enough to justify the flight here, and the menu at the Boat Landing is no exception, with an extensive repertoire of local vegetarian delights to entice even the most hardened meat-eater. Revolving around a few key components, from sticky rice to chicken noodle soups and the essential chilli pastes, meals are traditionally served on low, round rattan tables. After a day spent trekking or biking through the forests, few things can be more rewarding than feasting on such delights while watching the flow of life on the river, from locals fishing and children swimming, to iridescent birds and butterflies swooping over the languid, lazy waters.

Soneva Fushi Resort

Kunfunadhoo Island, Baa Atoll, Maldives
+960 660 0304 / www.sixsenses.com / reservations-fushi@sonevaresorts.com

THE mere concept of creating a luxury resort on a Maldivian island that conforms to ecological parameters may sound like a contradiction in terms. Surrounded by some of the most endangered marine habitats on earth, the low-lying Maldive islands are also more threatened than most by climate change. Add to this their geographical isolation, dependence on imported items and the ongoing human rights controversy surrounding the government, and one might wonder how a resort in the archipelago could ever be included in this book.

At first glance, Soneva Fushi could go unnoticed, but it's worth looking again. Sixty-five luxury villas are discreetly tucked among the natural landscape of Kunfunadhoo Island. Sandy cycling tracks wind through lush jungle vegetation, where the tentacles of giant banyan trees disappear into a thick carpet of leaf litter. This 40ha (100-acre) island is just one of the 1,190 sprinkled through the Maldives. Surrounded by a ring of dazzling beach and coral reef, and a stretch of water that slides from cool aquamarine to distant sapphire, Kunfunadhoo looks much like other islands in the region – but its accommodation sets it apart.

The Soneva strapline, 'intelligent luxury', conveys the essence of the resort's innovative and influential formula, and its parent company, Six Senses, is one of the few setting the pace for an environmental conscience within the luxury hotel industry. The challenge is Herculean. The

energy demands from a hotel of this calibre, for example, are formidable. Each villa has a TV, DVD player, stereo, fridge, air conditioning and a bewildering number of lights. Add to these the steam rooms, saunas, a desalination plant and a laundry that is in constant use, and its mission to be 'zero carbon' by 2010 sounds like a lost cause. However, by working closely with leading international eco-design consultants, the Soneva team is on course to achieve this ambitious goal.

For the last 15 years, Sonu and Eva Shivdasani (hence Son-Eva), the entrepreneurial couple who have driven the Six Senses group from its inception, have applied themselves to numerous local issues, from forcing a ban on turtle hunting to funding environmental education projects on neighbouring islands. The buildings themselves integrate locally made palm-frond thatch with recycled telegraph poles, driftwood, sustainably sourced teak, and timber from the island itself. Restaurants and bars are simple open structures, with squeaky-white sand on the floors to minimize the use of cement. The attention to detail is flawless, from the composting systems to the self-bottled water and employment of the majority of staff from neighbouring islands.

Although Soneva is still reliant on many imported foods, impressive steps have been made with vegetable and fruit gardens, the latter now home to a treehouse restaurant suspended above the canopy. Mushrooms are cultivated in a subterranean chamber, strict policies determine the selection of locally sourced fish, and even the caviar comes from the world's only sustainable source.

At Soneva, the barefoot media-free environment that comes with the 'No news, No Shoes' philosophy, combined with the low-frills yet elegant understatement that runs throughout, make the resort's concept of 'intelligent luxury' a reality. And, if it achieves its zero-carbon goal by 2010, the myth that sustainability equals deprivation will be on shakier ground than ever.

ECO**FILE**

Rooms: 65 luxury villas.
Rates: From Rf7,000 (US$540) per villa per night.
Location: The island is 227km (141 miles) north of the capital, Malé.
Best time to go: Year-round.
Getting there: From Malé, the transfer to the resort is 25 mins by seaplane.
CO_2 emissions: Rtn flight to Malé from New York 4.42 tonnes; London 2.45; Sydney 2.65. Rtn transfer 0.04.
Offset cost: $66.20; £18.65; A$50.20.

Responsibility: The Soneva experience of 'intelligent luxury' has to be congratulated for its innovation and commitment. The resort's proactive stance on issues ranging from the hunting of marine turtles to environmental education on neighbouring islands has further increased the respect it has fostered within the area. If its ambitious 'zero-carbon' goal is achieved and is replicated by others, a new day will have dawned in the luxury hotel industry.
Environmental: ∅∅∅∅∅
Social: ∅∅∅∅∅

Three Camel Lodge

Nomadic Expeditions, LLC Building 76, Suite 28, 1-40,000, Peace Avenue, Chingeltei District, Ulaanbaatar, Mongolia
+976 11 313 396 / www.threecamellodge.com / info@threecamellodge.com

THERE is something slightly surreal about enjoying this level of sustainable and sophisticated comfort in the Gobi Desert. Dwarfed by a volcanic outcrop dating back 54 million years and surrounded by the silence of sand dunes in a landscape filled with fossilized dinosaurs and ancient petroglyphic art, one feels humbled by the geologic timescales and infinitude of space. The desert has always been a mystical place and, at Three Camel Lodge, this is no exception. It's hard not to think about 'the big questions' when you are immersed in such an immense stillness.

The lodge itself is a masterpiece of Mongolian design, faithfully executed according to the traditional canons of local Buddhist belief and constructed without the use of a single nail. The solid stone walls store the heat of the day, radiating it back inside during the cool desert nights, and retain the warmth from the open central fireplace. The result is a cosy space that is the perfect place to congregate over drinks, comparing notes from a day spent undertaking one of the numerous activities on offer. The wooden porch and stone terrace outside allow for endless hours of star-gazing as one marvels at the array above, secluded from the light pollution that now denies such wonders to most of the world.

Accommodation is provided by 45 felted *gers*, traditional nomadic tents. These are each large enough for four and are tastefully decked out with indigenous furniture and painted wooden beds. The ambience is earthy – simplistic minimalism, but cosy. Wood-burning stoves provide ample warmth at night, and 24-hour electricity for lighting

comes from solar panels and a wind turbine. Bathrooms in the nearby lodge are fully fitted in western style and the waste is biologically treated. As a result, the footprints left here in the desert are as minimal as those of a traditional nomadic community. If the tents were removed, little would remain to suggest that there had ever been a hotel here.

In conjunction with its sister company, Nomadic Expeditions, Three Camel Lodge offers guests a whole host of adventurous trips through the Gobi, ranging from camel-trekking in the dunes and horseback riding in fertile valleys, to digging for dinosaur fossils at the Flaming Cliffs site with palaeontologists from the Mongolian Academy of Sciences. One excursion, for example, will take you trekking through the rolling green grasslands of the Gorkhi-Terelj National Park, kayaking on the crystal-blue waters of Siberia's ancient Lake Baikal and in search of Przewalski's horse, the world's only surviving species of wild horse.

By the time you are through with that, there will be much to discuss with your fellow travellers back by the fire at Three Camel Lodge. Few places on the globe can offer such an exhilarating and unusual experience, especially one that is supremely comfortable and ecologically sustainable at the same time.

ECOFILE

Rooms: 45 felted gers.
Rates: Standard ger MNT82,880 (US$70); Deluxe ger MNT118,400 ($100) per person per night, based on double occupancy, including meals.
Location: In the Gobi Desert, 640km (400 miles) from Ulaanbataar, next to the Gobi Gurransaikhan National Park, about 1.5 hours from the provincial capital of Bulgan Soum.
Best time to go: May–Sep.
Getting there: From Ulaanbataar, fly for 1.5 hours to Dalanzadgad, where pick-ups can be arranged.
CO2 emissions: Rtn flights to Dalanzadgad via Ulaanbataar from New York 2.99 tonnes; London 1.96; Sydney 2.98. Rtn transfer 0.04.
Offset cost: $47.20; £16.05; A$59.

Responsibility: The lodge has minimal impact on the desert, making use of renewable energies and biological sewage systems. It works with partner, Nomadic Expeditions, to create and sponsor ecological education events, and it trains guides and drivers in the principles of sustainable and responsible tourism.
Environmental: 𝄐𝄐𝄐𝄐𝄐
Social: 𝄐𝄐𝄐𝄐𝄐

Tiger Mountain Pokhara Lodge

GPO Box 242, Gongabu, Kathmandu, Nepal
+977 (0)1 4236 1500 / www.tigermountain.com / info@tigermountain.com

ECOFILE

Rooms: 19 in total, including doubles, twins, triples and family rooms.
Rates: From NRs13,000 (US$200) per person per night, including meals.
Location: Less than an hour's drive from Pokhara, and 175km (108 miles) northwest of Kathmandu.
Best time to go: Mar–May or Sep–Nov for the perfect balance of sunny skies and cool nights.
Getting there: From Kathmandu, fly 30 mins or take a 6-hour bus trip to Pokhara, where pick-ups can be arranged. Alternatively, drive 4.5 hours directly to the lodge.
CO2 emissions: Rtn flight to Kathmandu from New York 3.68 tonnes; London 2.07; Sydney 2.84. Rtn transfer by plane 0.08; by bus 0.03; by car 0.12.
Offset cost: $56.50; £16.45; A$55.40.

Responsibility: Tiger Mountain's commitment to responsible tourism is sincere. Numbers in groups are restricted, guides are expertly trained, waste is properly collected for disposal from its campsites, and solar technologies are incorporated where possible in its treehouses and bungalows. Organic local produce is sourced, staff are employed locally and local charities are supported.

Environmental:	∅∅∅∅∅
Social:	∅∅∅∅∅

WAKE up, pinch yourself and rejoice. You are as physically close to the heavens as most people will ever get, and that celestial clear view is suffusing your whole being with a sense of peace. Perfectly framed before you sit three of the highest peaks on the globe – Dhaulagiri, Manasulu and the famed Annapurna – all topping 8,000m (26,250ft).

Poised 300m (1,000ft) above the stunning Pokhara Valley, the most recent lodge to be added to the Tiger Mountain fleet is also its most dramatic and exclusive. Built from hand-cut stone, the 19 spacious rooms are contained within 13 bungalows, all strategically sited to maximize the breathtaking views while still enjoying the luxury of private gardens. The wooden floorboards, the sensual warmth of Tibetan wool carpets and the deep red monk's-robe bedspreads all create that snug sense of cotton-wool comfort so crucial for high-altitude luxury. Sit back, absorb the radiance of a Himalayan sunset, drink in hand, then wonder at how you were lucky enough to get here.

The Tiger Mountain company was originally founded back in the early 1960s, and Pokhara Lodge joins the Tiger Tops Jungle Lodge/Tented Camp and Karnali Lodge/Tented Camp to offer guests all the bells and whistles required for the complete Himalayan adventure. Elephant safaris, jungle treks, mountaineering, whitewater rafting, birdwatching, river exploration – it's all here and it's all off the charts. You can go in search of the one-horned rhinoceros, the sloth bear or the nocturnal royal Bengal tiger, or try to catch sight of some of the 450 species of bird found here. No previous experience is necessary for

the rafting, since the six nearby rivers offer waters graded from one to six. Adrenalin junkies will, however, head for the Jailhouse Rock and Inversion rapids on the Karnali, which are guaranteed to get the heart pumping.

After the exertions of the day, indulge in a shiatsu massage, do some gentle yoga with the resident instructor, or be tempted by the secluded pool above the Bijaypur River, where the reflected peak of Mt Machhapuchhare shimmers on the surface like a perpetual mirage. Once you have recovered from your intrepid forays through the roof of the world, there is always much to discuss by the main lodge fireplace, where the bar reassuringly stays open 'until the last guest retires'. For more sober stimulation, take in the library of Colonel Jimmy Roberts (one of the Tiger Mountain founders), an engrossing collection of Himalayan climbing literature and photographs. When sleep finally calls, amble back under starlit skies, through terraces of indigenous shrubs, bamboos and fruit trees, sit out on your veranda and try to remember that this is real.

251

Karma down

Following a week-long retreat at the Sri Lankan eco-village of Ulpotha to escape the pressures of civilization, **Rory Spowers** emerged cleansed and with a renewed sense of inner peace.

The time has come to embrace – dare I say it – your 'inner child'. Life at this Sri Lankan Neverland is as simple and carefree as a kid's. Whether you're frolicking on the freshwater lake, or climbing the hills and finding caves, Ulpotha encourages that joyful sense of wonder so frequently denied by modern lifestyles. It's bare and innocent, exotic and playful. Few places can boast such a subtle fusion of sybaritic indulgence and raw, ascetic comfort. Just when you feel the need for something – a drink, food to nibble on, a place to lounge beneath a majestic banyan tree – it miraculously appears, as if your every thought has been predetermined. Life here just flows, effortlessly.

To begin with, the transition from the urban West to a rural village in Asia proved quite a shock. Living without electricity, in

This page: Natural building materials are used throughout Ulpotha; ayurvedic spa treatment. Opposite: The *ambalama* (rest pavilion)

an open-sided mud hut, eating bizarre-looking local dishes and detoxing from a diet of strong espressos made me feel more than a little displaced. For some of my fellow visitors, these first two days were a bumpy ride, the jet lag combining with the shift in space-time to leave them looking a little bewildered. Hell, even the light seemed to be different. But once we adjusted to the pace of Ulpotha life, none of us ever wanted to leave. The village is Spartan but sophisticated; basic but opulent; bare but beautiful.

I started my days with some yoga in the breezy open pavilion. Ulpotha draws a steady stream of world-class teachers of all persuasions, from gentle Hatha to fluid, invigorating Ashtanga. All students are accommodated, from the novice to the adept. The vibe at Ulpotha precludes any sense of exclusion, so even if you have never navel-gazed or 'saluted the sun', do not be put off. The teachers set their own schedules, usually offering a class in the morning and again in the late afternoon. As with everything at Ulpotha, from meals to those indulgent daily massages and pamperings at the ayurvedic spa, yoga is part of the all-inclusive rate for your stay, so just take advantage when you wish. Nobody's going to raise an eyebrow should you decide to stay in bed or lounge in a hammock rather than work on your downward dog.

Breakfast is a relaxed come-and-go affair at the village *kade* (stall). Drink a mug of freshly brewed tea, feast on bananas that actually taste like bananas, or try rolled pancakes stuffed with coconut and jaggery, the brown sugar derived from the *kitul* palm. I developed a passion for *kola-kanda*, which looks like some science-fiction milkshake to guarantee superhuman strength, but is in fact a green-rice porridge made with *gotu-kola*, a herb renowned

for its anti-ageing properties and numerous health benefits.

Suitably stoked by my start to the day, I wandered down swept dusty paths to the *wedegedara*, or ayurvedic spa. During my free consultation, Dr Srilal, the resident ayurvedic physician, determined my body type, or *dosha*, then prescribed an appropriate diet and suggested possible courses of treatment for my stay. These packages are individually tailored to your needs and constitute the only extra cost to your stay, should you opt to take them. A minimum of one week is required, while the more involved programmes may require up to a month for their proper application. Traditional detoxification therapies range from soothing herbal baths and oil massages, to being steamed with herbs and spices inside a giant wicker basket. The fact that this looks like a torture chamber from a Bond film, and comprises a coffin that encloses the body and steams you with herbs heated in boiling clay pots below, should not cause alarm – it's quite safe and perfectly pleasant. Some of the elimination therapies, on the other hand, are not for the faint-hearted, involving enemas and enforced vomiting. You have been warned.

Lunch and dinner are served in the *ambalama* (rest pavilion) at the heart of Ulpotha. A stunningly diverse assortment of exquisite curries, all served in clay bowls, are beautifully arrayed on one huge woven mat. Rare red rice strains combine with the delicate spicing of pulses and vegetables, all grown at Ulpotha and washed down with ayurvedic teas or the medicinal juice made from the extraordinary wood apple. You will never have eaten meals like this, anywhere, ever. The *ambalama* also provides the focal point for the Ulpotha community, where guests converge for food, for conversation, or just to relax with a book on the sumptuous cushions and absorb the heady tranquillity that pervades life here. I soon felt like whole weeks had drifted by, entranced by passing butterflies during the day and fireflies flashing at night.

Physical activity is by no means restricted to yoga. Every day I went swimming and boating in the vast freshwater tank, surrounded by water lilies and iridescent dragonflies. On the far side, waterways disappear into overhanging jungle and expeditions can feel like an Amazonian adventure. I hiked the jungle trails to the *ulpotha*, or spring, that gives the location its name, and others went to visit practising shamans and ascetic monks in the local caves and temples that dot the hillsides. There is always the option to take a bicycle to the nearby village, or to venture farther afield on day-trips to ancient sites.

Most of us preferred to stay anchored to Ulpotha, the combination of the *ambalama*, the tank and on-tap massages proving too addictive to part with. A steady flow of western practitioners passes through over the two seasons, adding acupuncture, reflexology and other treatments to the repertoire, beyond pure ayurveda. Again, none of these requires dipping into your pocket so, in addition to media, electricity and cappuccinos, you can forget about money for a while.

If this sounds too virtuous and worthy for you, feel free to crack open your bottle of duty-free scotch or wine and dance all night, to sounds provided by local musicians and twinkling lights provided by nature. Ulpotha is not an ashram. It's about letting go, having fun and unleashing the Peter Pan that lurks within us all.

ECO**FILE**

Location: Ulpotha is 135km (84 miles) northeast of Colombo, close to the ancient city of Anuradapura.

Getting there: From Colombo airport, guests are collected and driven the 3 hours to Ulpotha by minivan taxi.

CO_2 emissions: Rtn flight to Colombo from New York 4.43 tonnes; London 2.51; Sydney 2.52. Rtn transfer 0.08.

Offset cost: $67.20; £19.45; A$48.70.

Staying there: There are 12 mud huts with double beds and a 3-bed family room.

Rates: SLRs145,000 (US$1,300) per person per week, all inclusive bar tailored ayurvedic treatment programmes (SLRs44,500/US$400) per week. Minimum stay of 1 week.

Best time to go: The 2 seasons are late Nov–end Mar and Jun–Aug.

Further information: www.ulpotha.com

Responsibility: Ulpotha is hard to fault. All staff are local, the organic food is grown on site and the village is self-reliant on water. There is no power; all waste is recycled and the net carbon footprint is virtually zero. The new ayurvedic clinic provides a free service to surrounding villagers, and rehabilitation of the watershed has transformed the lives of thousands of people who depend on it. To sum it up, Ulpotha has no electricity or mod cons, and maintains an intelligent use of natural resources.

Galapita

Buttala, Sri Lanka, Galapita, Sri Lanka
+94 (0)11 2508755 / www.galapita.com / paradiselanka@sltnet.lk

WHETHER it was karma, kismet or something written in the stars, Galapita was blessed from the outset. On a pilgrimage to Kataragama – a sacred site for Buddhist, Hindu, Muslim and indigenous Sri Lankan communities – gemmologist Rukman De Fonseka stumbled across the site of Galapita. Here, the force of the Menik Ganga, or 'River of Gems', is compressed by the narrow confines of a gorge and then spills and twists over waterfalls, creating natural Jacuzzis and whirlpools in sculpted rocks that are more than 2 billion years old. Rukman bought the land and set about building his own gem: a jungle retreat, only recently opened to visitors.

Your arrival at Galpita is understated. Vehicles are discarded at the end of a 1km (0.6-mile) dirt track and entry to the extensive gardens and grounds is through a wooden door in a simple mud wall. A short walk brings you to the river and a suspension bridge, best negotiated when sober.

On the far bank is your accommodation for the evening, in one of several sprawling mud-hut complexes. Seating and beds rest on sculpted mud platforms, covered in woven matting, bedding and cushions just begging for your attention. Local materials have been used throughout the structures, from the *illuk* thatch on the roofs to the twisted branch-

es that form the frames of the huts. All the rooms have fine views of the river, the gorge and the glorious stars. Families or groups may choose to stay in a villa that's separated from the main accommodation; while treehouses may tempt the romantic or adventurous.

There is minimal use of cement and no electricity, except for a small solar panel to power the 12-volt car stereo in the villa. Virtually all waste is composted and water is drawn from on-site wells. Meals are simple but nutritious and delicious, prepared from rice, vegetables, fruits and herbs all grown organically on site. The mineral-rich soil and dry-zone conditions here combine to add an extra intensity to the flavour of the tomatoes, mangoes and watermelons. Cooking is done over open fires using clay *chuttees* (cooking vessels), which Rukman claims accounts for at least 25 per cent of the flavour.

Rukman's attention to detail is reflected throughout. Little is there, but nothing is lacking, right down to a telescope for star-gazing. Trips can be arranged to nearby Yala National Park, to spot elephants, crocodiles and possibly leopard, or to the sacred sites in and around Kataragama. For an adrenaline rush, take a trip down the rapids in a rubber innertube when the river water is high.

Taking his connection with fine stones one step further, Rukman has now launched an ayurvedic mineral spa at Galapita, integrating various gemstones with ayurvedic treatments to tap their inherent healing energies. A consultation with the resident ayurvedic doctor may result in your treatment with herbal compresses combined with certain minerals, or bathed in lemon grass, kaffir lime, tamarind or frangipani leaves and uncut sapphires.

Rukman also encourages guests at Galapita to try their hand at 'panning' in the river with a wicker basket. Several uncut sapphires and cat's-eyes have been found, including one cornflower-blue sapphire weighing 18 carats. Since any stones you may find are yours to keep, it's easy to see why Galapita could prove a difficult place to leave.

ECO**FILE**

Rooms: Five simple open-sided buildings, 1 villa and 3 treehouses.
Rates: From SLRs8,000 (US$80) per person per night, including meals.
Location: Near the 31km (19-mile) post on the road between Buttala and Kataragama. Galapita is 280km (174 miles) from Colombo.
Best time to go: Year-round.
Getting there: From Colombo, hire a van and driver for the 6-hour journey to Galapita.
CO2 emissions: Rtn flight to Colombo from New York 4.44 tonnes; London 2.51; Sydney 2.52. Rtn transfer 0.17.
Offset cost: $68.50; £20.10; A$50.35.

Responsibility: Galapita has used local materials for construction, grows organic food on site and is self-reliant on water, making its ecological footprint negligible. All staff members are local and receive a percentage of profits according to their length of employment.
Environmental: ØØØØØ
Social: ØØØØØ

Samakanda Bio-versity

Nakiyadeniya, Sri Lanka
+94 (0)777 424 770 / www.samakanda.org / rory@samakanda.org

ECOFILE

Rooms: Two fully renovated self-catering bungalows.
Rates: From SLRs8,400 (US$75) per bungalow per night, including a daily meal of curry and rice. Minimum stay of 2 nights.
Location: A 40-min drive inland from the southern city of Galle. 140km (87 miles) from Colombo.
Best time to go: Dec–Apr and Jul–Aug.
Getting there: From Colombo, fly 15 mins by floatplane to nearby Koggala Lake, where pick-ups can be arranged, or drive 4 hours to Samakanda.
CO_2 emissions: Rtn flight to Colombo from New York 4.44 tonnes; London 2.51; Sydney 2.52. Rtn transfer by plane 0.04; by car 0.08.
Offset cost: $67.25; £19.50; A$48.75.

Responsibility: Although it is still in its infancy, the Samakanda Bio-versity has laudable aims and is grounded in good eco-credentials. When the course programme is fully established and the second-phase accommodation is complete, this will be a prime destination for those who wish to take home more than just memories.
Environmental: ⊘⊘⊘⊘⊘
Social: ⊘⊘⊘⊘⊘

WELCOME to 'bio-versity', a kind of university for the eco-conscious. This is a place to learn about sustainable lifestyles – and to see them in action. You won't get a degree, but you'll certainly get an education; and at the heart of all these learned aims, you will also find a wonderfully tranquil place to stay.

There's no denying that Samakanda (Peaceful Hill) is different. While acknowledging its attraction as an eco-tourism venture, it places equal emphasis on being an ecological learning centre, offering guests an educational experience in sustainable lifestyle solutions. With this in mind, the owners coined the term 'bio-versity', and created space for a shifting population of teachers and students.

The campus of this bio-versity is the 'bowl' at the heart of Samakanda, an edible landscape filled with a cornucopia of organic vegetables, rare red rice strains, tropical fruits, herbs and spices. The inspiration for the workshops and courses – whether they be ecological building techniques, permaculture design or ayurveda – is drawn from the concept of the natural intelligence of biological systems.

Samakanda is the vision of Rory and Yvette Spowers, who moved to Sri Lanka from the UK in 2004 to pursue their dream of living a largely self-reliant lifestyle. There they bought an abandoned 40ha (100-acre) tea estate that had reverted to thick jungle after ten years of neglect. The presence of pristine water sources, fertile soils and miles of immaculate stone terracing, combined with the fact that no chemical fertilizers or pesticides had been used on the site since it was abandoned, provided the perfect environment in which the couple could sow their organic ideas.

Samakanda opened in January 2007, offering accommodation in two renovated bungalows, with a second phase of three Eco-Pods (low-impact huts) to follow. The Eco-Pods will maximize the potential for passive cooling, harvest their own water, generate their own power and treat their waste biologically. The original three-bedroom Bungalow is perched on the crest of the estate's ridge and is fitted with solar hot water, high-speed Internet access, a kitchen and a modern bathroom. The two-bedroom Cottage, which overlooks the 'bowl' below, is solar-powered and similarly geared for self-catering. An outdoor shower is positioned within a spiral of bananas and fed by a bamboo pipe. Both buildings have wood-fired clay pizza ovens and, with their kids' camps and treehouse platforms, are ideal for families with young children.

The property is divided into seven zones, ranging from the cultivated 'bowl' and spice garden, to hiking and mountain-bike trails through a biodiversity refuge. This reserve covers the bulk of the land and will be preserved intact as a habitat for the numerous endemic birds, mammals and reptiles found here, including giant monitor lizards, porcupines and the rare nocturnal pangolin. A 'healing zone' is being developed around an area of giant boulders, caves and banyan trees, and has been planted with medicinal herbs and rare ayurvedic plants.

All those employed on the project live nearby, building materials have been sourced on site, and meals are prepared from Samakanda produce, from rice and curry to green salads and wood-roasted vegetables. There is no obligation for guests to take part in any of the courses, workshops or other activities offered at Samakanda – after all, lounging in a hammock, absorbing the views and natural tranquillity that surrounds you, is all part of the bio-versity experience.

Tree Tops Jungle Lodge

Buttala, Sri Lanka

+94 (0)777 036 554 / www.treetopsjunglelodge.com / treetopsjunglelodge@yahoo.com

SECURE in the knowledge that pachyderms don't climb trees, sleep comes easily here. From the vantage point of your treehouse, elephants can often be heard crashing through the jungle scrub that surrounds the lodge. Sometimes they can even be viewed under the monochrome light of the full moon. Owner Lars Sorensen calls this 'reality tourism': a full-on, totally authentic experience of raw jungle habitat. Even the approach to Tree Tops Jungle Lodge is an adventure itself, only safe during the heat of the day, when elephants will not stray across the bumpy potholed track that leads you in.

The project began in 1997 as a private nature retreat, with a proactive intention to protect the endangered wild Asian elephant, then opened for small groups of visitors in 2002. Prolonged periods of drought had forced local subsistence farmers to seek alternative sources of income, namely illegal hunting and logging, leading to biodiversity loss and deforestation. By laying the foundations for responsible tourism, Lars has not only provided for new livelihoods, but also created a natural security mechanism for protecting the area, as his staff keep an eye on illicit comings and goings.

The lodge's simple mud huts are almost invisibly integrated within the landscape. All the materials used in their construction were drawn from the immediate surroundings, from fallen trees to cattle dung and clay dug from the land – not a single tree was felled. The treehouse design mimics the traditional *chena* treehuts used by slash-and-burn farmers to watch over plots of land secure from encroaching elephants, but has been combined with fresh ideas for modern comfort and functionality. These include features such as sculpted mud seating, space for hammocks, and good-quality sheets and mosquito nets. There's no electricity, you bathe at the freshwater well, and local dishes are prepared in traditional clay *chuttees* over an open fire, the flavours seemingly intensified as a result.

The main reason for visiting Tree Tops is to make excursions through the jungle. These are undertaken on foot, with experienced local guides, in the early morning or late afternoon. In addition to almost guaranteed elephant sightings, the area is rich in sambur, chital deer, marsh crocodiles, armadillos, giant squirrels and wild boars, plus a plethora of birds, many of them endemic. This tropical dry evergreen forest is also filled with rare hardwoods, such as ebony, and a living jungle pharmacy of medicinal ayurvedic plants.

Culture vultures will be as much at home here as naturalists, since the surrounding region is peppered with some of the finest ancient sites in the country – from the crystalline limestone Buddha at Maligawila to the Arahat Kanda caves and the pilgrimage centre of Katargama. And for those worried about the proximity of roving pachyderms, rest assured that the lodge is well stocked with fire-crackers, ready to repel any intruder that ventures too close for comfort.

ECO**FILE**

Rooms: One double-bed treehouse and 1 double-bed mud hut.

Rates: SLRs6,700 (US$60) per person per night, including all meals but excluding activities. Three-night all-inclusive packages SLRs25,200 (US$225) per person.

Location: 9km (6 miles) from Buttala in southeastern Sri Lanka.

Best time to go: Year-round, although the rainy season (Oct–Jan) is best avoided. The jungle stays green and lush until the heat of May; Jun–Sep is best for elephants.

Getting there: From Colombo, hire a van for the 6-hour journey to Buttala. Check with Tree Tops for the status of the road to the lodge and the best time to travel.

CO_2 emissions: Rtn flight to Colombo from New York 4.44 tonnes; London 2.51; Sydney 2.52. Rtn transfer 0.17.

Offset cost: $68.50; £20.10; A$50.35.

Responsibility: With no electricity, water from a well, materials drawn from the land and not even a tree felled during construction, the low-impact design of Tree Tops is as minimal as it comes. Apart from the English-speaking manager, all staff are local, and systemic impacts on the community and ecology – from preventing poaching to policing illegal logging – combine to make Tree Tops a blueprint for responsible conservation tourism.

Environmental: ✐✐✐✐✐

Social: ✐✐✐✐✐

Gecko Villa

126 Moo 13, Baan Um Jaan, A Prajak Sinlapakom, 41000 Udon Thani, Thailand
+66 81 9180500 / www.geckovilla.com / info@geckovilla.com

THE long, canopied tunnel of swaying bamboo that brings you to Gecko Villa is like a green throat, swallowing you into nature. The path clears to reveal a tropical bolthole surrounded by mango, papaya and other fruit trees, organic vegetable gardens, grazing pasture and an expanding woodland reforestation project funded by previous guests.

Charles Coleman initiated Gecko Villa in response to the fragmentation of families he witnessed in Thailand's northeastern province of Isaan, as members were drawn south to find work but their original communities were deprived of this new economic prosperity. Built and owned entirely by local villagers, the project has enabled several families to remain intact and enjoy sustainable livelihoods. All services are sourced in the district and revenue from the project is disbursed locally. Starting with an area of drought-stricken disused paddy fields, a series of wells and ponds were dug to harvest and store the water that now feeds a fertile landscape, reversing the trend of widespread deforestation.

The villa itself is modern and fully equipped, with two air-conditioned double bedrooms with en suite bathrooms, a third fan-cooled twin room, a slick contemporary western kitchen with adjoining Thai-style kitchen, and a living room with TV and music system. Local artwork and handicrafts place the building firmly into context. An inviting swimming pool is directly outside, lined with hand-made tiles and surrounded by extensive wooden decking and seating, where barbecues and al fresco dining can be enjoyed to a backdrop of fireflies flashing through the surrounding foliage.

You can spend your time here just languidly soaking up the atmosphere, or you can opt to partake in a wide variety of activities that help

ECOFILE

Rooms: Three (2 doubles, 1 twin).
Rates: From 4,900B (US$150) per night for up to 2 guests, including all meals and transfers from Udon Thani.
Location: 20km (12 miles) southeast of Udon Thani in Isaan, northeast Thailand.
Best time to go: Year-round. Activities vary with the seasons.
Getting there: From Bangkok, fly 50 mins or travel by train for 9 hours to Udon Thani, where pick-ups can be arranged.
CO2 emissions: Rtn flight to Udon Thani via Bangkok from New York 4.51 tonnes; London 2.92; Sydney 2.27. Train figures for Thailand n/a.
Offset cost: $33.85; £21.90; A$44.40.

Responsibility: By identifying innovative possibilities for eco-tourism in a remote and untouched region, Gecko Villa has shown the way forward. It has responded well to local needs, and has created positive and sustainable opportunities for the community in the process.
Environmental: 𝄢𝄢𝄢𝄢𝄢
Social: 𝄢𝄢𝄢𝄢𝄢

to establish a sense of connection with the local community. You can have a go at planting or harvesting rice with the locals and then visit listed wetlands nearby, or learn to cook Thai dishes like green papaya salad and *tom yum kung*. Walking, mountain-biking and fishing trips can also be arranged, which take in the local flora, fauna and rich tradition of handicrafts. This level of interaction between guests and the community has had reciprocal benefits in terms of education, and has also generated a renewed pride in the local culture.

For an area where Charles says 'carbon footprints are generally imagined to be what are left on the ground when someone stumbles through the ashes of an old fire', Gecko Villa has encouraged an impressive variety of new community initiatives, from dealing with waste to planting trees. Although the modern materials and creature comforts of Gecko Villa may not scream eco-credentials at you, the project has created a benchmark model for the wider community, acting like a catalyst for deeper and more systemic impacts. Perhaps most importantly, it has shown the value for this kind of approach in a milieu that previously did not recognize such possibilities for tourism.

Australasia

Main picture: Wilpena Pound, South Australia. Left, from top: Jacky dragon; Paperbark Creek; Burrawang West Station; fishing at Cape Leveque; spa treatments at Jean-Michel Cousteau Fiji Islands Resort

Locator map & budget guide

- ● Budget (up to US$100)
- ● Moderate (US$100–250)
- ● Expensive (US$250–500)
- ● Blow out (more than US$500)

Prices are for a double room, or two people, per night

Accommodation

Malaysia

Indonesia

Darwin

❽

Broome

Great Sandy

❿

Desert

Perth

I N D I A N

O C E A N

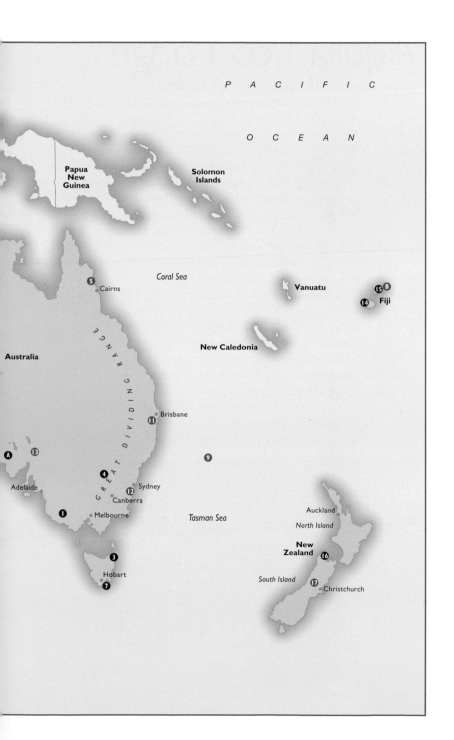

P A C I F I C

O C E A N

Papua
New
Guinea

Solomon
Islands

Coral Sea

5 Cairns

Vanuatu

15 **B**

14 Fiji

Australia

New Caledonia

11 Brisbane

A

13

9

4

Adelaide

12 Sydney

Canberra

1 Melbourne

Tasman Sea

Auckland

North Island

**New
Zealand**

16

3

South Island

17 Christchurch

Hobart

7

G R E A T   D I V I D I N G   R A N G E

Aquila Eco Lodges

Victoria Valley Road, Dunkeld, Victoria 3294, Australia
+61 (0)3 5577 2582 / www.ecolodges.com.au / ecolodges@ozemail.com.au

IT'S a taste of classic Australian bush that's on offer at Aquila Eco. Nestled in a hundred wild acres (40ha) amid the rumpled mountains and outlandish rock formations of Victoria's Southern Grampians, the property is in a world of grass trees, grevilleas and orchids that abound among the stringybark eucalypts, along with kangaroos, wombats, emus and at least 200 species of bird. As an added bonus, there are also echidnas – spiny mammals that look a little like hedgehogs yet lay eggs.

Aquila's land and network of hiking paths flow into the magnificent Grampians National Park. Surrounded by such natural abundance, the owners have approached things with a balance of taste and tact, working with the Trust for Nature to preserve the environment.

The property is home to four self-contained lodges based on two designs: the Loft and the Treehouse. All have been built with expansive windows angled to make the most of the view and the winter sun, while cutting down on the amount of sun during the hot summer. It goes without saying that each comes with a sense of seclusion.

The Lofthouse design can sleep up to six people, features a mezzanine level and has a touch of light-filled cathedral about it. The Treehouse design takes up to four people and, with warm hues provided by its earthy red gum flooring, rises three storeys to drink in the

views across the shimmering canopy and the Victoria Valley. A specially designed shower means you can even keep an eye on the wildlife while lathering up, though for those who feel shy about being in a state of undress around curious marsupials, there is a privacy blind.

All the lodges contain such essentials as a slow-burning wood heater, barbecue, fully equipped kitchen, DVD player and sheltered outdoor area. Stretched beneath a window that looks scarcely smaller than a cinema screen is a daybed, providing the perfect spot to kick back with a book – although that view means it's likely you'll be easily distracted.

The entire property is solar-powered, with a diesel generator as back-up. When the generator does have to be fired up, it is run partly on biodiesel produced at Aquila from recycled cooking oil, methanol and caustic soda. All lighting and appliances are of low wattage and guests are encouraged to con-serve energy, a process aided by the design of the lodges themselves, which incorporates insulation and passive heating and cooling.

As for water – an increasingly sensitive topic in Australia – this is collected from the rooftops and greywater is recycled to irrigate a bush-food orchard. Waste is sensitively treated, but like so many of the ecological measures here, it's something that just goes on quietly in the background while you focus on soaking in this lovely neck of the woods.

ECO**FILE**

Rooms: Two Loft lodges (up to 6 guests each) and 2 Treehouse lodges (up to 4 guests each).
Rates: From A\$220 (US\$180) per couple per night. Lodges are self-catering, but a breakfast hamper can be provided on request.
Location: Dunkeld, 288km (179 miles) from Melbourne, in the South Grampians, southwestern Victoria.
Best time to go: Avoid the sum-mer's heat and bushfires (Dec–Feb).
Getting there: From Melbourne, drive 3.5 hours to Dunkeld.
CO_2 emissions: Rtn flight to Melbourne from New York 5.50 tonnes; London 5.59; Sydney 0.18. Rtn transfer 0.17.
Offset cost: \$84.30; £43.25; A\$6.60.

Responsibility: Aquila's property is covenanted with the Trust for Nature for the preservation and study of its natural environment and species. The lodges have been built using local materials and labour (where possible), using designs that minimize environmental impact and energy consumption. Power is mainly solar. Recycling is performed, organic waste is composted, and levels of non-biodegradable waste are care-fully measured and recorded. Environmental restoration has seen the re-emergence of native orchids.
Environmental: ⌀⌀⌀⌀⌀
Social: ⌀⌀⌀⌀⌀

Bamurru Plains

PO Box R446, Royal Exchange, Sydney, New South Wales 1225, Australia
+61 (0)2 9571 6677 / www.bamurruplains.com / info@bamurruplains.com

WATER buffalo plod darkly as the early morning sun burns off the last
of the dawn mist draped across an ocean of spike rushes. The shore is
a quivering carpet of whistling ducks. Overhead, geese fly in tight
squadrons across the still orange sky. As the airboat comes to rest out
here in the middle of a floodplain vibrating with the honking of magpie
geese, frogs as small as thumbnails leap from the stems in sprays of
green and brown. Stilts, bright-eyed and white-feathered, wade with an
almost balletic elegance. Once in a while, the low serrated silhouette of
a crocodile breaks the surface in perfect silence.

But the high drama comes at a nearby magpie goose nest, as a band
of kites harries away the parents and plucks out a pair of newborn
chicks. The first is carried away, only for the victorious kite to be
ambushed by another. In the resulting chaos, the hapless chick is
dropped and plummets earthwards for a few seconds, then snatched
by another kite and stuffed into its beak. The only thing missing is the
voice of David Attenborough.

The floodplains are the quintessential – and most changeable – part
of the natural cycle in the Top End of the Northern Territory: rich,
floating meadow in the wet season, and, come the dry, an expanse of
cracked earth fringed by permanent waterholes festooned with lilies.
Bamurru – from the local Aboriginal name for the magpie goose – is
the perfect window on to this remarkable world.

Billed as wild bush luxury, Bamurru is a camp of simple (but not
Spartan) cabins spread along the edge of the floodplain in the midst of
a working buffalo farm. Just 20 minutes by small plane from Darwin (or
less than three hours by car in the dry), it feels like a world of its own.

ECO**FILE**

Rooms: Nine safari suites on raised decks.

Rates: A$850 (US$710) per person per night, based on double occupancy and including all meals and scheduled activities. Minimum stay of 2 nights.

Location: Close to the western edge of Kakadu near Point Stuart on the Mary River floodplain, 190km (118 miles) east of Darwin, Northern Territory.

Best time to go: The wet season (Feb–Mar) is when life is at its most dizzying; Mar–May is best for bird-watching; and the weather is drier and cooler from Apr. Closed Nov–Dec.

Getting there: From Darwin, fly 20 mins by light plane or drive 2.5 hours by 4WD to Bamurru. It's advisable to fly in the wet season.

CO2 emissions: Rtn flight to Darwin from New York 5.91 tonnes; London 6.33; Sydney 0.69. Rtn transfer by plane 0.03; by car 0.11.

Offset cost: $89.50; £48.30; A$15.10.

Responsibility: Bamurru is run almost entirely on a computerized solar-power system, has no TVs and does not promote air conditioning. Organic waste is composted, as much waste as possible is recycled and some kitchen herbs are grown on site. The buildings are made from termite-resistant timbers to reduce pesticide usage. Staff are passionate about the environment, and most are local (in a Northern Territory sense of the word). Local suppliers and labour are used where practical.

Environmental: ⌀⌀⌀⌀⌀

Social: ⌀⌀⌀⌀⌀

The heart of operations is the lodge, whose features include daybeds, coffee tables with transient decorations in the form of small frogs, and an open bar. The wall facing the floodplain is actually a screen that allows you to gaze straight out to the wooden deck – with its fireplace, infinity pool and cushioned seating – and beyond to the wallabies and the setting sun. Relax on the deck awhile and it won't be long before staff are descending upon you with small but perfect temptations like oysters and buffalo satay. These are but warm-ups to the main culinary events, not least of which is the locally caught mud crabs – crustaceans as round as dinner plates, more fearsomely equipped than an a medieval armoury, and fantastic with chilli.

There are no televisions and no telephones, just comfort and the sights and sounds of the floodplain. While air conditioning is an option (you'll have to ask staff for the remote control), it's better to acclimatize yourself to the delicious heat. Give or take the occasional topping up by the nearly silent generator, everything here is as solar-powered as the local crocs.

Bay of Fires Walk & Lodge

170 Leighlands Road, Evandale, PO Box 1879, Launceston, Tasmania 7250, Australia
+61 (0)3 6391 9339 / www.bayoffires.com.au / bookings@cradlehuts.com.au

GAZING out across the island remains of the land bridge that once connected Tasmania to mainland Australia, Mt William National Park is a place of diverse bushland, Rubenesque rockscapes, beaches of searing white granite sand and sea of the palest blue. It's also a place rich in both wildlife and sites of Aboriginal significance. As with so much of the Tasmanian wilderness, it is at once recognizably Australian (the battalions of wallabies and barrel-bodied wombats are a giveaway, for starters) and yet, at the same time, a world apart.

One of the best ways to experience Tasmania in general, and Mt

William National Park in particular, is on foot, and one of the most agreeable tramping routes is the Bay of Fires Walk, a four-day southward trek (with a spot of kayaking and more than a little snorkelling) along the coast to the Bay of Fires. It's a gently paced adventure in the care of expert local guides.

The first night is spent at Forester Beach Camp, a little kingdom tucked away in a secluded hollow behind the beach. The twin-share rooms have timber floors and canvas ceilings, along with composting

toilets and outdoor decks. It's a very attractive warm-up to the more advanced state of luxury at the Bay of Fires Lodge, the base for relaxation and local explorations on the third and fourth days.

With its long pavilions of glass and timber set on a hilltop 40m (130ft) above the sea, the lodge manages to avoid looking like it has been forced on the landscape, which, sad to say, makes for a drastic contrast with much of Australia's coastal development. And thanks to the strict laws of national parks, it is the only building for many miles around. Constructed from a mix of native hardwoods and plantation pines, all of which was either brought into the national park by helicopter or by hand, it combines a sense of openness and light with clean lines and simple elegance. The twin-share bedrooms come with a choice of sea or bush views, and the living area has a sweeping wooden deck and, importantly in Tasmania's cooler climes, an open fire. Lighting and hot water are courtesy of solar power.

All that walking, paddling and clean air tend to provoke a fierce appetite. Happily, meals are prepared from local ingredients – Tasmanian produce has a semi-exalted reputation in Australia – and all the wines on offer are also from the island. There's nothing quite like the sound of a local Pinot Noir burbling into your glass to the accompaniment of a crackling fire and the crashing surf below. If the unholy harmonies of a bunch of Tasmanian devils (resembling mouths on legs) are thrown in on top, you've got it made.

ECO**FILE**

Rooms: Ten twin-share bedrooms.
Rates: A$1,850 (US$1,540) per person for the 3-night tour, based on twin share and including accommodation, all meals, park and guide fees, and transfers from Launceston.
Location: Mt William National Park, Tasmania. Walking tour starts from Evandale, near Launceston.
Best time to go: Nov–Apr.
Getting there: From Melbourne, fly to Launceston or take a 9-hour ferry to Devonport and then drive for 75 mins to Launceston, where pick-ups are arranged.
CO$_2$ emissions: Rtn flight to Melbourne from New York 5.50 tonnes; London 5.59; Sydney 0.18. Rtn transfer by plane 0.13; by ferry and car 0.05.
Offset cost: $84.45; £43.60; A$6.75.

Responsibility: Both the camp and lodge are discreetly positioned, creating a sense of interaction with the land and seascape. Building materials were either helicoptered in or carried by hand to minimize disturbance. Rainwater is collected via the rooftops, and greywater is treated and reused. Toilets are composting. Lighting and water heating is solar-powered. Meals are prepared from local produce, and guides are local, knowledgeable and passionate.

Environmental: ∅∅∅∅∅
Social: ∅∅∅∅∅

Burrawang West Station

Ootha (near Condobolin), New South Wales 2875, Australia
+61 (0)2 6897 5277 / www.burrawangwest.com.au / bookings@burrawangwest.com.au

IT began life as the unlikeliest of follies – a slice of Australian rural life for Japanese salarymen out among the emus, black swans and kangaroos in the Lachlan River country of central NSW. It was the early 1990s, and the chief executive of Japanese construction giant Kajima Corporation had chosen a 5,000ha (12,000-acre) cattle station as the place to create a retreat based on the quintessential Australian homestead.

Architect Richard Johnston responded emphatically with a grazier's palace – a beautifully understated Georgian-style home with a wrap-around veranda, high ceilings and a rose garden. Walk inside and you'll find polished floorboards and lavish colonial styling, a grand piano, a

billiard table, an open bar and cavernous fireplaces, and a pleasingly eclectic art collection that ranges from colonial-era lithographs to Aboriginal bark paintings and a sheet-iron kimono sculpture.

Add to all this a 20m (22yd) swimming pool framed in sandstone, saunas, conference facilities, tennis courts and four

boutique lodges that look like woolsheds but between them house 12 plush suites (crisp sheets, fireplaces and clawfoot baths are only the beginning), and you might begin to wonder how any of those high-powered executives actually got any work done – especially on nights when they sat out on the veranda, eyes peeled for sugar gliders, watching a plump moon drifting over the river gums. It gives one possible hint as to why the Japanese economy eventually went off the boil, leaving a big company like Kajima obliged to sell off frivolities, no matter how appealing.

These days Burrawang is open to paying guests, and while local owners Graham and Jana Pickles and their team have carefully maintained the atmosphere of rural refinement (aided to some extent by a lavish kitchen and a wine cellar of almost galactic proportions), they've also been busy attending to their natural environment. One of the main missions has been the rehabilitation and protection of the property's 111ha (275 acres) of wetland. Working with environmental scientists, the Pickleses have removed the pretty but catastrophic willow trees and revegetated with native species, and they have erected more than 18km (11 miles) of fencing to keep out the property's prize cattle and their mud-churning hooves. The result has been clear water and a thriving ecosystem of native water plants and birds, native fish, platypus, countless invertebrates and two species of freshwater tortoise, including the enormous broadshelled tortoise, which sports a muscular neck almost as long as its body.

Guests can explore by foot or on quad bike, or mess about in boats in the wetland in the shade of the river gums. Among the optional extras are bush poetry performances (from the sublime to the delightfully dodgy) and the chance to experience local Aboriginal culture through staged dances (which double as way of keeping the youngest generation in contact with the culture of their parents), as well as some very interactive cultural workshops.

ECO**FILE**

Rooms: 12 suites.
Rates: From A$770 (US$640) per person per night, including all meals, beverages and transfers from Parkes (or Condobolin) airport.
Location: 435km (270 miles) west of Sydney, between Condobolin and Parkes, central NSW.
Best time to go: Avoid the height of summer (Jan–Feb).
Getting there: From Sydney, take a 1-hour flight or 7-hour coach trip to Parkes, from where pick-ups can be arranged for the 45-min transfer. Alternatively, drive 6 hours from Sydney to the station.
CO_2 emissions: Rtn flight to Sydney from New York 5.21 tonnes; London 5.63. Rtn transfer by plane and car 0.14; by bus and car 0.07; by car 0.10.
Offset cost: $79.60; £43.30; A$2.50.

Responsibility: The owners have carried out significant work in saving and protecting 110ha (275 acres) of ecologically rich wetland; that they've done it in the midst of a working station is a considerable feat. The Aboriginal cultural activities provide local indigenous children with an incentive to know and engage with their traditions. Rainwater is collected from roofs and stored in big underground tanks for drinking and cooking; at the time of writing, they had not once run out of water (a major feat in inland Australia). Wastewater is treated and used for cleaning and irrigation. External lighting is solar-powered. There is no excessive lighting. Waste is separated and recycled.

Environmental:	⬭⬭⬭⬭⬭
Social:	⬭⬭⬭⬭⬭

Daintree EcoLodge & Spa

20 Daintree Road, Daintree, Queensland 4873, Australia
+61 (0)7 4098 6100 / www.daintree-ecolodge.com.au / info@daintree-ecolodge.com.au

THE 15 villas of Daintree EcoLodge stand high on their wooden stilts above a gushing stream, blending in among the trees, staghorns and strangler figs of the world's oldest rainforest. The UNESCO World Heritage-listed Daintree exists in a peculiar microclimate that has seen it and its botanical Noah's Ark survive through the comings and goings of a long procession of ice ages; by the time the Amazon jungle finally got around to forming, the Daintree had already been in existence for a not-to-be-sneezed-at 40 million years.

Despite some efforts by our species in the past couple of centuries, the Daintree tropical rainforest is with us still, and the Daintree EcoLodge – an enterprise managed with exquisite ecological and cultural sensitivity – is just one hint that we might be starting to understand how we can co-exist. Part of that co-existence involves working closely with bodies such as the National Heritage Trust and the Wet Tropics Management Authority, and another part of it involves regular consultation with the local Kuku Yalanji Aboriginal people.

A growing number of Kuku Yalanji are also employed at the lodge to provide classes in Aboriginal art, and to run guided tours in the bottle-green light of the rainforest, giving an insight into the cultural and spiritual significance of this part of the world. You will begin to understand

how the natural environment provides a rich abundance of bush foods, medicine and art materials – ochre alone can be used in art, body adornment and, mercifully, to douse the itch of mosquito bites.

Other Kuku Yalanji are involved with the lodge's spa – one of the most lavishly praised in Australia – where local ingredients and Aboriginal massage techniques have been carefully incorporated into a deeply and deliciously sybaritic experience. Sometimes the massages are given where a waterfall plunges into a clear stone pool, which in turn feeds the stream that flows along the forest floor, beneath the stilted villas and into a pond by the lodge's Julaymba Restaurant.

It's here that the massed frog choirs are at their most impressive, providing an almost musical backdrop to your meal. The chef and kitchen crew avoid the usual spa cuisine, instead relying on local ingredients where possible to serve up such dishes as red-claw crayfish in garlic and native ginger, and kangaroo steaks with wattle-seed wild-rice risotto and a rosella-flower jus.

The lodge's balance of responsibility with a sense of indulgence extends to the villas themselves, from the crisp linen of the huge net-veiled beds to the Jacuzzis on the screened verandas high above the stream. Even as you sit in the bubbling water close to the rainforest canopy, you can keep an eye out for wildlife. In this part of the world, spotting almost anything – from electric-blue butterflies to Australia's second-largest bird, the flightless cassowary – is entirely possible.

ECO**FILE**

Rooms: 15 villas (up to 3 guests).
Rates: From A$550 (US$460) per standard villa per night, including breakfast.
Location: Near the village of Daintree, 110km (70 miles) north of Cairns in northern Queensland.
Best time to go: Year-round, although cyclones occur Dec–Apr.
Getting there: From Cairns, drive 1.5 hours north to the lodge.
CO_2 emissions: Rtn flight to Cairns from New York 5.65 tonnes; London 6.07; Sydney 0.44. Rtn transfer 0.07.
Offset cost: $85; £46.05; A$9.45.

Responsibility: The lodge works closely with organizations such as the National Heritage Trust. The area's Aboriginal people are consulted on cultural and ecological matters, and employment is provided for Kuku Yalanji in ways that help preserve and convey their customs, traditions and knowledge. The buildings are constructed from recycled and recyclable materials. Waste is carefully managed, and water- and energy-conservation measures are in place.

Environmental:	∅∅∅∅∅
Social:	∅∅∅∅∅

Walking on Eyre

James Jeffrey discovered a land of contrasts on South Australia's Eyre Peninsula, from the dazzling whiteness of the Gairdner salt lake to the marine abundance of its west coast.

When it makes its first half-blinding appearance, Lake Gairdner is the light at the end of the tunnel. We round a bend with a dust cloud erupting from the back of our 4WD like a comet's tail and squint as the salt lake appears in a searing flash of white; it makes for a strangely divine vision out here in the semi-desert. The dry salt stretches for 160km (100 miles). As we walk out onto its hard, brilliant surface, all we can see is but a small leg of it, but from where we stand it looks as vast and as white as the Siberian steppes.

I've been on the road with Geoff Scholz – local, guide, effective environmental activist and co-owner of Gawler Ranges Safaris – barely a couple of hours, travelling across South Australia's shark-tooth-shaped Eyre Peninsula. We crossed an archipelago of saltbush spread pale and blue across the orange sand to the Middleback Ranges, passing through such places as the small mining community of Iron Knob – a still life with houses and a public toilet proclaiming 'DUNNY' in huge, gleaming letters – and a property called Siam, which announced itself with a small sign and a Neighbourhood Watch poster. ('A lot of people smile at

This page: Geoff Scholz standing on the hard salt surface of Lake Gairdner

This page: Wildlife on the Gawler Ranges – a blue wren and Wallaroos, which can be found in abundance

that,' Geoff noted. 'But these guys really know what's going on.')

From Gairdner, we head off towards the Gawler Ranges – volcanically formed and now the site of one of Australia's youngest national parks – nearly 650km (400 miles) northeast of Adelaide. Our progress is marked by comically bounding flocks of emus. We cross dry riverbeds and pass mountains, umbrella-like myall trees and rocks shaped into cubes and organ pipes, casting shadows in which wallabies lie.

Wallaroos, western grey kangaroos and the towering, muscular reds all cross our path, some lounging in the pools of shade under the myall trees, some erupting in furry, bounding columns. Geoff keeps apologizing for their diminutive numbers ('Normally we'd see a couple of hundred in a day'), but he is, of course, talking from another perspective. He grew up in the outback, but the 70 or so we see strikes me as rather a lot.

And then we're in the wombat zone. A network of wombat trails fans out through the grey grass like a version of the Los Angeles freeway system writ small; I can't help imagining the wombat gridlock here during the homeward rush hour just before dawn. One of Australia's rarest mammals – a young, southern hairy-nosed wombat – eyes us from the top of its burrow.

This sprawling, extraordinary landscape was once a sheep station that happened to be home to a number of rare species. There was a growing push a few years back for the state government to buy the property and turn it into a national park, but there was an obstacle – which is where Geoff stepped in.

'We invited three politicians who were not going to sign the purchase of the property to tour with us,' Geoff says in his laconic

The deep red, native plant, Sturt's Desert Pea

are loosely clustered around a mess hut lined with corrugated aluminium from World War II-era beer cans. At Kangaluna Camp, gas is used for hot water and cooking, but the rest runs on solar power. Geoff gets busy working his magic on porterhouse steak and mango salad, sharing stories about Eyre Peninsula life as he goes.

Charles Carlow, the owner of Bamurru Plains (see pages 270–1) and founder of specialist travel company Wilderness Australia, which markets Gawler Ranges Safaris, considers Geoff the perfect host and guide – as well as a great exponent of responsible tourism. 'Geoff's lived [in the Gawler Ranges] all his life,' says Charles. 'He's pretty much responsible for getting the national park established there. Kangaluna is just three tents, but it's very natural. There's good food, good wine and during the day when you're out there in the ranges or along the Eyre Peninsula, it's a fantastic safari

way. 'This convinced them to sign the sale.' The Gawler Ranges National Park was declared in early 2002.

As the sun settles onto the horizon, we reach Geoff's home-away-from-home, Kangaluna. Just down the road from Geoff's actual home in the small farming town of Wudinna, the camp comprises three luxury safari tents set in a gorgeous patch of bush near a pair of dry lakes. The two-bedroom tents, which are fitted out with hand-made wooden furniture and beds that grant guests the sleep of the innocent, are placed far enough apart for a sense of privacy to prevail, and

Left to right: The tents at Kangaluna Camp; swimming with sea lions

experience. But the experience is very much Geoff. You can have the best camp in the world, but if you haven't got the personality to deliver the experience, you only get half way. Geoff is great.'

I could happily potter around Kangaluna for days, but we have an appointment to keep with Trish and Alan Payne at Baird Bay on the western Eyre Peninsula, a stretch of coast punctuated with places of death (Coffin Bay), love (Venus Bay) and inter-mediate sensations (Anxious Bay).

Equipped with short wetsuits, masks and snorkels, we join Alan on his boat. Out beyond the towering cliffs, the great white sharks lurk, but here in the sheltered bays the sea lions wobble their way in safety along the shoreline of a small island. There are mothers with pups and watchful bulls built like trucks. Heads surface as a squadron of bulls setting out on a hunt slows down to examine us.

Then it's our turn to join them and our local guides in the water. I slip beneath the surface and the sea lions magically transform into ballet dancers. They frolic, they drift as languidly as seahorses and they accelerate like missiles, propelling their hundreds of kilos of flesh out of the water and somehow missing us as their great bulks come splashing down.

I eventually emerge from the water cold but high, ready to shout the Eyre Peninsula's name joyfully to the heavens. Seeing the expression on my face, Geoff smiles. I suspect he knows exactly how I'm feeling.

ECO**FILE**

Location: Wudinna, 566km (354 miles) from Adelaide, on the Eyre Peninsula, South Australia.
Getting there: From Adelaide, fly to Port Lincoln, where you will be met for the 2.5-hour transfer to Wudinna. Alternatively, drive 6.5 hours to Wudinna via Port Augusta.
CO_2 emissions: Rtn flight to Adelaide from New York 5.68 tonnes; London 5.33; Sydney 0.27 Rtn transfers by plane and car 0.22; by car 0.34.
Offset cost: $87.60; £41.55; A$9.10.
Staying there: Accommodation is provided in safari tents.
Rates: A$1,538 (US$1,280) per person for the 3-day, 2-night Sea Lion and Outback Experience, including accommodation and all meals. Other tours are available.
Further information: www.gawlerangessafaris.com
Best time to go: Avoid the heat of Dec–Feb. No tours Jun–Jul.

Responsibility: Geoff Scholz is passionate and knowledgeable about the environment and he shares this with visitors. He works respectfully with other locals and helps generate income for businesses in the area. Kangaluna is run on a mix of solar power and gas. Waste is recycled and organic waste is composted. All impacts are minimalized.

Gunya Titjikala

Level 57, MLC Centre, 19 Martin Place, Sydney, New South Wales 2000, Australia
+61 (0)2 9211 2322 / www.gunya.com.au / bookings@gunya.com.au

AS the late-afternoon breeze blows across the desert, it ruffles the silvery puffs of spinifex and whistles around the poles of the tents at Gunya Titjikala. On their raised timber decks, the tents gently creak like boats on a rippled sea of red sand. It makes for a surprisingly nautical effect in the middle of the Australian outback, thousands of kilometres from the sea.

Then the breeze fades with the sun, leaving the sky to fill with the horizon-to-horizon blaze of the Milky Way; nowhere do starry skies shine with the same sense of majesty as in the middle of the desert. And among all those stars are the darker shapes of the Aboriginal constellations such as the emu and the hunter, forever locked in the chase. They won't stay a mystery though, as someone from the nearby

Aboriginal community of Titjikala will be able to help you see the night through indigenous eyes and talk you through an astrological system far older than the more familiar one dreamed up by ancient Babylonians.

Gunya Titjikala has a way of bridging cultures like that. Both a promising joint venture and an intriguing experiment, it's the result of Gunya Tourism joining forces with Titjikala to create an experience that not only introduces visitors to the indigenous cultures of central Australia in a surprisingly powerful way, but also galvanizes the community in the process, involving them at all levels and generating real income.

It is the locals who make the experience so memorable. Whether you're sitting around talking on the bank of a dry river, hearing stories, learning about art, going out in search of bush tucker, or travelling through the startling landscape and its diamond-edged light to places such as Chambers Pillar, you start to get at least an inkling of the profound attachment the people of Titjikala have to the land. Best of all, there is much that is happily idiosyncratic in the Titjikala experience and little that feels choreographed. Even after just a couple of days with them, there's a very real possibility you'll never look at the outback quite the same way again.

Back at the camp, the Gunya dining experience is a fusion of western cuisine and traditional bush food – often including ingredients collected by guests and their hosts – accompanied by Aboriginal stories over dinner.

At an accommodation level, things have been kept simple with an air of laid-back luxury. Each safari tent and its veranda is set on poles 2m (6ft) above the sand. Screen windows allow any breeze to pass through, keeping the interior surprisingly cool, even in the fierce heat of a desert midsummer day. Interiors include polished timber floors, sofas, king-sized beds that can become singles, and en suites that are partly open to the sky and equipped with bathtubs comfortable enough to lie in for hours, gazing up at the extraordinary spread of stars and the dark gas clouds intertwined with them.

ECO**FILE**

Rooms: Five double/twin safari tents with en suites.

Rates: A$1,300 (US$1,080) per tent per night, including all meals, community tour and cultural activities. Minimum 2-night stay.

Location: On the edge of the Simpson Desert, 120km (75 miles) south of Alice Springs, Northern Territory.

Best time to go: Autumn for mild temperatures; spring for desert wildflowers; or summer (Dec–Feb) for the vivid colours of the landscape.

Getting there: From Alice Springs, drive by 4WD for 2 hours.

CO_2 emissions: Rtn flight to Alice Springs from New York 5.66 tonnes; London 6.08; Sydney 0.45. Rtn transfers 0.07.

Offset cost: $85.25; £46.15; A$9.75.

Responsibility: Half your tariff is put directly into the Titjikala community to support health initiatives and school retention programmes, to provide meaningful employment, to reduce welfare dependence, to promote social stability and to encourage the practice of traditional culture. Gunya Titjikala is run as a genuine joint venture between Gunya Tourism and the Titjikala community. It also gives visitors a genuine glimpse of Aboriginal Australia. Electricity usage at the camp is minimal and locally generated.

Environmental: ⌀⌀⌀⌀⌀
Social: ⌀⌀⌀⌀⌀

Inala

320 Cloudy Bay Road, Bruny Island, Tasmania 7150, Australia
+61 (0)3 6293 1217 / www.inalabruny.com.au / inala@inalabruny.com.au

BETWEEN the Tasmanian devils and the deep blue sea, Bruny Island is a quietly special place. Clinging to each other like a pair of non-identical twins via a sandy isthmus, North and South Bruny are separated from the Tasmanian mainland only by the dark, narrow waters of D'Entrecasteaux Channel, but together they make up an island that feels like a world of its own. It's a Tasmania in miniature, with environments spanning from bucolic farmland and golden bays, to dripping temperate rainforests and a wild southern coast pounded ragged by the swells rising up from Antarctic seas.

It's also a place that, unusually for the natural world, seems to have a soft spot for blondes – rare albino forms of possums and carnivorous quolls, and white Bennett's wallabies bounding through the ferns like plump ghosts. Somehow Dr Tonia Cochran, who sports what looks like anything up to half an acre of blonde hair herself, fits right in.

A zoologist, botanist, conservationist and farmer, Dr Cochran is also the owner, host and main guide at Inala Sanctuary, a 200ha (500-acre) slice of South Bruny on the road to Cloudy Bay, a major haven for the island's wildlife and a major heaven for birdwatchers.

There are two choices of accommodation set amid Inala's pasture (cropped by Dr Cochran's cows) and bushland. There's the original farmhouse, a simple but very appealing three-bedroom cottage that was recently renovated and sports all the modern conveniences, views to the South Bruny Ranges and, on chilly winter days, a curl of smoke from the chimney. A more recent addition has been Nairana Cottage, a one-bedroom spa unit with thoughtfully large windows to make bird- and wildlife-spotting easier.

ECOFILE

Rooms: Three-bedroom cottage and a 1-bedroom spa unit.
Rates: From A$180 (US$150) per night for the 3-bedroom cottage, excluding guided tours.
Location: South Bruny Island, 87km (54 miles) and a short ferry ride south of Hobart, Tasmania.
Best time to go: Year-round.
Getting there: From Hobart, drive one hour south to Kettering, then take a 15-min ferry ride to Bruny Island and drive 45 mins to the lodge.
CO2 emissions: Rtn flight to Hobart from New York 5.46 tonnes; London 5.88; Sydney 0.25. Rtn transfers 0.05.
Offset cost: $81.90; £44.50; A$5.60.

Responsibility: Inala combines sustainable farming with serious conservation work. Ongoing projects here include replanting, protection of waterholes and the fencing off of rare plant life. Owner Tonia Cochran is a very active advocate of Bruny Island, the natural environment and ecotourism, setting an example in a state not famed for its environmental practices. She also creates business for her fellow islanders.
Environmental: ⌀⌀⌀⌀⌀
Social: ⌀⌀⌀⌀⌀

All around them stretch Inala's grounds. A fifth of this has been cleared for sustainable farming, but the rest is bush – mainly tall, wet eucalypt forest vibrating with at least 90 of Bruny's 141 bird species. Not least among them is the endangered forty-spotted pardalote; more than half of the world's remaining population of this species lives on Bruny, and Inala is home to one of the biggest colonies. It's not unusual to see them going about their business in the trees near the cottages.

Dr Cochran offers guided walks along the bush trails that wind their way through Inala. This allows visitors to experience both the beauty of the environment with the help of an expert's eyes, and to see some of the conservation work being carried out. There is also the option of tours beyond Inala and into the rainforest, and to spots like Adventure Bay. It lives up to its name, with a comprehensive roll call of early European visitors, including James Cook, Abel Tasman and William Bligh, not to mention the pods of whales that pass through each year.

But it's Dr Cochran's night tours that reveal some of the real magic of Bruny, from platoons of fairy penguins to rare gold-furred quolls bounding off into the darkness like creatures from a dream.

Kooljaman

PMB 8, Cape Leveque, via Broome, Western Australia 6725, Australia
+61 (0)8 9192 4970 / www.kooljaman.com.au / leveque@bigpond.com

ECOFILE

Rooms: Various options, from camping sites to safari tents.
Rates: From A$16 (US$13) per person per night for a camping site, to A$240 (US$200) per night for a safari tent (1 queen bed and 2 singles). Minimum 2-night stay.
Location: Cape Leveque, Dampier Peninsula, 225km (140 miles) north of Broome, Western Australia.
Best time to go: Apr–Oct for the dry season; Jul–Oct for the whale season.
Getting there: From Perth, take a 2.5-hour flight to Broome then drive north by 4WD for 3 hours, or fly 1 hour by light plane to Cape Leveque.
CO2 emissions: Rtn flight to Broome via Perth from New York 6.75 tonnes; London 4.98; Sydney 0.74. Rtn transfer by car 0.12; by plane 0.06.
Offset cost: $102.05; £38.25; A$16.

Responsibility: All members of the local One Arm Point and Djar-indjin communities are shareholders in Kooljaman, and all profit goes to them. The camp creates local jobs, it works with conservation bodies on projects such as revegetation, waste is recycled, and electricity is used only for lighting and refrigeration.
Environmental: ⌀⌀⌀⌀⌀
Social: ⌀⌀⌀⌀⌀

IT'S a long and bumpy road that leads to Kooljaman's front door, a gash of red dirt stretching 225km (140 miles) north from Broome in Western Australia's Kimberley region. More delicate souls may prefer to go by light plane, but in a 4WD this road is a quintessential outback experience.

The journey is well worth it, because, facts be faced, Cape Leveque is a stunning. Jutting from the tip of the Dampier Peninsula in the northwest corner of Australia, this is where the paprika red of the interior collides with the luminous blue of the Indian Ocean and the white of the beaches; beaches, it might be added, that are almost entirely empty, thanks in part to that long dirt road.

There are worse ways to start the day than surveying the beach from the deck of one of the safari tents at the Aboriginal-owned Kooljaman. The camp offers a range of accommodation, from camping sites and basic (but fun) beach shelters made from palm fronds, to log cabins and those luxury safari tents, which perch on raised timber decks and

have balconies, kitchenettes and en suites. There is also a restaurant, a 'bush butler' service for those who prefer to dine at 'home', and the proper Australian answer to the question of matters culinary: barbecues – the ideal place to cook the fish you just caught.

Kooljaman is jointly owned by members of two local Aboriginal communities – One Arm Point and Djarindjin – both of which are part of the Bardi nation. Their mission to create a low-impact development that both generates employment and shows visitors this weepingly beautiful region through Bardi eyes has been an award-scooping success.

Many of the activities on offer involve the expert guidance of the locals. They include Aboriginal cultural tours of the area – we're talking here about one of the oldest living cultures amid one of the planet's most geologically ancient landscapes – as well as fishing and crabbing expeditions, and tours of the old mission ruins and coral reef of nearby Sunday Island. For fun with altitude, there are scenic flights over the Buccaneer Archipelago – a sight of arresting pulchritude – and the Horizontal Waterfalls, where the Kimberley's massive tidal forces work their wild, foaming magic through a series of pink and orange chasms.

Then there are the simple pleasures of puttering around in a dinghy or lolling in the bath-like sea. Kooljaman's owners are keen to empha-

size that, uncharacteristically for the Kimberley, crocodiles and stinger jellyfish have never posed a problem in these waters. Humpback whales, on the other hand, do put in regular appearances from July to October, often passing close to the beach with their newborn calves as they migrate south for the Antarctic summer.

Lord Howe Island

New South Wales 2898, Australia
+61 (0)2 6563 2114 / www.lordhoweisland.info / lhi.visitorcentre@bigpond.com

WITH the twin peaks of Mt Gower and Mt Lidgbird looming moodily over its southern tip, Lord Howe Island overcomes its diminutive size to present one of the most visually striking landscapes Australia has to offer. It's close enough to the mainland to be able to pop over for a short visit, yet far enough for an air of carefree isolation and a lingering sense of a bygone Australia where cars were few and no one bothered locking their doors.

Arguing that Lord Howe has the best of a whole bunch of worlds isn't the trickiest of assignments. It's warm enough to have palm trees, the world's southernmost coral reef, and swarms of green turtles, butterfly fish and rays as big as table tops – but without the crushing humidity, box jellyfish and crocodiles that can so enliven jaunts to the tropics. At just under 11km (7 miles) long and curled delicately around a shimmering lagoon; it's small enough to feel intimate, yet somehow

manages to squeeze in epic scenery and a smorgasbord of environments, from clownfish-dotted reefs and sublime beaches to shadowy banyan groves and mist-draped cloud forests. Just to cap things off, the world's tallest rock spire – Ball's Pyramid – thrusts 562m (1,844ft) out of the sea nearby like a giant fang.

Between the landscape and the extraordinary profusion of wildlife, it shouldn't come as

much of a surprise to learn that Lord Howe gained UNESCO World Heritage status back in 1982, the same year as the Galápagos Islands. Thanks to careful management and the sensitivity of the islanders, it has fared the best of the two.

For starters, you can't just turn up. Accommodation has to be booked from the mainland and there's a strict limit on the number of visitors at any one time – a very civilized 400, which matches the number of full-time residents – so Lord Howe never feels crowded. Once here, almost everyone gets around on foot or by bicycle.

Rare species have found sanctuary here, and some – like the Lord Howe Island woodhen – have been pulled back from the brink of extinction, thanks to careful revegetation programmes and the eradication of feral animals. Much of the credit for these successes lies with the islanders themselves, who are generally from families that have been here for generations and are in touch with their environment to an extraordinary degree. They know they have something special and are keen to see it stay that way; it's an entire community living according to World Heritage rules.

Accommodation spans the full spectrum, from self-catering units to luxury lodges. The longest lived of them all is the venerable Pinetrees resort, which has been in the hands of one family for more than a century – an achievement of some magnitude in a country as young as Australia.

ECO**FILE**

Rooms: Range from self-contained units to suites at luxury lodges.

Rates: Rooms at Lorhiti Apartments start at A$90 (US$75) per couple per night, including airport transfers. At the other end of the scale, a night at the Capella Lodge starts from A$550 (US$460) per person per night, including breakfast, dinner and airport transfers.

Location: In the Tasman Sea, 663km (411 miles) east of Port Macquarie, New South Wales.

Best time to go: Oct–May, though birders will be best rewarded in Oct–Nov, when the migratory seabirds begin arriving.

Getting there: From Sydney, fly to the island in just under 2 hours.

CO2 emissions: Rtn flight to Sydney from New York 5.21 tonnes; London 5.63. Rtn transfer 0.23.

Offset cost: $80.40; £43.70; A$3.65.

Responsibility: The locals are protective and proud of their island. Programmes are in place to preserve local species and to restore native vegetation. Businesses and accommodation are mainly locally owned and run. Recycling and careful waste management protocols are followed. Visitor numbers are limited to 400, and the main forms of transport are bicycle and walking.

Environmental: ∅∅∅∅∅

Social: ∅∅∅∅∅

Should I buy Aboriginal art?

ABORIGINAL Australia is responsible for some powerful and striking imagery, the flowering of the world's longest continuing art tradition. Who wouldn't want even a little piece of that for themselves?

But in recent years, the tradition of at least 40,000 years has also become a boom industry, one crowded with frauds and cowboys, sharks, speculators and cultural thieves. Northern Australian writer Nicolas Rothwell describes the scene as one of moral decay.

Whether it's the bona fide artists, or the imposters cranking out fakes and junk for souvenir shops, most of the money gets scooped up by retailers and middlemen. For the successful artists, things can get complicated amid the tangles of obligation and responsibility in their remote communities. The pressure from family and community members – not to mention the dealers – to produce art at a

conveyor-belt rate can ultimately prove overwhelming for both the artists and their art.

What makes things worse is the almost complete absence of meaningful criticism of Aboriginal art, partly because most art critics are unable to come to grips with what is an alien symbolic universe.

But the situation isn't completely dire. Start by visiting websites such as www.aboriginalart.org, which provides links to many Aboriginal-owned and operated art centres, and www.ankaaa.org.au – the website of the Association of Northern, Kimberley and Arnhem Aboriginal Artists – for a more detailed guide to purchasing Aboriginal art.

Art should come with a certificate of authenticity. This should provide information about the artist (name, language group), the artwork (title, the story behind it, when and where it was made), and, ideally, a statement from the artist.

When you're planning to buy, ask the dealer or art centre operator more questions about the work, the artist, the cultural context of the work, and also about how the artist is paid. This way it can be possible to buy Aboriginal art in a culturally ethical way that brings maximum benefit to the artists and their communities.

Ningaloo Reef Retreat

PO Box 471, Exmouth, Western Australia 6707, Australia
+ 61 (0)8 9949 1776 / www.ningalooreefretreat.com / info@ningalooreefretreat.com

A WHOLE continent away from the traffic, crowds, pontoons and cheap souvenir shops of the Great Barrier Reef lies an altogether more enticing coral experience. Remote even by Australian standards, and only just being discovered by the eastern states, Ningaloo Reef stretches 420km (260 miles) along the North West Cape of Western Australia's central coast. Ningaloo is home to some 250 species of coral and at least 500 species of fish. Some of the bigger creatures include dugongs, manta rays, whales and, for a few months each year as they pass through on their enigmatic annual migration, whale sharks.

Ningaloo Reef Retreat has a front-row seat for most of the action. A kilometre (half a mile) along a walking trail from its unmarked car park, it's discreetly tucked away among sand dunes and comprises a series of smart wilderness tents. The rugged limestone Cape Range provides the backdrop, while the front yard is a long and splendidly empty beach that slopes into the ultramarine water in a radiance of white sand and orange pebbles.

And then there's the reef. For those used to the Great Barrier Reef, where access to the coral generally involves long trips in boats, Ningaloo comes as a surprise. Here, the reef begins just 10m (11yds) from the beach. With snorkelling gear provided by the retreat, it's easy to feed yourself into the gentle current that helpfully swishes along the

reef like a liquid conveyor belt parallel to the beach. Thanks to this current, you're able to drift with little effort or movement, allowing you to focus more on the wildlife. This includes technicolour parrot fish, lionfish with their fins arranged in a burlesque array of feathers and fans, turtles dozing among coral shelves and giant clams. It's a world of constant movement and kaleidoscopic, almost overwhelming colour, all enhanced by the shimmering clarity of the water. To make some sense of it all, guided snorkelling and kayaking tours are offered – and they are knowledgeable affairs.

When you're ready to work on your land legs again, trails meander from the camp up through the wildflowers, past emus and kangaroos, into the gorges of the Cape Range.

The camp itself is loosely clustered around a central dining and kitchen tent. Each tent is set on a wooden deck with a small veranda and, crucially, a hammock. Inside are queen-sized beds and en suites that are open to the elements but kept private with carefully positioned shade cloths. The showers are solar-powered and the toilets are of the composting variety.

As dinner is prepared at night, you can appreciate the isolation in a different way. With no pollution and the nearest town almost an hour's drive away, the night sky is so clean and undiminished by ambient light, you can watch Venus setting into the sea.

ECO**FILE**

Rooms: Wilderness tents with en suites.

Rates: From A$440 (US$370) per single tent per night, or A$720 (US$600) per double tent. Low-price packages are also available.

Location: Cape Range National Park, 60km (37 miles) from Exmouth, Western Australia.

Best time to go: Apr–Jun is the peak of the whale shark season; humpback whales are commonly seen Aug–Oct; and Oct–Feb is the best time to see turtles nesting.

Getting there: From Perth, take a 1.5-hour flight to Exmouth, where you are collected for the 1-hour drive to the camp.

CO_2 emissions: Rtn flight to Perth from New York 6.37 tonnes; London 4.60; Sydney 0.72. Rtn transfers 0.35. **Offset cost:** $100; £37.15; A$20.65.

Responsibility: Ningaloo Reef Retreat is visually discreet, and raised decking and walkways minimize the impact on the fragile dune environment. Lighting and showers are solar-powered and toilets are waterless and composting. The retreat offers scholarships to postgraduate students in a variety of disciplines, including ecotourism, marine biology and anthropology. It also recruits local Exmouth-based staff annually, providing training in marine tourism.

Environmental: ⬤⬤⬤⬤◯
Social: ⬤⬤⬤◯◯

O'Reilly's Rainforest Retreat

Lamington National Park Road, via Canungra, Queensland 4275, Australia
+61 (0)7 5502 4911 / www.oreillys.com.au / reservations@oreillys.com.au

IT'S barely more than an hour's drive from the glitz and high-rise jungle of Surfer's Paradise, but you'd never know it. Surrounded by nearly 20,000ha (50,000 acres) of subtropical rainforest, O'Reilly's may as well be on an entirely different planet. It's been open since 1926, an accidental guesthouse that was born when the dairy farming O'Reilly family — five brothers and three cousins — refused to sell the land they'd bought from the Queensland state government just a few years before.

The government had changed its mind about farming and wanted to turn the area into a national park. As current managing director Shane O'Reilly explained, 'There was no way eight young hot-headed Irish people were going to agree on the time of day, let alone the price of land, so they didn't sell.'

More than 80 years later, the farm is gone, but the O'Reilly clan is still well and truly in place and that guesthouse has grown into a small village in the heart of the UNESCO World Heritage-listed Lamington National Park. A green pioneer long before the word ecotourism was ever coined, O'Reilly's offers tours of some of the most beautiful rainforest in the country. There's also an expansive network of walking trails, including a skywalk stretching 180m (200yds) through the trees some 15m (50ft) above the forest floor.

During the eight decades the guesthouse has been in operation, the accommodation options have expanded to include 66 rooms in a range of styles. The grandest of them all are the two-bedroom Canopy Suites, created when one of the original O'Reilly family homes was converted into two units. Each is distinguished by warm hues from floors of polished timber, cedar shutters and furniture handcrafted from Queensland maple. There are two bedrooms – one equipped with a four-poster king-sized bed – as well as a living room, fireplace, a spa bath on the deck, and the sort of view across the rainforest canopy to the McPherson Ranges that would suck the breath out of most lungs.

There are also one-bedroom Canopy Suites with similarly epic views, four-poster beds and floors of polished, recycled timber. The spa bath is inside, but located next to a huge picture window. The Mountain View rooms are smaller but still generous with their space. Again, timber is the dominant theme, including exposed beams across raked ceilings. The balcony is the perfect spot to watch the sun sink behind the McPherson Ranges in a blaze of saffron.

The Garden View Rooms are basically tastefully done motel-style rooms with cedar shutters and maple furniture and, as the name suggests, views of the luxuriant gardens. For those travelling solo, there's the option of the Bithongabel single rooms. From 2007, the Lost World Spa will also be part of the O'Reilly's menu.

ECO**FILE**

Rooms: 66 rooms, ranging from the luxurious 2-bedroom Canopy Suites to motel-style digs.

Rates: From A$155 (US$130) per single room per night, including morning and afternoon teas, to A$680 (US$570) for the 2-bedroom Canopy Suites. Check the website for frequent discounts.

Location: Lamington National Park, 100km (60 miles) south of Brisbane, southern Queensland.

Best time to go: Year-round, though orchid lovers should focus on Sep–Oct. O'Reilly's altitude of 900m (3,000ft) means it's always a little cooler here than on the coast.

Getting there: From Brisbane, drive south for 2 hours to the lodge.

CO_2 emissions: Rtn flight to Brisbane from New York 5 tonnes; London 5.43; Sydney 0.19. Rtn transfer 0.06.

Offset cost: $75.25; £41.20; A$4.65.

Responsibility: The O'Reillys incorporate three generations of accumulated knowledge into their operation and into educating their guests. Green features of the lodge include an environmental management plan; reduction policies for waste, recycling, water and energy usage, and greenhouse gas emissions; and support for research into the natural environment of Lamington National Park. Recycled materials are used where possible in construction. O'Reilly's also has a policy of hiring local staff and purchasing from local suppliers whenever possible.

Environmental: ⌀⌀⌀⌀⌀
Social: ⌀⌀⌀⌀⌀

Paperbark Camp

PO Box 39, Huskisson, New South Wales 2540, Australia
+61 (0)2 4441 6066 / www.paperbarkcamp.com.au / info@paperbarkcamp.com.au

ONE of the more entertaining ways to wake up is to the sound of a bird engrossed in conversation with itself in your bathroom mirror. This is always a possibility at Paperbark Camp, where the en suite bathrooms in the African safari tents are partly open to the sunshine and the breeze – as well as the inquisitive birdlife. Just wait for it, as you gently drift out of your morning dreams to a gentle tap-tap-tapping against the glass, then a long and involved twittering that sounds like a catch-up between long-lost friends.

Birdlife is just one of the wonderful things Paperbark Camp has in spades. Set among the woods by the banks of Currambene Creek near Jervis Bay, Paperbark is the result of the passion and bloody-minded persistence of owners Irena and Jeremy

Hutchings, who were obliged to push their way through more than four years of bureaucratic inertia to realize their dream.

The result is Paperbark, a camp of 12 safari tents surrounded by eucalypts and the ubiquitous parchment-skinned paperbark trees. There are trails through the wallaby-dotted woods to cycle on, and a broad, languid creek to canoe the few kilometres down to the great glittering sweep of Jervis Bay, home to some of the whitest sand in Australia.

The heart of Paperbark is the Gunyah, the chic main building and restaurant, which stands on stilts and, come night-time, appears to float among the trees. With its high, raked ceilings, a blazing fire on wintry nights and outdoor tables (with roving possums) during summer, the Gunyah is an attractive environment in its own right. And it has a menu to match, for it has established a reputation as the finest restaurant in NSW south of Sydney, which covers quite a lot of distance.

As you glance out from the Gunyah, you might have to remind yourself that there's a whole camp around you. None of the tents are far away, but each has been beautifully hidden at the end of a bush path that's softly lit at night. It meanders under a Milky Way so bright that an upward glance gives the impression of trees encrusted with stars. You can keep an eye on the constellations and the abrupt magnesium flare of shooting stars from the balcony of your tent or, come daytime, stretch out for an hour of massage.

The tents are perched on stilted wooden platforms above the forest floor and have solar-powered lighting, comfortable beds and indoor/outdoor en suites with showers. The two deluxe tents also offer corruptingly comfortable daybeds – the perfect spot from which to watch sunsets and moonsets – as well as a claw-foot bath, where you can soak in starlit water. Cotton sheets and sumptuously stuffed duvets keep you toasty even on the coldest nights, allowing you to fall asleep to the soft hooting of owls and the occasional plop of fish in the nearby creek.

ECO**FILE**

Rooms: Ten double safari tents and 2 deluxe safari tents, all with en suites.
Rates: From A$344 (US$290) per standard tent, including breakfast, or A$816 (US$680) for a 3-night stay.
Location: Near Huskisson, Jervis Bay, 200km (125 miles) south of Sydney, New South Wales,
Best time to go: Year-round. Oct–Mar is best for swimming.
Getting there: From Sydney, drive 2.5 hours south to the camp.
CO2 emissions: Rtn flight to Sydney from New York 5.21 tonnes; London 5.63. Rtn transfer 0.12.
Offset cost: $79.25; £43.15; A$2.25.

Responsibility: Paperbark Camp is visually discreet, and all buildings/tents are raised off the ground to minimize impact. Only a small amount of land had to be cleared for its construction, and that was done by hand to minimize disturbance. Lighting in the accommodation is solar-powered and hot water is heated on request only and by gas. Sewage and wastewater are pumped off site to protect the creek. Staff and owners are knowledgeable about local plants and animals, and guests are encouraged to interact with, and learn about, the natural environment.

Environmental: ⵁⵁⵁⵁⵁ
Social: ⵁⵁⵁⵁⵁ

Rawnsley Park Station

Wilpena Road, via Hawker, South Australia 5434, Australia
+61 (0)8 8648 0030 / www.rawnsleypark.com.au / info@rawnsleypark.com.au

WHEN first glimpsed from the air, Wilpena Pound – an amphitheatre of mountains thrusting out of the earth in the Flinders Ranges – can look strangely like a giant mouth, reaching up either to kiss the heavens or suck them down whole. The German-Australian artist Hans Heysen, on the other hand, looked to the ancient, worn ranges of this corner of the South Australian outback and declared them to be 'the bones of the earth laid bare'. With all its rich browns and ochres, this land has a very different sort of beauty to the Red Centre, but one that's scarcely any less dramatic. The artists keep coming, and so do the travellers.

A good few of them will have met Tony and Julieanne Smith, fifth-generation locals who have transformed what was a struggling sheep station in the shadow of Rawnsley Bluff at the southern end of Wilpena Pound into a successful tourism venture. For more than 20 years, the Smiths have offered camping sites, holiday units and even a caravan park (in a red earth gully, no less), but they took a new step in 2006 with the addition of four eco-villas.

Designed by Adelaide architect Paul Downton – a specialist in environmentally sustainable buildings – the villas perch on a ridge away from the hub of the station, with magnificent views of Wilpena Pound (and, come dusk, the local kangaroo population) generously framed by floor-to-ceiling windows. They come complete with that important outback accessory, the wrap-around veranda, and are the full luxury

experience: high raked ceilings, flat-screen televisions, artworks by local Aboriginal artists, South Australian wine, big en suites with deep tubs, towels of almost supernatural fluffiness, polished timber floors, solid timber furniture, and huge, scrumptious beds. There's even a large sky-light above the bed behind the retractable canvas ceiling, providing an all-too-rare opportunity to fall asleep in starlight.

What isn't so immediately apparent is the care that has gone into the design. Built from ren-dered straw bales, the villas use a host of pas-sive solar principles and natural ventilation to keep energy use to a minimum. Each has a rainwater tank and effluent is treated using a natural composting and filtration system.

Of course, it's not all fluffy towels and space-age toilets. There's a magnificent wilder-ness to explore, one rich in wildlife, light, vivid colours, vast silences and eagles' cries. Rawnsley Park Station's adventure menu includes 4WD safaris, scenic flights, treks on horseback and hiking tours. There are also mountain bikes available for hire, and then there's a swimming pool and restaurant back at the station to recover in afterwards.

ECO**FILE**

Rooms: Eco-villas, as well as camp-ing sites, caravans and units.

Rates: From A$320 (US$270) per eco-villa per night; from A$104 (US$90) per couple in a deluxe en suite unit; A$50 (US$42) per couple for an onsite caravan; A$10 (US$8) per person for a camping site.

Location: South of Wilpena Pound and 435km (270 miles) north of Adelaide, in the Flinders Ranges, South Australia.

Best time to go: Anytime other than summer (Dec–Feb).

Getting there: From Adelaide, drive 4–5 hours north to the station.

CO2 emissions: Rtn flight to Adelaide from New York 5.68 tonnes; London 5.33; Sydney 0.27. Rtn transfer 0.26. **Offset cost:** $88.25; £41.90; A$9.90.

Responsibility: The eco-villas have been built in a sustainable, low-impact and energy-efficient way. The owners are locals with a passion for and an extensive knowledge of the region. They work closely with the South Australian Department for Heritage and Environment to preserve the area's biodiversity, and recently turned 1,000ha (2,500 acres) of their property into a private wildlife reserve. They also create employment in a region where the farming sector is suffering.

Environmental: ∅∅∅∅∅
Social: ∅∅∅∅∅

Tribal welfare

James Jeffrey investigated a ground-breaking project in which 'tribe' members are recruited online to create a low-impact eco-village on a Fijian island. Is this the future of ecotourism?

We should be thankful Ben Keene and Mark James elected to use their powers for good instead of evil. When they dreamed up their scheme to recruit a 'tribe' over the Internet and create a community on a small Fijian island with secret beaches and so-called pirate caves, it could have been the start of a tacky reality TV series. But what they have on their hands instead is an audacious social and ecological experiment that might just result in the birth of an exciting new form of responsible tourism.

Despite a diverse array of adversity thrown their way in the early months – fire, tropical cyclone and even a military coup – Keene,

James and their ever-expanding tribe are succeeding in their mix of adventure, audacity and dreams made real. It is, as Keene puts it, 'people making history on a tiny ripple of rock, jungle and sand in the South Pacific'.

The heart of the Tribewanted project is Vorovoro, 80ha (200 acres) of picture-perfect island paradise off the northern coast of Vanua Levu, the second biggest of Fiji's islands.

Keene and James have rented the island until 2009 from Tui Mali, a local chief who, along with members of fishing communities on nearby islands, is consulted on all the tribe's actions and has become a major fan of the project. As he explained in an interview with the *Guardian* in early 2007, 'My people were worried about what was happening here, but once they heard that visitors were wearing *sulus* and trying to build like we do, everyone wanted to see.' Mali and his small family had been the sole inhabitants of

Vorovoro until the new tribe began arriving.

The plan is to develop the island in an ecologically and socially responsible way – no swimming pools, no air conditioning and not even a passing resemblance to Club Med – with the involvement of a tribe of 5,000. A maximum of 100 are allowed on the island at any one

This page, opposite and pages 302–3: Vorovoro island, home to a remarkable experiment in eco-tourism that combines low-impact island life with Internet technology

301

ECO**FILE**

Location: Vorovoro Island, off the north coast of Vanua Levu, Fiji.

Getting there: From Nadi on Viti Levu, fly to Labasa on Vanua Levu, where you are collected for the boat transfer to the island.

CO2 emissions: Rtn flight to Nadi from New York 3.96 tonnes; London 5.32; Sydney 0.70. Rtn transfers 0.09.
Offset cost: $60.20; £40; A$13.25.

Staying there: Accommodation on the island is in basic huts – the great *bure*, bunk house, or in tents.

Membership rates:
£120 (US$240) for 'nomads' staying for 1 week; £240 (US$480) for 'hunters' for 2 weeks; £360 (US $720) for 'warriors' for 3 weeks.

Further information:
www.tribewanted.com

Responsibility: The environmental impact of all actions is minimized and carefully measured. Toilets are composting, recycling and stringent waste management are practised, and there is no electricity. Local communities are carefully consulted and involved, and cultural interchanges take place between locals and tribe members. Community projects are supported with money and volunteer labour, and the project creates employment for Fijians. All carbon emissions generated by the tribe are offset.

time (although the number may be lowered), but tribe members stay involved via the Internet, keeping tabs on what's going on, voting and having their say in what happens on the island. It's an Internet community with real life consequences.

Anyone aged 18 and over can join, with membership fees starting at £120 (US$240) for 'nomads', who are entitled to a week on the island, ranging up to £360 (US$720) for 'warriors', who get three weeks. Once there, members live in the evolving village, which is centred around a communal *bure*, or Fijian thatched hut. Along with some requisite tropical island lazing, snorkelling and the like, tribe members pitch in with the help of a small army of paid locals from a neighbouring island. No one is under any obligation to do anything more than wash up their own plate, but there's work to be done – as well as discussed with the rest of the Vorovoro community online.

When we caught up with Keene in May 2007, he was taking some time out from island activities like 'dancing around the pig's head' to work on a book he's writing about the Tribewanted experience.

'A lot has happened since the "first-footers" arrived on the island on September 1st 2006,' he said. 'A basic village infrastructure has been built including 50,000 litres (13,000gal) of rainwater storage, compost toilets, bucket showers, a great *bure* (large community house). We've now got a kitchen with oven, we've got composting, a recycling unit and wormery, outdoor dining tables, a family *bure*, a chief's *bure*, super-shed, treehouse, farm, football park, and landscaped gardens.'

By this stage, 1,170 tribe members had joined from 35 countries, and of those 250 had already visited Vorovoro. Nearly 50 votes had been cast online and more than 15,000 posts made by members, ranging from detailed musings about how to improve the composting system to plans for the first Tribewanted wedding. A library had been built for the local school and filled with more than 500 books brought to the island by members.

'We have had our challenges,' Keene explained. 'Organizing the community online and on island has been complex but worth the effort, a fire on the island in the first month was interesting, a coup in Fiji almost closed down the project, and a cyclone in February almost smashed up the village. But it didn't and we're here and it's an experience of a lifetime for all involved.'

As for the future and the possibility that the Tribewanted concept could spread beyond this small, intimate corner of the Fijian archipelago, Keene said it was all a bit of a question mark.

'For me it's about getting it right here on Vorovoro first. We're on our way but we're not there yet. If it works here then it could work elsewhere. For me the two biggest successes of the project so far have been one, the involvement of travellers in their holiday destination before, during and after their stay. They are as knowledgeable about this place and culture as I expect they have been about any of the places they have travelled

to, and many of them haven't even been here yet.

'Two, that the focus of the project on embracing and protecting the local culture seems to have reawakened a local interest in their own heritage, be it through *mekes* (traditional dances), *bure* building, or the relationship with their chief.

'At the end of the three-year project it will be up to the island chief, Tui Mali, as to what happens. He and his community will own everything that has been built on the island. The purpose of the online community is to extend the island experience beyond members' physical stays on Vorovoro and to build a democratic decision-making system that influences the sustainable development of Vorovoro.'

Jean-Michel Cousteau Fiji Islands Resort

Savusavu Bay, Vanua Levu, Fiji
+1 415/788-5794 (reservations office) / www.fijiresort.com / info@fijiresort.com

WHEN a star oceanographer falls in love with an island, you know it's got something going for it, especially when that oceanographer happens to be none other than Jean-Michel Cousteau, son of Jacques. This 9ha (22-acre) resort was born of Cousteau's all-embracing love affair with Fiji, resulting in an experience that combines luxury with natural beauty, strong and meaningful interaction with the local community, and some revelations about the intricacies of life on a coral reef.

Guests stay in a range of 25 refined *bures* (thatched houses) just a few steps from the water. Each has cathedral ceilings, four-poster beds, daybeds, rattan furniture, polished floors and bathrooms with Italian tiles. To improve natural airflow, each *bure* is elevated and has windows fitted with wooden louvres. As an extremely thoughtful finishing touch, they have neither telephones nor televisions.

The resort offers a range of spa and massage treatments, and dining is either by the candlelit pool or in the open-air restaurant; some of the menu items come from the resort's gardens, which are designed to be edible rather than just ornamental.

With Cousteau directing and shaping the resort's programmes, ecology and local culture are the twin driving forces here. To this end there

is both a marine biologist and a cultural officer on staff, and both are heavily involved in making guests more aware of the world they are immersing themselves in.

The cultural programmes include guided trips to villages, markets and church services, as well as storytelling sessions, kava ceremonies and traditional craft demonstrations. Less visibly, the resort has established the Savusavu Community Foundation, which works to protect the local environment, ecologically educate the local community, and provide medical services – including regular eye clinics – free to locals.

The marine biologist leads expeditions among the local coral reef and by boat out to spots such as the Namena Marine Reserve, which is just over 10km (6 miles) away and is regarded as one of the top ten dive spots in the world. Expeditions are tailored to the skill of the diver, but it's a good idea to have completed all theory and pool work before heading to Fiji; that way, you'll spend more time in the water.

Mangrove and rainforest tours, slide shows, seminars and even night-time snorkelling adventures are also on offer. There's a real desire to get across the richness, the diversity, the complexity and the delicacy of the world of the reef, and how it all ties in with Fijian cultural life. Cousteau doesn't want you to head home a happy diver; he wants you to go back out into the world as an ambassador.

ECO**FILE**

Rooms: 25 *bures* (thatched houses).
Rates: From F$620 (US$575) per night. Minimum stay of 3 nights.
Location: Savusavu Bay, Vanua Levu.
Best time to go: Year-round, though the water is warmest (around 28°C/83°F) Dec–May.
Getting there: From Nadi, fly 50 mins by turboprop to Savusavu, where you will be collected.
CO_2 emissions: Rtn flight to Nadi from New York 3.96 tonnes; London 5.32; Sydney 0.70. Rtn transfer 0.07.
Offset cost: $59.90; £40.40; A$14.30.

Responsibility: Among other initiatives, the resort minimizes its impact through recycling, using solar power, ensuring energy efficiency, treating wastewater and using it for irrigation, and putting organic waste into its gardens. Guests and locals are ecologically educated, and guests are introduced to local culture. Locals make up 98 per cent of the staff and are paid well above standard wages, local communities are regularly consulted and they are also provided with free health measures. In addition, a fund has been set up to benefit both the environment and the community.
Environmental: ⵁⵁⵁⵁⵁ
Social: ⵁⵁⵁⵁⵁ

Sonaisali Island Resort

PO Box 2544, Nadi, Viti Levu, Fiji
+679 670 6011 / www.sonaisali.com

IT may be one of the shorter boat rides in the world – just a three-minute zip across a lagoon in a launch from Fiji's main island of Viti Levu – but it takes you to the self-contained world of Sonaisali, a 42ha (105-acre) sliver of green and the very image of a quintessential South Pacific resort. Here, palm trees, caster-sugar sand, thatched beach umbrellas, crystalline swimming pools and a limpid blue sea are all infused with the easy warmth of service for which Fiji has gained such a reputation.

At the pleasant if relatively ordinary end of the accommodation options are 32 hotel rooms along the beachfront, complete with picture windows and balconies with views across the water. They are fully kitted out with just about everything, from air conditioning to satellite television. Families who want to travel together but maintain an element of privacy, can opt for interconnecting rooms.

But it's the *bures* (thatched houses), with their thatched roofs, high vaulted ceilings, plantation shutters and wooden decks, that give more of a South Pacific feel. All the *bures* are either on the beach or, at the very least, afford fine views of the shatteringly blue sea. There are three family *bures*, each with two bedrooms, a separate living room, satellite television and all the rest of it. The ocean *bures* are set back a little farther, but with water extending as far as the eye can see, while the beachfront spa *bures* go the extra distance, with spa baths set in their timber decks.

The main dining options are the Sunset Terrace, whose buffets are an open-air affair, and the Plantation, with air conditioning, silver service and a menu to match. At least some of the meal is likely to have come from Sonaisali's own hydroponic farm.

There is some exposure to Fiji's traditional culture in the form of dancing and firewalking performances, as well as some less staged dancing put on by staff and their relatives from the nearby village of Korovuto. Other activities span the spectrum from the sybaritic (spa treatments) through to the aquatically genteel (catamaran sailing and canoeing), the laddishly incongruous (paintball) and the Hemingwayesque (game fishing).

But it's the diving that has to be one of the main drawcards, particularly on the coral reefs among the Mamanuca Islands, a volcanic archipelago 20 minutes away by boat. There are day and night dives into this world of caves, wrecks, kaleidoscopic sealife and reef formations. Sonaisali, as a founding member of the Mamanuca Environment Society, is actively working to protect the environment here with money and with education for both staff and guests. Considering the many threats faced by coral reefs around the world, any friends they can get are valuable indeed.

ECO**FILE**

Rooms: 32 hotel rooms, 42 ocean-view *bures* (thatched houses), 46 beachfront spa *bures*, 3 beachfront family *bures*.

Rates: From F$485 (US$800) per night for a hotel room, based on double occupancy and including breakfast, to F$803 (US$1,330) for a family *bure*.

Location: Sonaisali Island, just off the west coast of Viti Levu, Fiji.

Best time to go: Year-round, but the water is warmer Dec–May.

Getting there: From Nadi, take a 15-min taxi ride to the jetty and then a 3-min boat ride to the resort.

CO2 emissions: Rtn flight to Nadi from New York 3.96 tonnes; London 6.33; Sydney 0.70. Rtn transfer 0.01.

Offset cost: $60.20; £39.95; A$13.25.

Responsibility: The resort is a founding and active member of Mamanuca Environment Society. Continual efforts are made to reduce waste, energy and water consumption, produce is grown hydroponically on the property and non-biodegradable chemicals are being phased out. Employment is created for locals, with special consideration going to villagers from nearby Korovuto, and staff are educated in ecotourism principles.

Environmental: ∅∅∅∅∅
Social: ∅∅∅∅∅

Awaroa Lodge

PO Box 163, Takaka, Golden Bay 7110, New Zealand
+64 (0)3 528 8758 / www.awaroalodge.co.nz / stay@awaroalodge.co.nz

SECRETED away in the Abel Tasman National Park at the northern
end of New Zealand's South Island, Awaroa is mercifully far from any
roads, leaving guests the arrival options of small plane, helicopter,
cruiser or aqua taxi. But those who want to take time to absorb the
landscape properly and radically slash their carbon emissions can kayak
in or hike along the Abel Tasman Track through the kanuka forest.

An absence of cars is usually four-fifths of tranquillity. Add in the
sweep of a golden bay, the blue Pacific and rugged hills cloaked in lush
forest, and the remaining fifth is pretty well in hand. Keeping true to this
atmosphere, the accommodation at Awaroa is stylish without ever being
over the top, decked out either in earthy or cool, almost Scandinavian
tones. Interiors and exteriors are marked by clean, simple lines.

Four open-plan family rooms each include a mezzanine level and
enough beds for eight people (a number that might put a slight dent
in that tranquillity). Most of the deluxe rooms can accommodate three
or four people, while the superior studio suites – which are more spacious, and include private decks and views of the forest and wetland –
fit up to three. In a blissful move, no televisions have been included;
there is, after all, a sense of isolation to be maintained, give or take the
wireless broadband.

Among the highlights of the restaurant are fresh seafood and fine
meats, along with wines from the nearby Nelson and Marlborough
regions. A large proportion of the fruit, herbs and vegetables used is
grown on the property, and organic waste that would once have been

ECOFILE

Rooms: Four family rooms, 10 deluxe rooms, 12 superior suites.
Rates: From NZ$235 (US$165) per room per night.
Location: Awaroa Bay, Abel Tasman National Park, at the northern tip of South Island.
Best time to go: Nov–Mar when the sea is warmer, or Mar–May to avoid the crowds.
Getting there: From Nelson, drive 1 hour or take a bus to Marahau, then catch a water-taxi 1.5 hours to the lodge. Alternatively, fly 20 mins by light plane directly to the lodge, or drive 2.5 hours to Totaranui and then walk for 2 hours or kayak for 45 mins to Awaroa.
CO_2 emissions: Rtn flight to Nelson via Auckland from New York 4.63 tonnes; London 6.36; Sydney 0.62. Rtn transfer by car to Marahau and water-taxi 0.01; by plane 0.02; by car to Totaranui 0.07.
Offset cost: $69.85; £48.20; A$12.85.

Responsibility: Feral pest animals are being eliminated, allowing the native bird population to recover, and the 4ha (10-acre) wetland has been restored to its pre-European state. Organic waste is composted and used to help grow food. Solar power is used for heating water, recycling is practised and environmentally friendly products used. Guests are offered exposure to Maori history, knowledge and traditions. Awaroa also contributes to the Nelson-Tasman Sustainable Tourism Charter.
Environmental:
Social:

expensively shipped away is now composted and put on the 750sq m (8,000sq ft) of organic garden; isolation is the mother of invention. It also means the menu is partly dictated by the seasons, and anyone who has weaned themselves away from supermarket produce knows this is a good thing.

Beyond the lodge, choices beckon from all directions. Awaroa is all but surrounded by forest thick with walking trails and the beach is scarcely more than 300m (984ft) away. If one beach isn't enough, there are sea-kayaks and sailing boats with which to explore the bay-scalloped coast.

Your perceptions of this world can be expanded with one of the Maori-guided tours on offer, which share the indigenous take on the forest and the coast. Whether you choose to go walking through the woods or kayaking among the islands and seal colonies off Awaroa, your guide will introduce you to the natural world as the Maori see it with the benefit of centuries of accumulated knowledge.

Wilderness Lodge Arthur's Pass

PO Box 33, Arthur's Pass, Canterbury, New Zealand
+64 (0)3 318 9246 / www.wildernesslodge.co.nz / arthurspass@wildernesslodge.co.nz

ECOFILE

Rooms: 20 Mountain View rooms, 4 Alpine Lodge rooms.
Rates: From NZ$290 (US$200) per person per night, including breakfast, dinner and nature tour.
Location: 16km (10 miles) east of Arthur's Pass on SH73, in South Island's Canterbury region. 130km (80 miles) from Christchurch.
Best time to go: Jun–Oct for skiing; otherwise year-round.
Getting there: From Christchurch, take the TranzAlpine train 2.5 hours to Arthur's Pass, or drive 1.5 hours to the lodge.
CO2 emissions: Rtn flight to Christchurch from New York 4.67 tonnes; London 6.50; Sydney 0.47. Rtn transfer by car 0.08. Train figures for New Zealand n/a.
Offset cost: $70.60; £49.30; A$10.20.

Responsibility The ecologically knowledgeable owners work closely with the NZ Department of Conservation to protect flora and fauna. Sheep farming is carried out in a sustainable way, maintaining traditions and providing employment while reducing impact. Buildings are oriented to maximize passive solar heating in winter and cooling in summer to reduce power consumption.
Environmental: ⊘⊘⊘⊘⊘
Social: ⊘⊘⊘⊘⊘

THE Maoris who came here first knew this part of the world in the bosom of New Zealand's Southern Alps as Te Ko Awa a Aniwaniwa, or the 'Valley of the Mother of Rainbows'. Confronted with the same scene centuries later, British settlers opted to call it the more prosaic Arthur's Pass.

One can only presume that Arthur was an unusually prepossessing man, as this is a place of monumental beauty. Wilderness Lodge Arthur's Pass sits in the thick of it, pulling off the tricky feat of uniting the disparate worlds of sheep farming, environmental protection, and some truly serious birdwatching.

Set on 3,000ha (7,500 acres) amid southern beech forests, lakes and rivers, and beneath soaring snowcapped mountains that would look familiar to anyone who's seen the cinematic version of *The Lord of the Rings*, the lodge is owned by ecologists Gerry McSweeney (who doubles as president of New Zealand's Royal Forest and Bird Society) and Anne Saunders.

Accommodation at the lodge is characterized by soft, earthy tones, big windows and huge views, along with the traditional high-country blend of stone, wooden beams and corrugated iron. The newest part comprises the four Alpine Lodge rooms, which are set in a secluded clearing with such essentials as a gas log fire, spa bath and a bed almost big enough to land a helicopter on.

The menu in the lodge's restaurant focuses on the sophisticated end of hearty (say venison or fillet of groper), which suits the crisp climate at this altitude, but vegetarian options are always available. Then there's a communal log fire to repair to afterwards.

Not surprisingly, walking is the main form of voluntary exertion here, and the lodge's property alone has 30km (20 miles) of trails ranging from the easy stroll to the strenuous. A daily hour-long guided nature trip is included in the tariff, and covers just about everything from the ecology of the beech and thorn forests and the wonderfully peculiar birdlife, to astronomy and the workings of the lodge's merino sheep farm. If you've ever wanted to shear, here's your chance.

The merinos' superfine wool is sent from here to the fashion houses of Italy and stands a decent of chance of coming back as, say, a Zegna suit. McSweeney and Saunders keep the farming sustainable by working on improving soil fertility and the quality of the pasture, thereby reducing the size of the area needed.

They also work with New Zealand's Department of Conservation to protect the environment, discovering rare plants in the forest near the lodge and nurturing populations of avian species such as the bellbird and the kea. The latter is one of the world's few alpine parrots and possibly the only one with a taste for sheep flesh, a habit that often used to place it at the wrong end of farmers' guns.

For an extra fee (ranging from NZ$88/US$61 to NZ$170/US$118), there are guided adventure tours that go farther into the wilds of the Southern Alps to explore rivers, caves, glaciers, moss forests, alpine wetlands and – snow bunnies take note – ski fields.

Contributors

Foreword

RICHARD HAMMOND writes a column on eco-travel for the *Guardian* and is the editor of the green travel website, greentraveller.co.uk. He edited Alastair Sawday's *Green Places to Stay* and has contributed to many publications including *BBC Wildlife*, *Geographical*, *Green Futures*, *New Consumer*, the *Observer*, *Resurgence*, the *Times*, and *Wanderlust*. Richard has also written several weighty tomes on responsible tourism. He helps judge the Responsible Tourism Awards and the *Guardian*'s Ethical Travel Award. Richard has recently been the Contributing Editor of the UK Travel Channel's new six-part series 'How to Holiday Greener'.

Main authors

REBECCA FORD is an award-winning travel writer with a keen interest in ecology and animal protection issues. She contributes regularly to UK publications such as the *Daily* and *Sunday Express*, as well as the *Evening Standard*, *Independent on Sunday* and Scotland's *Sunday Herald*. Rebecca is the author of several guidebooks to Italy and Wales. She specializes in writing about Britain, Italy, rail journeys, walking and wildlife, and is the main author of the Europe chapter.

JAMES JEFFREY is an award-winning travel writer for Australia's national newspaper, the *Australian*. Having grown up surrounded by wilderness and wildlife, James has long been an advocate of the natural environment. He has written for many other publications including the *Moscow Times*, the *Australian Review of Books*, the *Daily Telegraph* in Australia as well as Lonely Planet's *Code Green*. His recent book, *The Paprika Paradise,* is described as a true-life story of love, lard and family in provincial Hungary. James is the main author of the Australasia chapter.

NICK MAES is a travel writer, novelist and broadcaster. He writes regularly for the *Guardian*, *Intelligent Traveller* and the *Daily Mail*, as well as writing and presenting travel documentaries on BBC Radio 4. Nick writes a lot about Africa – a speciality – but is just as happy to be anywhere else on the globe. Ideally he would prefer to be found nosing around bazaars in East Africa or chilling on Himalayan mountain passes rather than at home in London. Nick has written two novels, *Not Dark Yet* and *The Africa Bar*. He is the main author of the Africa & the Middle East chapter.

RICHARD NEWTON has been involved in conservation his entire working life. He has worked as an education officer at Marwell Zoological Park, and as a wildlife officer for the Department of National Parks and Wildlife in Malawi, but since 1989 he has been a freelance writer and broadcaster, specializing in wildlife and sustainable tourism. Richard has a particular interest in wildlife of North America and the Caribbean and has won many awards for his writing. Richard is the main author of the North America & the Caribbean chapter, and contributed to the Africa chapter.

ALEX ROBINSON is a travel writer and photographer who has written extensively about green issues in Mexico, Central and South America in the British and Latin American press. His book on the Amazon, written together with his Brazilian wife Gardenia, was the first to cover nature-based and community tourism throughout the Amazon basin. Alex is the author of several guidebooks to Brazil and Rio de Janeiro. He is the main author of the Central & South America chapter, and also contributed to the North America chapter.

RORY SPOWERS is a writer and broadcaster who lives near Galle in Sri Lanka, with his wife and two sons. His most recent book, *A Year in Green Tea and Tuk-Tuks*, follows the creation of 'Samakanda', the transformation of an abandoned tea estate into a tropical 'forest garden', ecological learning centre and eco-tourism destination. Rory is also the author of *Rising Tides: A History of Ecological Thought*, as well as *Three Men on a Bike*, a bizarre tale of cycling though Africa with friends. Rory is the main author of the Asia chapter.

Contributing authors

ROBIN BARTON was born in England and raised in New Zealand, before travelling the world as a freelance writer and editor. He specializes in adventure sports and travel and contributes regularly to the *Independent on Sunday*. He is an occasional contributor to the *Guardian*, the *Observer*, the *Evening Standard* and the *Financial Times* and has written and edited several guidebooks. Robin wrote the features on sea-kayaking in Mexico and cycling in Scotland.

RUPERT ISAACSON divides his time between writing and working for the land rights of indigenous peoples. Rupert is the author of *The Healing Land: the Bushmen and the Kalahari*, and has written guide-books to African countries, India and elsewhere. He writes regularly for the *Daily Telegraph* and *Conde Nast Traveler*. His organization, the Indigenous Land Rights Fund, recently helped win the largest indige-nous land claim in African history on behalf of the Gana and Gwi San or Bushmen of Botswana's Central Kalahari Game Reserve. Rupert wrote the feature on hunting with the Kalahari Bushmen in Namibia.

Further information

The following organizations are good starting points for further information on responsible tourism:

- Association of Independent Tour Operators *www.aito.co.uk*
  Tourism industry association that requires its many members to adhere to responsible tourism guidelines.
- Ecotravel.com *www.ecotravel.com*
  Directory of eco-travel holidays around the world, with information on policies and practices.
- Equations *www.equitabletourism.org*
  A non-profit organization working towards holistic tourism in India.
- Ethical escape *www.ethicalescape.co.uk*
  Directory of responsible travel holidays and accommodation around the world.
- Ethical Traveler *www.ethicaltraveler.org*
  Educates travellers about the social and environmental impact of tourism.
- Green Traveller *www.greentraveller.co.uk*
  For green places to stay and tips on how to have a greener holiday.
- International Centre for Responsible Tourism (ICRT) *www.icrtourism.org*
  Based at Leeds University in the UK. Runs conferences and courses on responsible tourism.
- International Ecotourism Society (TIES) *www.ecotourism.org:*
  US-based responsible tourism organization with extensive online resources.
- International Tourism Partnership *www.tourismpartnership.org*
  A responsible business programme whose members include some of the big brands in hospitality and tourism.
- Nature Conservancy *www.nature.org*
  US-based NGO with international volunteer conservation programmes.
- Planeta *www.planeta.com*
  Database of information about eco-tourism and conservation projects.
- Responsible Travel *www.responsibletravel.com*
  Online travel agency with responsible holidays around the world.
- Responsible Ecological Social Tours (REST) *www.rest.or.th*
  Thai NGO offering community-based tourism in rural Thailand.
- Sustainable Travel International *www.sustainabletravelinternational.org:*
  US-based website with valuable advice on sustainable tourism.
- Tourism Concern *www.tourismconcern.org.uk:*
  UK-based charity that champions ethical and fair-trade tourism, and campaigns for human rights. Publishes the *Ethical Travel Guide* (see page 318).
- The Travel Foundation *www.thetravelfoundation.org.uk:*
  UK-based charity encouraging responsible and sustainable tourism.
- World Tourism Organization *www.unwto.org*
  A specialized agency of the United Nations and the leading international organization in tourism. Acts as a forum for tourism policy issues.
- World Wide Fund for Nature (WWF) *www.wwf.org*
  International conservation organization. Website includes information on responsible tourism.

Features and dilemmas

The features and ethical travel dilemmas in this book deal with a range of responsible-travel issues. They are listed below under related subject areas.

Active travel

Cycling (see pages 146–9)
- Sustrans www.sustrans.org.uk
- 7stanes mountain bike trails www.7stanes.gov.uk

See also
- Cycle Campaign network www.cyclenetwork.org.uk
- Cyclists' Touring Club www.ctc.org.uk
- Freecycle www.freecycle.org

Seakayaking (see pages 28–31)
- Baja Outdoor Activities www.kayakinbaja.com
- Journey Latin America www.journeylatinamerica.co.uk

See also
Advice for outdoor enthusiasts
- Leave No Trace www.lnt.org

Walking (see pages 132–5)
- ATG www.atg-oxford.co.uk
- Explore www.explore.co.uk
- Headwater www.headwater.com
- Inn Travel www.inntravel.co.uk
- The Ramblers Association www.ramblersholidays.co.uk
- Village Ways www.villageways.com (see pages 228–231)

See also
Everyday walking
- Walk to School www.walktoschool.org.uk
- WalkingBus.com www.walking bus.com
- Sustrans: Safe Routes to Schools www.saferoutestoschools.org.uk
- Living Streets www.livingstreets.org.uk

Yoga (see pages 252–5)
- Ulpotha www.ulpotha.com

Carbon offsetting (see pages 154–5)
The Carbon offsetting market is still developing and has been working on ways to increase its credibility as a means to reduce climate change. The Gold Standard, launched in 2003 for the CER market (Certified Emissions Reduction – for governments aiming to meet their Kyoto agreements), is considered the most stringent certification for carbon credits. In 2006 the Gold Standard launched a new version of the standard, applicable to projects in the VER market (Verified Emissions Reduction – for offsetting projects that exist in addition to the Kyoto Protocol emission reduction schemes). *Ethical Consumer*'s report on carbon offsetting, 'Enron Environmentalism?' found that, of the top carbon offsetting companies, those who can provide Gold Standard carbon credits included:
- Atmosfair www.atmosfair.de
- My Climate www.myclimate.org
- Climate Friendly www.climatefriendly
- Pure www.puretrust.org.uk

Those projects being assessed for the Gold Standard included:
- Carbon Neutral www.carbonneutral.com
- Carbon Offsets www.carbon-offsets.com
- Climate Care www.climatecare.org

Those without Gold Standard projects included:
- Climate Trust www.carboncounter.org
- Co2balance www.co2balance.com
- Driving Green www.drivinggreen.com
- Equiclimate www.ebico.co.uk
- Global Cool www.global-cool.com
- NativeEnergy www.nativeenergy.com

See also
- CDM Gold Standard www.cdmgoldstandard.org
- Choose Climate www.chooseclimate.org/flying

Further information

- 'Enron Environmentalism?' *Ethical Consumer*, Issue 106, May/June, 2007
- Tufts Climate Initiative *www.tufts.edu/tie/tci/carbonoffsets/*
- UK Department of Environment, Food and Rural Affairs *http://www.defra.gov.uk/environment/climatechange/uk/carbonoffset/faqs.htm*
- FoE, WWF and Greenpeace joint statement *www.foe.co.uk/resource/briefings/carbon_offsetting.pdf*

Train travel as an alternative to flying
- Man in Seat 61 *www.seat61.com*
- Rail Europe *www.raileurope.co.uk*
- National Rail (UK) *nationalrail.co.uk*
- Countrylink (Australia) *www.countrylink.com.au*
- Amtrak (USA) *www.amtrak.com*

Cars
Car hire (see pages 52–3)
- Bio-beetle *www.biobeetle.com*
- EV Rental *www.evrental.com*
See also
Greener motoring
- Environmental Transport Association *www.eta.co.uk*
- Australian Government's Green Vehicle Guide *www.greenvehicleguide.gov.au*
- UK Department for Transport, Act on CO2 *www.dft.gov.uk/ActOnCO2*
- Car Fuel Data *www.vcacarfueldata.org.uk*
Reducing Reliance on cars
- Car Free Cities *www.carfree.com*
- Autoholics Anonymous *www.autoholics.org*
- World Carfree Network *www.worldcarfree.net*
- Cutting Your Car Use *www.cuttingyourcaruse.co.uk*
- Greenergy *www.greenergy.co.uk*
- Veggiepower *www.veggiepower.org.uk*

Community tourism
Favela (slum) tourism (see pages 90–3)
- Be a Local *www.bealocal.com*
- Favela Tours *www.favelatour.com.br*
- Rio Hiking *www.riohiking.com*

Kalahari safaris (see pages 184–7)
Responsible tour operators
- Okavango Tours *www.okavango.com*
- Safari Drive *www.safaridrive.com*
Kalahari peoples
- Indigenous Land Rights Fund *www.landrightsfund.org*
- Kalahari Peoples Fund *www.kalaharipeoples.org*

Food
Wine and cheese (see pages 120–3)
- Ridge View *www.ridgeview.co.uk*
- Breaky Bottom *www.breakybottom.co.uk*
- Wensleydale Creamery, Hawes *www.wensleydale.co.uk*
- Northumberland Creamery *www.northumberlandcheese.co.uk*
- Caws Caerfai *www.cawscaerfai.co.uk*
- Pant Mawr Farmhouse Cheese *www.pantmawrcheeses.co.uk*
- Caws Cenarth Cheese *www.cawscenarth.co.uk*
- Lowna Dairy *www.lownadairy.com*
See also
- Specialist Cheesemaker's Association *www.specialistcheesemakers.co.uk*
- The Soil Association *www.soilassociation.org*
- The Greens–European Free Alliance *www.greens-efa.org*
- Compassion in World Farming *www.ciwf.org.uk* farm animal welfare
- National Farmers' Retail and Markets Association (FARMA) *www.farmersmarkets.net*
- Slow Food *www.slowfoodusa.org* *www.slowfood.com*

Human rights and human welfare

Poverty relief (see pages 208–9)
- Department for International Development *www.dfid.gov.uk*
- Oxfam International *www.oxfam.org*
- UNICEF *www.unicef.org*

Human Rights (see pages 242–3)
- Burma Campaign, UK and US *www.burmacampaign.org.uk* *www.uscampaignforburma.org*
- Voices for Burma *www.voicesforburma.org*
- Friends of the Maldives *www.friendsofmaldives.org*
- Tourism Concern *www.tourismconcern.org*

See also
- Amnesty International *www.amnesty.org*
- Human Right Watch *www.hrw.org*

Indigenous art (see pages 290–1)
- Aboriginal Art *www.aboriginalart.org*
- Association of Northern, Kimberley and Arnhem Aboriginal Artists *www.ankaaa.org.au*

See also
- Aboriginal Art Online *www.aboriginalartonline.com*
- Yothu Yindi Foundation *www.garma.telstra.com*
- Nyinkka Nyunyu Art and Culture Centre *www.nyinkkanyunyu.com.au*

Local experiences

World music (see pages 172–5)
- Gnaoua Festival, Morocco *www.festival-gnaoua.co.ma*
- Festival in the Desert, Mali *www.festival-au-desert.org*
- Busara Music Festival, Zanzibar *www.busaramusic.com*

See also
- World of Music, Art and Dance (WOMAD) *http://womad.org*

Local tours and eco-tourism projects (see pages 278–281, 300–3)
- Gawler Ranges Safaris *www.gawlerrangessafaris.com*
- Tribewanted *www.tribewanted.com*

Volunteering and conservation

(see pages 198–201)
- Discovery Initiatives *www.discoveryinitiatives.co.uk*
- Earth Watch *www.earthwatch.org*
- Biosphere Expeditions *biosphere-expeditions.org*

See also
- Action Without Borders *www.idealist.org*
- Green Volunteers *www.greenvol.com*
- United Nations Volunteers *www.unvolunteers.org*
- World Volunteer Web *www.worldvolunteerweb.org*
- The Conservation Foundation *www.conservationfoundation.co.uk*
- Blue Ventures *www.blueventures.org*
- World Wide Opportunities on Organic Farms *www.wwoof.org*
- World Conservation Union *www.iucn.org*

Wildlife-watching

Bear-watching (see pages 38–41)
- All Alaska Tours *www.alaskatours.com*

See also
Responsible bear-watching holidays
- Valhala Wilderness Society *www.vws.org*
- Responsible Travel *www.responsibletravel.com*

Jaguar-spotting (see pages 80–3)
- Fundación Amigos de la Naturaleza (FAN) *www.fan-bo.org*
- Neblina Forest *www.neblinaforest.com*
- Ruta Verde *www.rutavedebolivia.com*

See also
- Tribes Travel *www.tribes.co.uk*

Further information

Responsible tour operators
- Adventure Company
  www.adventurecompany.co.uk
- Camino Travel *www.caminotravel.com*
- Discovery Initiatives
  www.discoveryinitiatives.co.uk
- Exodus Travel *www.exodus.co.uk*
- Explore Worldwide *www.explore.co.uk*
- Intrepid Travel *www.intrepidtravel.com*
- Rainbow Tours *www.rainbowtours.co.uk*
- Sunvil *www.sunvil.co.uk*
- Tribes Travel *www.tribestravel.com*
- Wilderness Explorers
  www.wilderness-explorers.com.

Awards and accreditation
There is currently no one globally accepted accreditation body that can be used to compare green accommodation around the world. Hundreds of eco-tourism labels exist, all with varying criteria, making it difficult for travellers to separate the green from the greenwash. Some organizations are currently working towards developing a single internationally accepted standard for green holidays. In the meantime, major schemes around the world include:
Australia
- Ecotourism Australia (Australia)
  www.ecotourism.org.au
Central & South America
- Certificate in Sustainable Tourism
  www.turismo-sostenible.co.cr
Europe
- Voluntary Initiatives for Sustainability in Tourism *www.visit21.net* includes:
- Green Tourism Business Scheme (UK)
  www.green-business.co.uk
- Green Key (France, Sweden, Greenland, Estonia) *www.green-key.org*
- Legambiente (Italy)
  www.legambiente.eu
South Africa
- Fair Trade in Tourism South Africa
  www.fairtourismsa.org.za

General
- Green Globe *www.greenglobe.org*
The following awards also indicate and a commitment to responsible tourism:
- Responsible Tourism Awards
  www.responsibletourismawards.com
- Tourism for Tomorrow Awards
  www.tourismfortomorrow.org
- IH&RA Green Hotelier of the Year

Recommended reading
- Duffy, R (2002) *A Trip Too Far: Ecotourism, Politics and Exploitation,* Earthscan Publications
- Flannery, T (2006) T*he Weather Makers: The History and Future Impact of Climate Change,* Text Publishing
- Honey, M (1999) *Ecotourism and Sustainable Development: Who Owns Paradise?* Island Press
- Hickman, L (2007) *The Final Call: In Search of the True Cost of Our Holidays,* Guardian Books
- Hickman, L (2005) *A Good Life: The Guide to Ethical Living,* Guardian Books
- Pattullo, P (2006) *Ethical Travel Guide,* Earthscan Publications
- Fennell, D (2003) *Ecotourism: An Introduction,* Routledge

Magazines
- Green Hotelier *www.greenhotelier.com*
- Green Futures *www.greenfutures.org.uk*
- Ethical Consumer
  www.ethicalconsumer.org
- The Ecologist *www.theecologist.org*
- New Consumer
  www.newconsumer.org
- Resurgence *www.resurgence.org*

Websites
- Treehugger *www.treehugger.com*
- Green Biz *www.greenbiz.com*
- No Impact Man
  http://noimpactman.typepad.com/blog/
- Web of Hope *www.webofhope.com*

Index

Index

Acknowledgements

The Automobile Association would like to thank the folllowing photographers, companies and picture libraries for their assistance in the preparation of this book.

Abbreviations for the picture credits are as follows: (t) top; (b) below; (c)centre; (tl) top left; (tr) top right; (tc) top centre; (bl) below left; (br) below right; (bc) below centre; (cla) centre left above; (clb)centre left below; (cra) centre right above; (crb) centre right below.

2tl: Gecko Villa, Thailand; **2tr:** Base Camp Travel; **2cla:** Hôtel de la Paix, Cambodia; **2cra:** Anjajavy l'Hôtel, Madagascar; **2clb:** Daintree EcoLodge & Spa, Australia; **2crb:** Bay of Fires, Australia; **2bl:** James Jeffrey; **2br:** Gunya Titjikala, Australia; **6l:** AA/R Newton; **6r:** Wilderness Lodge Arthur's Pass, New Zealand; **7l:** Hoopoe Yurt Hotel, Spain; **7r:** Kalmatia Sangam Himalaya Resort, India; **9l:** AA/A Mockford & N Bonetti; **9r:** AA/A Baker; **10l:** Darren Leal/O'Reilly's Rainforest Retreat, Australia; **10r:** Bespoke Experience Ltd/Oliver Pilcher; **11l:** Whitepod, Switzerland; **11r:** Anjajavy l'Hôtel, Madagascar; **12:** AA/D Henley; **13:** AA/S L Day; **14:** Kalmatia Sangam Himalaya Resort, India; **15bl:** AA/S L Day; **15br:** AA/L K Stow; **17t:** Black Sheep Inn, Ecuador; **17c:** Black Sheep Inn, Ecuador; **17b:** Vamizi Island, Mozambique; **20tl:** Bathurst Inlet Lodge, Canada; **20cla:** Tiamo Resort, Bahamas; **20clb:** Maho Bay Camps & Estate Concordia Preserve, US Virgin Islands; **20bl:** The Colony Hotel, USA; **20–21:** AA/Clive Sawyer; **25:** Banff Park Lodge, Canada; **26–7:** Bathurst Inlet Lodge, Canada; **28–31:** Robin Barton; **32l:** Balamku, Inn on the Beach, Mexico; **32r:** AA/Clive Sawyer; **34–5:** Hotel Eco Paraíso Xixim, Mexico; **36–7:** Villas Ecotucan, Mexico; **38, 39t, 40:** Getty Images/Photodisc; **39b:** Wolfgang Kaehler/Alamy; **41t:** Mira/Alamy; **43:** The Colony Hotel, USA; **44–5:** Dobson House, USA; **46:** The Fairmont Chicago, USA; **48–9:** Hotel Triton, USA; **51:** Inn Serendipity, USA; **52–3:** Bio-Beetle ECO Rental Cars; **54–55:** Tiamo Resort, Bahamas; **56:** Papillote Wilderness Retreat, Dominica; **58:** Maho Bay Camps & Estate Concordia Preserve, US Virgin Islands; **60tl:** Yachana Lodge, Ecuador; **60cla:** Black Sheep Inn, Ecuador; **60clb:** Black Sheep Inn, Ecuador; **60bl:** La Quinta Sarapiquí Country Inn, Costa Rica; **60–1:** AA/B Davies; **64:** James Strachan/Robert Harding; **65:** Upperhall Ltd/Robert Harding; **67:** Steppingstones, Belize; **68–9:** Finca Rosa Blanca Country Inn, Costa Rica; **70–1:** AA/C Sawyer; **72:** Hotel Punta Islita, Costa Rica; **74–5:** Lapa Rios, Costa Rica; **76–7:** La Quinta Sarapiquí Country Inn, Costa Rica; **78–9:** M Spanowicz/Chalalán Ecolodge; **80:** Gardenia Robinson; **81–4:** Alex Robinson; **86–7:** Fazenda San Francisco, Brazil; **88–93:** Alex Robinson; **95:** Black Sheep Inn, Ecuador; **96:** Kapawi Lodge, Ecuador; **98–9:** Yachana Lodge, Ecuador; **100–1:** Alex Robinson; **102–3:** Pantiacolla Lodge, Peru; **104–5:** Tambopata Research Centre and Posada Amazonas, Peru; **106:** Suriname Vacations; **108tl:** Locanda della Valle Nuova, Italy; **108cla:** Hoopoe Yurt Hotel, Spain; **108 clb:** Anna's House, Northern Ireland; **108b:** Casa del Grivo, Italy; **108–9:** AA/D Tarn; **113:** Bedruthan Steps Hotel, England; **114–15:** Rebecca Ford; **116–17:** The Eco-lodge, England; **118–19:** The Hen House, England; **120t:** Jim Wileman/Alamy; **121l:** Ashley Cooper/Corbis; **121r:** AA/N Setchfield; **122:** Rebecca Ford; **124–5:** Primrose Valley Hotel, England; **126–7:** Strattons Hotel, England; **128–9:** L'Auberge les Liards, France; **130–1:** Perché dans le Perche, France; **133t, 133b:** AA/T Harris; **134tl:** AA/T Mackie; **134cl:** AA/T Harris; **136–7:** mitArt,

Germany; **139:** Rebecca Ford; **140–1:** Casa del Grivo, Italy; **142–3:** Locanda della Valle Nuova, Italy; **144–5:** Anna's House, Northern Ireland; **146:** Robin Barton; **147:** AA/J Smith; **148:** Forestry Commission/Andy McCandlish; **150–1:** Aqua City Resort, Slovakia; **152:** Hoopoe Yurt Hotel, Spain; **154:** Digital Vision; **156–7:** Holistic Destinations; **158–9:** Whitepod, Switzerland; **160–1:** Yediburunlar Lighthouse, Turkey; **162tl:** Buffalo Ridge Safari Lodge, South Africa; **162cla:** Kasbah du Toubkal, Morocco; **162clb:** Bespoke Experience Ltd/Oliver Pilcher; **162bl:** Anjajavy l'Hôtel, Madagascar; **162–3:** AA/C Sawyer; **166–7:** Base Camp Travel; **168–9:** Campi ya Kanzi, Kenya; **171:** Anjajavy l'Hôtel, Madagascar; **172–4:** Gnaoua World Music Festival; **176:** Kasbah du Toubkal, Morocco; **178–9:** Lalla Mira, Morocco; **180:** Bespoke Experience Ltd; **182:** Vamizi Island, Mozambique; **184–7:** Rupert Isaacson; **188–91:** Wilderness Safaris; **192:** Buffalo Ridge Safari Lodge, South Africa; **194–5:** Hog Hollow Country Lodge, South Africa; **196:** Vuyatela, South Africa; **198:** AA/P Kenward; **199:** AA/E Meacher; **200:** AA/S McBride; **201l:** AA/P Kenward; **201r:** AA/C Sawyer; **202l:** Hal Thompson/Chumbe Island Coral Park, Tanzania; **202r:** Heinz Heile/Chumbe Island Coral Park, Tanzania; **204–5:** Fundu Lagoon, Tanzania; **206–7:** Conservation Corporation Africa; **208l:** Peter Turnley/Corbis; **208–9c:** Paul W Liebhardt/Corbis; **209br:** David Turnley/Corbis; **210:** Classic Representation; **212l:** fl online/Alamy; **213r:** Rob Howard/Corbis; **214–5:** Wild Jordan/RSCN; **216tl–cla:** Kalmatia Sangam Himalaya Resort, India; **216clb:** Gecko Villa, Thailand; **216bl:** Boat Landing Guest House, Laos; **216–7:** Kalmatia Sangam Himalaya Resort, India; **220–1:** Hôtel de la Paix, Cambodia; **222:** Steve Bloom/steve-bloom.com; **225:** Cardamom House, India; **227:** Kalmatia Sangam Himalaya Resort, India; **228–30:** Villageways, India; **232–3:** Orchid Hotel, India; **234–5:** Wildernest Nature Resort, India; **236–7:** Yogamagic Canvas Ecotel, India; **238–9:** Nihiwatu, Indonesia; **240–1:** Linda Garland/Panchoran Retreat, Indonesia; **242:** Yann Arthus-Bertrand/Corbis; **243l:** Marcin Suder/Corbis; **243r:** Yann Arthus-Bertrand/Corbis; **244–5:** The Boat Landing Guest House, Laos; **246–7:** Six Senses Resorts & Spas; **248–9:** Nomadic Expeditions; **251:** Tiger Mountain Pokhara Lodge, Nepal; **252cl:** AA/L K Stow; **252–4:** Ulpotha Retreat, Sri Lanka; **256–7:** Galapita, Sri Lanka; **259:** Richard Powers/Samakanda Bio-versity, Sri Lanka; **260:** Tree Tops Jungle Lodge, Sri Lanka; **263:** Gecko Villa, Thailand; **264tl:** James Jeffrey; **264cla:** Burrawang West Station, Australia; **264clb:** Kooljaman, Australia; **264bl:** Jean-Michel Cousteau Fiji Islands Resort, Fiji; **264–5:** AA/M Cawood; **268–9:** Aquila Eco Lodges, Australia; **270–1:** Bamurru Plains, Australia; **272–3:** Bay of Fires, Australia; **274:** Burrawang West Station, Australia; **276–7:** Daintree EcoLodge & Spa, Australia; **278–81:** Geoff Scholz; **282:** Gunya Titjikala, Australia; **285:** Inala, Australia; **286–7:** Kooljaman, Australia; **288t:** John Carnemolla/ Corbis; **288–9:** Kevin Schafer/Corbis; **290:** John Van Hasselt/Corbis; **291:** Penny Tweedie/Corbis; **292–3:** Ningaloo Reef Retreat, Australia; **294–5:** O'Reilly's Rainforest Retreat, Australia; **296–7:** Paperbark Camp, Australia; **298–9:** Rawnsley Park Station, Australia; **300–1:** Tribewanted.com; **304–5:** Jean Michel-Cousteau Fiji Islands Resort, Fiji; **306–7:** Chris McLennan/Alamy; **308–9:** Awaroa Lodge, Abel Tasman National Park, New Zealand; **311:** Wilderness Lodge Arthur's Pass, New Zealand.

Front cover: Paperbark Camp, Australia
Back cover, left to right: Nihiwatu, Indonesia; Yediburunlar Lighthouse, Turkey; Anjajavy l'Hôtel, Madagascar

Special thanks also to Bettina Koller at Climate Care for her assistance in preparing the carbon offset figures throughout this book, and to Tourism Concern for the use of their Avoid Guilt Trips guidelines.

Editor
Beth Hall

Design
Catherine Murray

Cover design
Nora Rosansky

Picture research
Sarah Hopper

Cartography
Mapping Services Department of AA Publishing.
Mountain High Maps® Copyright© 1993 Digital Wisdom, Inc.

Contributors
Rebecca Ford, James Jeffrey, Nick Maes, Richard Newton, Alex Robinson, Rory Spowers
(main authors); Robin Barton; Richard Hammond; Rupert Isaacson (contributing authors);
Susi Bailey (copy editor); Lisa Regan (proofreader); Marie Lorimer (indexer).

ISBN 978-1-4000-0753-0

FIRST EDITION

Important tip
Time inevitably brings changes, so always confirm prices, travel facts, and other perishable
information when it matters. Although Fodor's cannot accept responsibility for errors, you can
use this guide in the confidence that we have taken every care to ensure its accuracy.

Special sales
This book is available for special discounts for bulk purchases for sales promotions or premi-
ums. Special editions, including personalized covers, excerpts of existing books, and corporate
imprints, can be created in large quantities for special needs. For more information, write
to Special Markets/Premium Sales, 1745 Broadway, MD 6-2, New York, NY 10019 or email
specialmarkets@randomhouse.com.

The paper used for this book has been independently certified as
coming from well-managed forests and other controlled sources according
to the rules of the Forest Stewardship Council.

This book has been printed on GardaMatt Art manufactured by Cartiere del
Garda, an environmentally sustainable company,
ISO 14001-certified and EMAS-registered.

Colour separation MRM Graphics.

Printed and bound in Italy by Printer Trento S.R.L., an FSC certified
company for printing books on FSC mixed paper in compliance with the
chain of custody and on-products labelling standards.

WIP AO3314   10 9 8 7 6 5 4 3 2 1